D1545656

GOETHE
AND
ROUSSEAU

Carl Hammer, Jr.

GOETHE
AND
ROUSSEAU

Resonances of the Mind

THE UNIVERSITY PRESS OF KENTUCKY

To my wife, Mae

ISBN: 0–8131–1289–3

Library of Congress Catalog Card Number: 72–91665

Copyright © 1973 by The University Press of Kentucky

A statewide cooperative scholarly publishing agency serving Berea College, Centre College of Kentucky, Eastern Kentucky University, Georgetown College, Kentucky Historical Society, Kentucky State University, Morehead State University, Murray State University, Northern Kentucky State College, Transylvania University, University of Kentucky, University of Louisville, and Western Kentucky University.

Editorial and Sales Offices: Lexington, Kentucky 40506

Contents

Foreword

The initial plan of the following study proposed a comparison of *Die Wahlverwandtschaften* with *La Nouvelle Héloïse*. It soon became apparent that a re-examination of the entire Goethe-Rousseau problem was advisable. Many circumstances (among them, frequently, "the challenge of the day," to quote Goethe) combined to delay completion of the investigation; nevertheless, it has thereby acquired a broader scope and profited from numerous publications of recent date.

Direct quotations of prose passages are given in English translations which, with occasional minor exceptions, are my own. In the case of titles, verse, and short expressions of special import, the original is retained. For Goethe, except as otherwise noted, I have followed the Weimar edition (containing all his extant references to Rousseau, outside of those reported in the conversations or correspondence of others). I have used the Du Pont edition of Rousseau's works, because of its readable print, in preference to the more usually quoted Hachette version.

Completeness of bibliography—so immense in the case of both writers—plainly defies attainment. Still, I believe that in my search extending through two decades I have missed relatively few pertinent items, and hardly any that would have altered the picture essentially.

To the late Professor Albert W. Aron, of the University of Illinois, I am indebted for his having inspired me to undertake this investigation. I gratefully acknowledge generous research grants from Louisiana State University and Texas Tech University. It is a pleasure to express my obligation to the librarians of the following universities: Columbia, Harvard, Princeton, Texas, Tulane, and Yale, and of the Library of Congress for their assistance. With sincere appreciation I mention the perennial encouragement received from two former colleagues, Professor John G. Frank, formerly of American University, and Dr. John T. Krumpelmann, Professor Emeritus of German, Louisiana State University, as well as from my present colleague, Professor Theodor W. Alexander. Finally, I thank the sponsors of the Kentucky Foreign Language Conference for honoring me with the first annual Conference Award.

Explanation of Page References

Sources of quotations from Goethe and Rousseau are indicated (usually in the text) as follows:

W.A. I = "Weimarer Ausgabe," first section (*Werke*, or literary works). Volume and page numbers are listed by Arabic numerals, with a colon between them; e.g., 16:301. W.A. I, 16:301 is therefore a typical reference to Goethe's creative writings, except that line numbers are given for quotations from poems and verse dramas. A superscript means that the volume has two parts; thus W.A. I, 25^1 signifies volume 25, part 1. W.A. II (containing the scientific works) is similarly quoted. For the diaries (W.A. III), letters (W.A. IV), and conversations (from various sources), only the dates are cited. In exceptional instances the "Gedenkausgabe" is listed, as for example, G.A., 6:240.

In the case of Rousseau, O.C. = "Œuvres complètes," edited by Musset-Pathay, with designation of volume and page like that for Goethe's works; viz., O.C., 9:442. On occasions when the Musset-Pathay edition was not accessible, single-volume texts of the "Classiques Garnier" were quoted (as C.G.).

Introduction

Within the scholarship of comparative literature there is, of course, a plethora of "influence studies," so much so that one hesitates to add another such item to the bibliography. The cultural relationship between such giants as Goethe and Rousseau is of such obvious importance, however, that it merits investigation, despite the critical dangers involved.

The linkage has been attempted before and remains a debated topic of Franco-German literary relations. For more than a century the popular view held that Goethe's interest in Rousseau ended with the "Sturm und Drang" era, and echoes of this now outmoded notion still persist. Rousseau remained a vital inspirational force for Goethe during Goethe's entire lifetime, as comparative study of Goethe's post-*Werther* works will demonstrate. The review of literature on this subject reveals the limited scope and fragmentation of previous research, despite the clash of viewpoint, and highlights the timeliness of a comprehensive treatment.

Fortunately, changes in the contemporary images of Rousseau and Goethe simplify a discussion of Rousseau's lifelong importance for Goethe. The *Rousseaubild* of our time, created by Bernard Groethuysen,[1] Jean Guéhenno,[2] Léon Émery,[3] and others, is more sympathetic than the nineteenth-century image depicted by Saint-Marc Girardin,[4] Jules Lemaître,[5] and Georg Brandes.[6] The gradual trend toward a better understanding of Rousseau received new impetus from the founding of the Société Jean-Jacques Rousseau at Geneva in 1905.[7]

Likewise, today's concept of Goethe is more realistic than that of 1900. Late nineteenth-century scholars of the positivistic school too often represented Goethe as conforming to their own moral stringency. To a "human, all-too human" portrait of the author of the *Confessions* they opposed an "Olympian" Goethe, whose foibles had to be glossed over, if not ignored completely. That mistaken idea, though long in vogue, is now wholly outdated in favor of a Goethe no longer elevated to Jovian heights, but viewed instead on a more human level.[8] Emil Staiger,[9] Heinrich Meyer,[10] Barker Fairley,[11] and Albert Fuchs,[12] to name but a few, have helped to make this change.

To chase after direct influence, as Erich Schmidt and his contemporaries were fond of doing, contradicts the whole mode of thinking of a man like Goethe, who derogatorily used the foreign word "Influenz" instead of the German "Einfluss." The octogenarian Goethe assured Eckermann (December 16, 1828) that the question of a famous author's originality was ridiculous, insisting: "We indeed possess inherent capabilities, but we owe our development to a thousand influences of a great world from which we appropriate what we can and what is suited to us. I owe much to the Greeks and the French; I have become infinitely indebted to Shakespeare, Sterne, and Goldsmith. Yet the sources of my culture are not established by that; it would lead one endlessly afield, and would not be necessary, either. The important thing is that one should have a soul that loves the true and takes it where it finds it."

This quotation indicates that Goethe was strongly aware of a problem which is still controversial in comparative literature circles and reminds us that one might well essay a medial objectivity toward the extreme poles of opinion about the extent of Rousseau's impact upon Goethe. Ulrich Weisstein summarizes the dangerous aspects of influence-seeking, calling the concept of literary influence the "Schlüsselbegriff" of all comparative investigations. It presupposes the existence of two works: the one from which it proceeds and the one it affects.[13] Weisstein insists that one cannot speak of influence in the literal sense of studies of analogies and parallels, since at most it is a matter of affinities (p. 95), and he urges observance of an equilibrium between *rapports extérieurs* and *rapports intérieurs* (p. 102).

This book attempts to preserve that equilibrium. The introductory discussions of the *Rousseaukult* in Goethe's Germany, Geothe's acquaintance with eighteenth-century French literature, and his recorded comments about Rousseau constitute *rapports extérieurs*. The correspondences between the actual works of the two writers, especially affinities where there is no indication of direct influence, lend a balance as *rapports intérieurs*.

It seems advisable, then, to subdivide the term "influence" by separating probable but less easily provable points of contact from those which Goethe recognized and acknowledged. We shall deal here with: 1) general similarities in personal experience and character as well as in style, motifs, and characterization; 2) instances of Goethe's adopting specific ideas to which Rousseau gave currency, but which may have

2

reached Goethe indirectly; 3) Goethe's specific admission of conscious use of Rousseau's ideas, formulations, and phraseology.

When Goethe's first novel, *Die Leiden des jungen Werthers*, appeared in 1774, many readers at once associated it with *La Nouvelle Héloïse*. That verdict gradually became an international tradition; thus *Werther* was inevitably regarded as the focal point for whatever inspiration Goethe might have received from Rousseau. In Erich Schmidt's noted monograph *Richardson, Rousseau und Goethe*,[14] published in 1875, there was a virtual crystallization of the assumption that the influence of the Citizen of Geneva hardly extended beyond the *Werther* period.

Erich Schmidt's book was considered such a monumental feat of scholarship that it was reprinted after half a century without any change whatever.[15] Usually at long intervals, there were a few brief reminders that Erich Schmidt had not uttered the last word on the subject, but it largely remained for the Goethe bicentenary of 1949 and its aftermath to produce more tangible proofs of an about-face, with French scholars playing an increasingly prominent role.

How did it happen that research concerning this relationship advanced so little in the course of three generations? There is a strong possibility that the belief in Rousseau's diminished impact after "Sturm und Drang" was encouraged by the index to the Weimar edition of Goethe's works (of which Erich Schmidt was one of the editors). For the earlier writings, Rousseau is sometimes listed even where he is not mentioned in the text, merely because Goethe writes about nature. Hence *La Nouvelle Héloïse* is actually suggested "als Vorbild" for the entire *Werther* (W.A. I, 55:272).[16] References for the subsequent literary productions were omitted, despite the fact that they would often seem equally justifiable. This negative attitude not only stubbornly persisted but gained ever-increasing weight through repetition.

Of course Erich Schmidt did not always meet with absolute acceptance. For example, in that same year of 1875 Lucien Lévy-Bruhl published a monograph on Rousseau's influence in Germany, in which he lauds Schmidt but asks whether one must assume that *Werther* proceeded from *La Nouvelle Héloïse*.[17] He concedes Goethe's acquaintance with Rousseau's writings and thought, yet he doubts any strong influence upon "the most objective of writers"; even if Goethe had wished it, "he could not have been inspired by Rousseau." The one, according to Lévy-Bruhl, is the type of the "proud ego," the other that of the "restless ego." Goethe, he continues, is capable of marvelous exactness of depiction. Thus a kind of reflected image causes us to recognize Rousseau on nearly every page of the novel; in spite of appearances, Werther is "less a sign of Rousseau's effect upon the mind of Goethe himself than a decisive testimony to his influence on the youth of the time in Germany" (p. 343). There is no mention of the works after Werther.

Although Lévy-Bruhl's concept of a "reflected image" is in keeping with Goethe's own penchant for "Wiederspiegelung," it was the age of positivism, with "sources" the chief concern. Thus Wilhelm Scherer, in his famous German literary history, remarks that Rousseau is not included among those named as Werther's favorite authors; as a reason he suggests "Goethe's disinclination at that time toward French literature, even on intrinsic grounds." Yet Scherer immediately adds that Rousseau to some degree "secretly" played a part in the development of Werther. In no book of earlier literature, he says, does one find such exact affinity with Goethe's novel as in La Nouvelle Héloïse, namely, "an analogous hero, analogous motifs, an analogous language, analogous tendencies."[18] The chief emphasis again lies on Werther, with only fleeting reference to other works, even those of Goethe's youth.

Jules Barbey d'Aurevilly, who labels Goethe and Diderot as "minds of an identical nature," finds Rousseau reflected in Torquato Tasso. The latter, he maintains, is neither the historical Tasso nor a creation of Goethe: "No! it is Rousseau, of whom the world was full at the time when Goethe wrote . . . . It is Rousseau, passed over the double stamp of the imbecile Platonism of the Renaissance and German idealism . . . ."[19] A more sympathetic appraisal is that of John Grand-Carteret, who calls attention to Goethe's commendation of Rousseau in Dichtung und Wahrheit and to his criticism of the Encyclopedists, particularly Holbach's Système de la nature.[20]

Joseph Texte was widely considered to be the authority on the Richardson-Rousseau problem following Erich Schmidt.[21] His 1895 treatment of the Goethe-Rousseau complex is of a more general nature. Texte holds that it was given to Rousseau "to cause the best of what was in the English spirit to pass over into the French spirit"; what Richardson and others had partially accomplished, Rousseau completed. At the same time, he states that Jean-Jacques belongs only halfway to the French, being a

Swiss with extensive German Pietistic influences in his religious background, and that foreign critics regard him "as the most German of the
French, if not as the most English"; he is at the very least "a cosmopolite"
(p. 110). Texte states in his introduction that Frenchmen who read
Werther or Schiller's play *Die Räuber* could find there a proof of the relationship of Rousseau's genius with the Germanic genius (p. XVI). *Werther* is the stopping point for Texte, as well as for Virgile Rossel, who
characterizes that novel as "a bit of Jean-Jacques recast by the hand of a
great artist."[22] Rossel, in quoting Erich Schmidt's connection of *Werther*
with *La Nouvelle Héloïse* approvingly, follows well-worn paths (p. 436).
Several brief sketches dating from the late nineteenth century are of a
generally positive tone but add scarcely anything new; e.g., the survey by
Armand Caumont (dealing almost exclusively with the young Goethe)[23]
and the catalog-like listing by C. Sachs.[24]

Isaac Benrubi's long article represents the most noteworthy contribution to the Goethe-Rousseau problem among the works published during the Rousseau bicentennial year of 1912. Goethe, according to Benrubi,
admired and loved Rousseau from his tenderest youth until his death, and
he nearly always mentioned him with sympathy.[25] From his childhood
Goethe lived in a Rousseauistic milieu because his mother brought him
up according to principles of education very near to those of Rousseau
(p. 442). Despite a sometimes extreme enthusiasm, Benrubi gives a valuable résumé of Goethe's early preoccupation with Rousseau, and—what
is more important—he insists on the continuity of Rousseau's stimulus
beyond *Werther*. For example, Benrubi considers it certain that *Dichtung
und Wahrheit*, "one of the most remarkable works of Goethe's maturity,"
cannot be properly understood without reference to Rousseau's autobiography (p. 443). While expressly forgoing a detailed consideration of
Rousseau-like elements in *Egmont*, *Tasso*, *Iphigenie*, *Hermann und
Dorothea*, and *Die Wahlverwandtschaften*, Benrubi implies that such research would be rewarding; in fact, he attempts it to a limited extent with
Wilhelm Meister and *Faust* (pp. 444–449).

Benrubi's challenging appraisal attracted little notice at the time of
its appearance and thereafter. During the subsequent quarter of a century
there is seldom an allusion to it, even in bibliographical references. Louis
Reynaud designates the extensive influence of Rousseau which he sees in
Goethe's works as imitative, from *Werther* ("a direct imitation of *La
Nouvelle Héloïse*") to *Faust*.[26] This attitude represents a step backward

from the position taken by Benrubi. Equally devoid of any progress a decade later is Max Kommerell's verdict that only in the case of *Werther* do Rousseauistic elements occur in Goethe's writing.[27] Herbert Smith, disregarding the majority of Goethe's own comments, questions whether Rousseau had any "fundamental influence on him at all," even before 1775.[28]

Meanwhile, Eduard Spranger had issued his anthology of selections from Rousseau, entitled *Kulturideale*,[29] which suggests a relationship between Jean-Jacques and Goethe inasmuch as they both strove for "cultural ideals." Spranger characterizes *La Nouvelle Héloïse* as brilliantly colorful, despite its strong didacticism, as well as psychologically and intrinsically profound, and calls it the prototype of *Werther* and *Die Wahlverwandtschaften* (p. 19). Many passages by Rousseau read (in the German translation by Hedwig Jahn) strikingly like Goethe.

In his generally admirable book on Goethe and France, Hippolyte Loiseau retains the widely accepted theory of an intense early interest in Rousseau, but he takes the familiar negative position toward any post-*Werther* influence.[30] Loiseau believes this so strongly that he disregards some of Goethe's most significant statements about Rousseau, such as those in *Dichtung und Wahrheit*, the very work in which Goethe alludes to him most often.

For all its vast body of commemorative and critical writings, the "Goethe Year" 1932 brought few contributions to a deeper understanding of the role played by Rousseau in Goethe's evolution as a poet and thinker. German and English publications for that occasion mostly deal with other aspects, and those which do refer to the issue in question tend to reiterate the time-honored standpoint that Goethe lost his interest in Jean-Jacques after "Sturm und Drang." The same is true of the somewhat fuller discussion by the American scholar, E. Preston Dargan, who largely follows Loiseau.[31]

A more comprehensive treatment of the subject is found in the French doctoral thesis of Valentin Brunet, which seems to have passed almost unnoticed at the time of its appearance in print.[32] Like others before him, Brunet stresses the alleged fervor of the Strassburg student for Rousseau and adduces numerous instances of his apparent effect on Goethe's youthful writing. Brunet maintains that after 1791 Goethe, alarmed by the revolutionary movement and made wise by study and experience, cherished in Rousseau's works whatever ideas are of a con-

6

servative, pacifying nature—concepts reflected especially in Goethe's unfinished dramas of the French Revolution (p. 30). There are only sparse
references to Hermann und Dorothea, the most eminent of Goethe's
works concerning the upheaval in France. Chief attention is given to
Werther, a moderate amount to Wilhelm Meisters Lehrjahre, and very
little to the later novels, Die Wahlverwandtschaften and Wilhelm Meisters Wanderjahre.

In 1936 Albert W. Aron published the most sweeping reassessment
of the Goethe-Rousseau question up to that time, calling attention to the
singular lack of progress in research caused by the canonical acceptance of
Erich Schmidt's book and to the perpetuation of his viewpoint through
reissuance of that volume after fifty years.[33] Aron's article subjects Loiseau's then recent study to a critical examination, as far as it concerns
Rousseau. He shows by quotations from the letters, diaries, and conversations, as well as from the literary and scientific works, that Loiseau un-
derestimated Goethe's sympathetic comments in some cases, overlooked
important passages in others, and sometimes even misinterpreted the
German text (pp. 171–179). Attributing this procedure to Loiseau's uncritical acceptance of Schmidt's position, Aron urges a re-examining of
the mature works, especially Die Wahlverwandtschaften, as part of a reconsideration of the whole relationship (pp. 181–182).

Bertram Barnes' useful book on Goethe and French literature (which
appeared a year after Aron's essay) devotes a chapter to Goethe's comments about Rousseau which is misleading through the omission of some
of Goethe's most significant remarks.[34] Again one encounters the assumption that Goethe's concern during his later decades was virtually confined
to Rousseau the botanist. Although obviously wishing to be objective,
Barnes betrays a lack of sufficient information about previous Goethe-
Rousseau investigations.

In the introduction to his monograph on Rousseau and the Romantic movement in Germany, Rudolf Buck quotes first Kommerell's denial
of Rousseau's meaningful effect on Goethe, even in Werther, then the
conflicting opinion of Oskar Walzel.[35] Examples of related concepts cited
by Buck do not go beyond the "Sturm und Drang" epoch. He evidently
knew nothing of Aron's essay published only three years before his own.

Among the more discerning Goethe books of the 1940's are René
Michéa's comparison of the respective Italian experiences of Rousseau
and Goethe[36] (followed a year later by a reconsideration of their com-

munity of botanical interests[37]) and, especially, the brilliant work of Albert Fuchs, who with rare penetration reaffirms the role of Rousseau in the young Goethe's development.[38] (Unfortunately, the initial volume, which has not been followed up, ends with the pre-Weimar Goethe.) The evaluations by Fuchs, conceived as a *biographie intérieure*, indicate not merely external resemblances, but rather a kinship of thought and sentiment such as Michéa has demonstrated for the *Italienische Reise* of later date. For instance, Fuchs maintains that between Goethe the "Stürmer" and Goethe the classicist there is less a difference of proportioning of moral and mental forces than a difference of temperature, temperament, pace, and dynamism (p. 243).

Several studies which appeared in or around 1949, the year of the bicentennial, demonstrate the persistence of the late nineteenth-century notion that Goethe renounced Jean-Jacques before going to Weimar. An example is Fritz Strich's excellent work on Goethe and world literature, which, aside from a single quotation from *Dichtung und Wahrheit*, scarcely takes any cognizance of Rousseau in connection with Goethe after the *Werther* era.[39] Roy Pascal likewise reiterates the supposed rejection of Rousseau by the mature Goethe in an essay contrasting the autobiographies of the two men.[40] Since Pascal regards Goethe's reading of the first six books of the *Confessions* in 1782 as marking the end of his enthusiasm for Rousseau, he doubts Rousseau afforded any appreciable inspiration in the genesis of *Dichtung und Wahrheit*.

Edmond Vermeil, in his acute reappraisal of the Goethe-Rousseau relationship, declares that Rousseau's impact on European thought has been mistakenly belittled, especially through its confinement to "Sturm und Drang" by Erich Schmidt and others.[41] According to Vermeil, a careful, objective analysis of *La Nouvelle Héloïse* combined with an unprejudiced interpretation of the Genevan's "mysticism" will show that this is one of the elements which helped shape Goethe's thought and gave him a sort of "program" for his own literary creation (p. 70). The failure to interpret Rousseau's work adequately gave rise to the narrow view that he exerted no further effect than that of an individualistic, sentimental, or revolutionary kind. The paradox that nature and civilization are incompatible merely prefaces *La Nouvelle Héloïse*, *Émile*, and the *Contrat social*, which are seen by Vermeil as parts of a grandiose attempt to bring about individual and social recovery (p. 70).

Vermeil regards *La Nouvelle Héloïse* and Shakespeare's plays (to which he devotes part of his essay) as the archetypes of Goethe's great works, which form their prolongation, their survival amidst his prodigious culture and his creative genius (pp. 69–70). Instead of conscious borrowing or precise imitation, Vermeil continues, there is a repercussion, with Goethe's originality preserved. He considers analogies between Rousseau's characters and those of Goethe to be as valid for the latter's mature dramas and novels as for his earlier works. Vermeil attempts to establish a spiritual kinship between Julie, the heroine of Rousseau's novel, and Goethe's Iphigenie, assuring us that the same procedure could be carried out even more readily in the case of *Wilhelm Meisters Lehrjahre* and *Die Wahlverwandtschaften* (p. 65). Finally, together with Shakespeare and others, Rousseau is designated one of those inspirational forces which, "swathed in a vast philosophy," find expression in the works of Goethe's old age, especially in his *Westöstlicher Divan*, *Wilhelm Meisters Wanderjahre*, and the Second Part of *Faust* (p. 74).

In 1957 Vermeil slightly elaborated his thesis of the archetypal function of *La Nouvelle Héloïse* in Goethe's creative writings.[42] A year later Maurice Bémol published an article on the relationship of *Faust* to Rousseau which shows its author in essential agreement with Vermeil.[43] Bémol's discussion of the Second Part, although brief, outlines some important points of contact with Jean-Jacques. In his opinion, both the *Rêveries du promeneur solitaire* and the *Confessions* are of fundamental importance for the proper comprehension of Goethe's greatest work (p. 17).

From the foregoing summary it should be evident that the past several decades have witnessed noteworthy progress in the evaluation of the mature Goethe's concern with Rousseau. Such affirmative estimates as those of Aron, Vermeil, Bémol, and others invite a fuller treatment, which is attempted in the chapters that follow.

I

The Cultural
Background

As a background to an understanding of the Goethe-Rousseau relationship, the first part of this chapter deals with the reception of Rousseau's works in Germany during the third quarter of the eighteenth century, the period of Goethe's youth, and the second offers a résumé of Goethe's knowledge of French literature, particularly that of his own century, in which Rousseau played a momentous role.

1. ROUSSEAU'S IMPACT ON EIGHTEENTH-CENTURY GERMANY

A frequently repeated story tells how Immanuel Kant became so absorbed in reading Rousseau's Émile that he forgot to take his daily walk, by which the citizens of Königsberg were said to have set their clocks. It is probably as apocryphal as most anecdotes related about famous men; also, as Ernst Cassirer points out, it is not needed, since Kant's own testimony gives far more impressive evidence of the profound influence which Rousseau exerted upon him.[1] It typifies, nonetheless, the great enthusiasm with which Jean-Jacques' teachings were greeted in Germany. There, as he himself realized, he had "plus de réputation qu'en France."[2]

Yet, after two centuries, there is still no extensive general treatment of that reception. The promising beginnings made several decades ago by

Wolfgang Liepe were never carried to completion. We find thus far nothing comparable to Roland Mortier's book *Diderot en Allemagne, 1750–1850*[3] or Jacques Voisine's work *J.-J. Rousseau en Angleterre à l'époque romantique*[4] and few, if any, articles as comprehensive and penetrating as Herbert Dieckmann's "Goethe und Diderot."[5] Voltaire also has fared better than Rousseau in estimates of their respective roles in the Teutonic world. As Karl S. Guthke remarks, a history of Rousseauism in Germany would be an undertaking fraught with difficulties, many of which have not received appropriate consideration in the multitude of individual studies.[6] As a result, appraisals of Rousseau's impact upon German literature and thought often contradict each other strikingly. Very often, Guthke continues, no clear distinction has been made between Rousseau and the "Zeitstimmung" of Irrationalism, of which he became the exponent. For not every anti-intellectual or irrationalistic trend, not every criticism of the civilization of that age was obliged to stem from Rousseau. Through failure to realize the existence of a common spirit akin to that of the Philosopher of Geneva, one tends to represent German "Geistesgeschichte" as "Rousseauism," at least from the last third of the eighteenth century until well into the nineteenth. Consequently, says Guthke, a far too vague and general criterion becomes an "Einflusskonstruktion," which in a number of instances has been questioned by more searching investigation of later date (p. 384).[7]

Although destined to be idolized a few years later by the young "Stürmer und Dränger," Rousseau did not at first meet with an unqualified welcome in Germany. When his first *Discours* appeared in 1750, it was soon translated by a member of the Gottsched circle at Leipzig and published with a refutation such as could be expected from that bastion of the "Aufklärung." But Lessing, on whom Rousseau's "männliche Beredsamkeit" and "erhabene Gesinnungen" made a profound impression, printed an excerpt in the April (1751) number of *Das Neueste aus dem Reiche des Witzes*.[8]

Much more of a furore was occasioned among adherents of the German Enlightenment by the appearance in 1755 of Rousseau's *Discours sur l'Origine et les Fondements de l'Inégalité parmi les hommes*. Frederic C. Tubach, who has succinctly dealt with the effect of that essay's central concept of "perfectibilité" upon several of the leading "Aufklärer," points out that the cultural pessimism of Rousseau and his longing for an ideal state of nature rest upon a deep-seated dualism which is foreign to the

11

Enlightenment.[9] For the adherents of the "Aufklärung," the development of culture evolves naturally from the primitive state, since human development proceeds according to a principle of Reason ("Vernunftsprinzip") which expresses itself everywhere and which Man realizes in his culture. Rousseau, however, rejects natural Man's progress by means of civilization. Having lost faith in the power of Reason, Rousseau looks backward toward Man's original nobility in his natural state. For Rousseau, therefore, the idea of "perfectibilité," so well suited to the Enlightenment concept of cultural progress, assumed a different dimension in viewing progress as the restoration of Man's primitive state. It is necessary to remember that the second *Discours* forms only one phase in the development of Rousseau's thought. It must be linked with the *Contrat social* of eight years later, where a compromise is attempted between natural Man and human society, which in the second *Discours* appeared irreconcilable. Some thinkers of the German Enlightenment, however, among them the Swiss Iselin and even Wieland, looked to the cultural pessimism of the second *Discours* without considering the new view expressed in the *Contrat social* (Tubach, pp. 145–146).[10]

Lessing's review of July 10, 1755 was the first German discussion of the second *Discours*. As in the case of the first *Discours*, the tone is general but approving, with Rousseau characterized as "noch überall der kühne Weltweise."[11] Presumably Lessing encouraged his friend Moses Mendelssohn to translate it; at any rate, he showed much interest in that effort. In the course of his translation, Mendelssohn gradually found himself at odds with Rousseau's dualism. On January 10, 1756, he wrote that he could disagree with Rousseau on very few points. But in his *Sendschreiben an den Herrn Magister Lessing in Leipzig*, which he published together with his German version of the second *Discours*, he expressed regret that Rousseau had not employed his divine eloquence for a better cause.[12] For Mendelssohn, culture (or civilization, in the deeper sense) is the consequence of a "perfectibilité" already assigned to Man in his natural state, a quality which Mendelssohn regards as the source of human happiness. If Mendelssohn, while exploiting Rousseau's concept of "perfectibilité," tries to restore the unity of Man in his development from the state of nature to a state of culture, Lessing does not find this unity endangered by Rousseau's idea. Rather, he neutralizes that concept of Man's progress toward a cultural state to a quality common to all things in the world, and absolutely necessary for their continuance (Tubach, p. 147).[13]

From Tubach's summary it becomes apparent that the "Aufklärer" oppose Rousseau's dualism and seek to restore a harmony in human nature. They differ thus in their premises: in contradiction to Rousseau, Mendelssohn sets up the principle of a harmony of laws; Lessing refers to Man's identity with "perfectibilité," even in the state of nature; and Wieland and Iselin deny the existence of "perfectibilité" in the natural state of humankind as understood by Rousseau, since they consider it a capability only of civilized Man (Tubach, p. 151).

Meanwhile, Kant enthusiastically encouraged the student Herder to read Rousseau. As Hans M. Wolff points out, it is the youthful Herder whose fervor over Rousseau is most unmistakable as witnessed by his early poem "Der Mensch." [14] On different occasions Herder expressed extremes of admiration and disapproval; for instance, after his first reading of *Émile* in 1763, he composed a poem entitled "Der Entschluss" for Kant which ends: "Komm! sei mein Führer, Rousseau!" [15] Four years afterward he characterized that tribute as "the belch of a stomach overloaded from reading Rousseau." [16] Robert T. Clark, in his important critical biography *Herder: His Life and Thought*, attributes this negative attitude to the ambivalent position of Hamann, Herder's other mentor at Königsberg. [17] Clark has shown that nineteenth-century literary scholarship overstressed the influence of Rousseau upon Herder, and that the twentieth-century American critics known as the "New Humanists" were misled by the assumption—devoid of historical basis—that Rousseau was the originator of primitivism (p. 47).

Herder's early essay *Über den Ursprung der Sprache* follows Rousseau's analogy of the development of language to the growth of Man: language displays "childhood, youth, manhood, and old age" (p. 63). But the revision of the *Fragmente*, Clark maintains, shows less dependence on Rousseau (p. 74). In his *Reisejournal* of 1769 Herder outlines educational plans far beyond the scope of *Émile* (p. 103). Later, in his correspondence with his fiancée, Caroline Flachsland, he cautions her against oversentimentality resulting from her enthusiasm for Rousseau. Nevertheless, he admits rereading the latter's works. It is Clark's opinion that Herder's advice to Caroline to read *Émile* (for which purpose she dutifully learned French) stems less from admiration for Jean-Jacques than from the desire to counteract the sentimentalism of *La Nouvelle Héloïse* with a work of more rationalistic character (p. 120). On another occasion Herder calls Rousseau's Man of Nature "a degenerate creature," which he equips on the one side with "réflexion en puissance," on the other with "perfecti-bilité" (p. 134). In his historical theories Herder repeatedly takes issue with Rousseau and the latter's pupil, Iselin, though he too neglects the Middle Ages (p. 192). With these and other illustrations, Clark shows that Herder was not the unswerving disciple of Rousseau, as some for-merly supposed. Still, it is evident that he was stimulated (or irritated) by Rousseau's wealth of ideas—if only, as often happened, to attack them or adapt them to his own ends, for Herder's universe was as broad and diverse as that of Rousseau.

As already observed, Wieland was repelled by the second *Discours*, but according to Friedrich Sengle, he was "no absolute antagonist" to Rousseau's world of ideas as a whole. His attack on Rousseau, according to that same biographer, was "more a pretext than a goal"; it was a means of starting a discussion and of expressing a feeling of the inadequacy of all philosophical systems.[18]

Quoting a passage from Wieland's *Araspes und Panthea*, "eine moralische Geschichte" (1760), Victor Michel asks whether the "tone of Wertherism" is not already present here, even before *La Nouvelle Héloïse*. Carried away by passion, conscience is set adrift, and Panthea becomes for Araspes "the soul of his soul."[19] Sengle considers the novel *Agathon* an intermediate stage between its Western European models and Goethe's *Werther*, which was inspired in turn by Rousseau. The Danae of the second edition is seen as "sentimentally painted over" after the manner of Rousseau's heroine. She now functions as one who has always remained essentially "eine schöne Seele," and who finally, like Agathon himself, yields to renunciation.[20] It is especially significant that Wieland appar-ently first occupied himself with political and social problems while under the impact of Rousseau's ideas. His reckoning with Rousseau in matters of state and society is obvious in the novel which won his appointment as preceptor for the two young princes of Sachsen-Weimar: *Der goldene Spiegel, oder Die Könige von Scheschian* (1772). To be sure, Rousseau is but one of a number of thinkers who contributed to Wieland's stock of ideas expressed in that book, but his theories are easily recognizable; for example, the Genevan talks in terms of a small state, and Wieland, too, presents the picture of an ideal little nation living in voluntary seclu-sion from the world at large. Idyllic and pastoral elements in Rousseau's philosophy appealed strongly to Wieland; an idealized rustic life à la Jean-Jacques is further described in the *Geschichte des Philosophen*

Danischmende, and there are echoes of it in the *Grazien* and even in the second canto of *Oberon*. The effect of Rousseau's *Pygmalion* upon Wieland as the author of "Singspiele" has been variously pointed out.[21] Finally, his *Teutscher Merkur* for 1780 contains an essay expressive of Wieland's admiration for Rousseau as a human being,[22] and in a letter to Fritz Jacobi written December 2, 1781, he calls *La Nouvelle Héloïse* "a divine book, of which the century is not worthy."[23]

Sophie von La Roche, the chief woman novelist of Germany in the "Sturm und Drang" era and Wieland's friend and sometime fiancée, was even then hailed as the pupil of Rousseau (and Richardson). Her novel *Die Geschichte des Fräuleins von Sternheim* (1771), which Goethe held in high esteem, proved especially important for the dissemination of Rousseau's ideas in Germany. Country life as she depicts it is identical with that encountered in *La Nouvelle Héloïse* and *Émile*, even to the planting of trees in the English style. Colonel von Sternheim is particularly concerned with improving schools, providing judicious pastoral care, agricultural innovations, aid to the poor, and instilling in young people of noble birth a humane, benevolent attitude toward their subordinates. His wife devotes herself to eighteenth-century philanthropic concepts.[24] Kuno Ridderhoff considers La Roche to be a more enthusiastic devotee of Rousseau in her subsequent and less well-known work, *Rosaliens Briefe*. Ridderhoff believes that Goethe, himself an ardent admirer of Rousseau, must have directed her attention to the Genevan, since the actual elevation of Frau Sophie's style does not begin until the fiftieth and fifty-first letters, hence after she had received a copy of *Werther*. Although she disapproved of the novel's content and ending, she admired the language as well as the feeling for nature and the poetic charm which pervade it. Even if the great similarity between *La Nouvelle Héloïse* and *Werther* had not been evident to her, says Ridderhoff, she could hardly have doubted for a moment that it was Rousseau who had rendered her young friend capable of so great a creation.[25]

Max Kommerell refers to Wilhelm Heinse's calling himself "einen feinen Rousseauisten" and "einen armen Thüringer Jean-Jacques."[26] In his two aesthetic novels, *Ardinghello und die glückseligen Inseln* and *Hildegard von Hohenthal*, Heinse combined a strong emphasis on feeling suggestive of Rousseau with the sensuality of classical antiquity. He even followed Rousseau's steps in Italy. Kommerell also calls attention to striking correspondences between their respective works on music. Heinse echoes Rousseau's preference for Italian compositions and operas in the Italian style and, like Rousseau, he admires Petrarch and Metastasio above all other Italian poets. In the same manner as Saint-Preux and Julie, Kommerell continues, the real Heinse studies "this music of speech and tones" with his likewise unattainable inamorata, Frau von Massow (p. 47).

At numerous points the "meteorically" tragic career of Jakob Michael Reinhold Lenz displays likenesses to Rousseau's inward struggles, and his works reveal the literary inspiration of Rousseau as well. It is generally assumed that Lenz' dramas, such as Der Hofmeister and Die Soldaten, represent the application of Rousseau's criticisms of society, although Heinz Kindermann cautions against overstressing the Genevan's influence.[27] Kommerell states that Lenz, as the actual theorist of "Sturm und Drang" literature, transplants Rousseau's social philosophy to the sphere of aesthetic judgment; for him the two sources of art are observation and imitation of nature (p. 55). In Lenz' novel fragment Moralische Bekehrung eines Poeten, the hero tells how, after reading about the death of Julie in La Nouvelle Héloïse, he has a dream portending the demise of his own beloved, similar to that experienced by Saint-Preux.[28] Just as Rousseau seeks to win the exiled King Stanislaus of Poland over to utopian ideas, says Kommerell, Lenz appeals to Duke Karl August of Weimar with a like objective (p. 56). An atmosphere reminiscent of Rousseau pervades the long poem Die Liebe auf dem Lande, which reminds us that Lenz tried unsuccessfully to woo Friederike Brion after Goethe's departure, but nevertheless lived an idyl at Sesenheim worthy of Goethe or of Jean-Jacques. Lenz remained in Rousseauesque seclusion at Bad Berka while writing his novel Der Waldbruder, which, like La Nouvelle Héloïse, is written in epistolary form. Kommerell, in fact, calls Lenz the one among all the "Kraftgenies" who most resembled Rousseau (p. 57).

The passage in Dichtung und Wahrheit (W.A. I, 28:254) where Goethe depicts his friend Friedrich Maximilian Klinger as an ardent disciple of Rousseau has been quoted with uncommon frequency. Kommerell, who (like Erich Schmidt[29] and F. A. Wyneken[30] before him) has pointed out numerous Rousseau-like features in Klinger's works, considers him the most perfect embodiment of the "Geniepersönlichkeit" of the 1770's. For instance, Kommerell sees the idyllic part of Otto as expressive of its author's delight in childhood, a delight awakened by Émile (p. 50). A reflection of this attitude occurs also in Klinger's zealous opposition to women who are overeducated in literature or philosophy to the point of becoming unnatural (p. 50). In Paris he became so enthusiastic about *Le Devin du village* that in his "Rahmenerzählung" *Der goldene Hahn* he connected it with the magic of Italy, which he visited six years before Goethe's famed pilgrimage (p. 51). Klinger's reasoning in *Giafar* in support of immortality is reminiscent of that employed by the Vicar of Savoy, although Henry Wood argues that in his "Faust novels" Klinger repudiates the firm reliance of Rousseau on "the inner voice" as the means by which God communicates with the heart of Man.[31] The *Geschichte eines Deutschen* not only contains direct praise of *Émile*, but as H. M. Waidson indicates, it also illustrates the conflict of the divided soul through the "parallel careers" of two boys, the passionate, worldly Ferdinand and the reflective, morally sensitive Ernst, who are reared together by a tutor named Hadem on principles derived from Rousseau.[32] Especially discerning is Hans M. Wolff's analysis of the similarities between *Das leidende Weib* and *La Nouvelle Héloïse*. Klinger, we read, is most nearly in agreement with Rousseau in a readiness to excuse, but not to defend, the lovers' wrongdoing. This is an acknowledgment of reason, its laws, and the duties which it imposes. Feeling is what draws the lovers to each other; the separating element is their reason, which makes them realize that in this case the voice of feeling must not be followed.[33]

Johann Georg Hamann, the "Magus des Nordens," early became interested in Rousseau, and, as Rudolf Unger states, he published his principal appraisals of the Genevan's writings (particularly in the *Hirtenbriefe* and *Chimärische Einfälle*) during the period ending in 1763.[34] According to Unger, any influence of Rousseau upon Hamann was by that time assimilated and surmounted, although his interest in Jean-Jacques the man and the writer continued. Hamann found much to criticize in Rousseau's *Discours* and, later, in the *Contrat social* and *Émile*; he was especially displeased with the theological tenets of the Savoyard Vicar (p. 341). Years afterward, the *Confessions*, which he had eagerly awaited, disappointed him (p. 397). *La Nouvelle Héloïse*, however, appealed strongly to Hamann, both aesthetically and because of the moral and religious feeling it expressed; he considered it unsurpassed as the novelized history of a passion (p. 347).

Hamann's praise of Rousseau's novel appears, then, to have contributed to the book's popularity and to its author's fame in Germany, although Unger is less inclined to attribute such a role to the "Magus" than is Hans M. Wolff in his article on Justus Möser and Rousseau, which demonstrates how Möser continued Rousseau's opposition to Rococo artificiality.[35] Wolff reminds us that in eighteenth-century Germany Rousseauism was above all a literary movement in which even the spirit of efforts at political reform became transmuted into literature. He maintains that Möser, whose importance also remained principally literary (aside from his activity in Osnabrück), should not be regarded as an uncritical "Rousseauist." Instead, his relation to Jean-Jacques rests chiefly on the fact that he, like Rousseau, identified the Rococo trend with "Verfall" (p. 117). At the time when Rousseau began to write, the Rococo movement in Germany had not yet moved beyond the Anacreontic stage; thus the "Aufklärer" failed to comprehend the import of his attack (p. 115). It was Möser who recognized the significance of Rousseau's struggle and the necessity for a parallel movement in Germany. In Wolff's opinion, Hamann transmitted an understanding of the form and Möser a comprehension of the content of Rousseau's works. United, the two are decisive for the genesis of Rousseauism in Germany during the 1770's. Möser's literary significance lies less in any contribution of new ideas to the "Sturm und Drang" than in the fact that his little narratives opened the eyes of the young "Genies" to the value and fruitfulness of Rousseau's philosophy (p. 124). In matters of religion, as Ludwig Bäte emphasizes, Möser differed with the views expressed by Rousseau through his Savoyard Vicar.[36]

Hermann Hettner stresses the far-reaching effect of Rousseau upon Friedrich Heinrich Jacobi, who unfailingly speaks of him with profound reverence. In a letter to Wieland he calls Rousseau "that greatest genius who ever wrote in the French language." Jacobi's early novels, *Allwill* and *Woldemar*, exhibit the influence of Rousseau's thought and his later, really philosophical works display a strikingly close relationship to *Émile*, particularly with regard to religious beliefs.[37]

Divergent opinions have been expressed concerning the importance of Rousseau for Schiller. Isaac Benrubi represents an instance of the above-mentioned "Einflusskonstruktion" in describing Rousseau's influence on the young Schiller as very great. He quotes the poet himself as saying that in Rousseau his indignation at the misery of his time found content and form, realization and aim.[38] Benrubi believes that the philosophical writings and later dramas confirm his contention that in the third part of Schiller's life he overcame his former extremes of sentimentalism, influenced by Goethe and antiquity as well as by his horror at the excesses of the French Revolution (p. 456). Nevertheless, he continued to fight with the same energy for an ideal of true liberty and culture. In that sense, says Benrubi, Hettner was right in maintaining that *Wilhelm Tell* represented a deepened and purified return to the poetry of Schiller's youth (p. 456), and to that extent Schiller can be considered a "continuator" of Rousseau (pp. 459–460).

The opposite standpoint is represented by Wolfgang Liepe. Schiller, he says, did not acquire a first-hand acquaintance with Rousseau's ideas until after he had left the Karlsschule; initially he derived a mythical image from Johann Georg Jacobi's "sentimental hymn" to the dead Rousseau.[39] Schiller read Rousseau in the original only after he had written *Die Räuber* and the poem "Rousseau," and then he saw only the "Kulturverneiner" (p. 309). Liepe thinks that, despite Rousseauistic coloring, the trend of ideas which begins with Schiller's "Akademieschriften" and *Die Räuber* leads uninterruptedly to *Don Carlos* and rests primarily on social and political views of Montesquieu and the "Aufklärung" (p. 328). Liepe does concede that the essay *Über das gegenwärtige deutsche Theater* (1782) shows verbal dependence on Rousseau in its utterance of misgivings concerning the aesthetic paralyzing of moral feeling by the stage. In his theater treatise of 1784, in which Liepe finds a lingering echo of the first mythical image of Rousseau, Schiller says: "Der härteste Angriff, den sie (die Schaubühne) erleiden musste, geschah von einer Seite, wo sie nicht zu erwarten war . . ." (p. 328). A more recent article by Roger Ayrault concerning the genesis of *Die Räuber* suggests that the true position of the young Schiller regarding Rousseau lies somewhere between the respective viewpoints of Benrubi and Liepe.[40] Recalling how Schiller later reduced his poem "Rousseau" from fourteen stanzas to two, Ayrault states that Schiller derives his understanding of how Rousseau sought to make men out of Christians from the last chapter of the *Contrat social* (p. 98). He attributes Karl Moor's final desire to give his life as testimony of his reconciliation with the "offended laws" entirely to the inspiration which Schiller drew from Rousseau (pp. 99–100).

In the judgment of E. L. Stahl, Schiller's aim of awakening "a new sense of dynamic values," which he expresses in the prefaces to *Die Räuber* and *Fiesco*, represents an ideal originating unmistakably from Rousseau. Still, his protest in *Die Räuber* is merely directed against modern "enfeeblement of life" and does not take into consideration the totality of Rousseau's thought. Instead of being concerned with problems of a specifically political nature, Schiller confined himself to depicting "comparatively rudimentary and social conflicts."[41]

Joachim Ulrich sees not only the influence of Goethe, but also the spirit of Rousseau in Schiller's characterization of the "Zeitgeist" in the fifth letter *Über die ästhetische Erziehung des Menschen*.[42] William F. Mainland asserts that the mature Schiller by no means renounced Rousseau and regards it as unfortunate that mention of Rousseau's importance for Schiller is generally confined to the early plays. Mainland finds this notion especially misleading because it implies that Rousseau followed a uniformity of thought such as he in reality never observed.[43] Mainland remarks that Schiller's partially adverse criticism of Rousseau in his essay *Über naive und sentimentalische Dichtung* (where he states, among other things, that Rousseau's writings have an undeniably poetic content, since they treat an ideal, but that Rousseau does not know how to make use of that content in a poetic manner) has sometimes been interpreted as confirmation of the assumption that the mature Schiller "abandoned" Rousseau's doctrines. Therefore one did not bother to inquire whether Schiller later occupied himself with Rousseauistic ideas such as the "elaborate analysis of liberty." But in *Wilhelm Tell*, according to Mainland, Schiller comes to terms with Rousseau's concept of the "general will"; he accomplishes his demonstration of it through "diversity of dramatic action," in contrast to Rousseau's concentrated argumentation in the *Contrat social* (p. 116).

Chronologically, the significance of Rousseau for the younger German writers who came into prominence around 1800 lies beyond the scope of this introductory survey; even Schiller, with whom it ends, apparently acquired his full awareness of Rousseau after the latter's death. Brief mention should yet be made, however, of some studies dealing with several of the most outstanding figures. The momentous role played by Rousseau in Jean Paul's development as a novelist and thinker, especially along educational lines, was set forth in considerable detail a few decades ago by Max Kommerell (whose work has already been cited above, in connection with various "Sturm und Drang" authors).[44] Oskar Ritter von Xylander pursued a similar aim in his 1937 study of Heinrich von Kleist and Rousseau.[45] The impact of Rousseau upon Friedrich Hölderlin's lyric poetry and his great unfinished "Briefroman" *Hyperion* has often been noted,[46] while the ill-starred love of Hölderlin and Susette Gontard seems itself a reincarnation of the luckless passion that befalls Saint-Preux and his Julie. More recently, Bernard Böschenstein has treated the "transfiguration" of Rousseau in German literature around the beginning of the nineteenth century. In addition to his own exposition of Hölderlin's indebtedness to Rousseau, he reconsiders the relationship of Rousseau to Jean Paul and Kleist, with special reference to the above-mentioned monographs of Kommerell and Xylander.[47] Closely related to Böschenstein's essay is Jacques Voisine's penetrating article concerning the impact of *La Nouvelle Héloïse* on the generation of Werther.[48] The "Sturm und Drang" writers, he says, largely missed the novel's deeper meaning concerning the education of Man by his own efforts and by life. Rather, it became the task of the succeeding generation to interpret adequately Rousseau's concept of the soul's development. He cites Goethe's *Wilhelm Meister*, Jean Paul's *Titan*, and Novalis' *Heinrich von Ofterdingen* as a few examples (p. 133). Voisine's inclusion of Goethe's novel is indicative of the increasing attention that recent scholarship has paid to the question of what Rousseau meant to Goethe; an answer to this question is attempted in the subsequent chapters of this book.

2. Goethe's Perspective of French Literature

Next to his mother tongue, French was the language Goethe knew best. In his eighth year he began taking lessons from a certain Mademoiselle Gachet. Shortly after his tenth birthday the French occupation of Frankfurt occasioned the quartering of the "Lieutenant du Roi" Thoranc in the Goethe household for some two and a half years. The story of how the boy Wolfgang became fluent in the spoken idiom through numerous contacts with Frenchmen, especially with young people, and through attending the French theater is fascinatingly told in *Dichtung und Wahrheit* (W.A. I, 26:141–152). Formal instruction under the supervision of a language master named Pfeil followed, after which Goethe's father sent him successively to Leipzig, called in *Faust* "ein klein Paris," and to bilingual Strassburg. Goethe's later experience in court circles brought a renewal of conversing and writing in French. No less a person than Madame de Staël admired his ability to speak it, when she came to Weimar in 1804.[49] One also recalls Goethe's conversations with Napoleon in 1808 and his pleasant association with Louis Bonaparte, Comte de Saint-Leu (sometime King of Holland), long afterward at Karlsbad. Especially in his later years he received visits from numerous prominent Frenchmen (e.g.,

Cousin, Ampère, and David d'Angers) and corresponded extensively with others. His ever greater interest in the language caused him to begin studying Old French at sixty-eight.

Goethe's overall acquaintance with the literature of France likewise extended well beyond his knowledge of other foreign belles-lettres—even that of English authors. At Strassburg he read with admiration the leading sixteenth-century writers, Montaigne, Amyot, Marot, du Bartas, and Rabelais (W.A. I, 28:52). Apparently he did not care for Ronsard and the other poets of the "Pléiade."[50] In his boyhood in Frankfurt he had frequently seen masterpieces of the great classical dramatists performed by French players. Throughout his life Goethe retained his esteem not merely for Racine and Molière (as some have claimed), but also for Corneille.[51] He likewise witnessed productions by that same theatrical troupe of many eighteenth-century plays, including pieces by Destouches, Diderot, Favart, Lemierre, Marivaux, Nivelle de la Chaussée, Palissot, Rousseau, and Voltaire. Goethe's wide reading in his later years ranged from Marie de France and Joinville to Victor Hugo, Dumas père, and Mérimée; indeed, the number of early nineteenth-century French authors in his ken is remarkable. During his old age he also read an amazing wealth of critical, historical, philosophical, and scientific works in French. He maintained a lively interest in Le Globe for years, until that journal became too strongly political for his taste. But it was French literature of the eighteenth century—the age of which he himself was a product—that Goethe knew best, from the great masters, Voltaire, Diderot, and Rousseau and such lesser figures as Prévost and Beaumarchais, to a host of minor ones, too numerous to mention here. Among the more prominent names not already cited are: Crébillon, Fréron, Le Sage, Mercier, Piron, Restif de la Bretonne,[52] and Bernardin de Saint-Pierre. When Heinrich Leopold Wagner translated Mercier's treatise Du Théâtre, ou nouvel essai sur l'art dramatique (1773) as Neuer Versuch über die Schauspielkunst (1776), Goethe furnished an appendix entitled "Aus Goethes Brieftasche" (W.A. I, 37:311–315). D'Alembert and Buffon interested him in the realm of scientific inquiry and in the philosophical and political sphere he admired Montesquieu, Mirabeau, and the Duc de Saint-Simon. The significance of Prévost (so greatly admired by Rousseau) for the stylized quality of Dichtung und Wahrheit is discussed in the fourth chapter. It is well known that the Mémoires of Beaumarchais served as the inspiration and source of Goethe's drama Clavigo, while the published recollections of Stéphanie, Princess de Bourbon-Conti, prompted him to write *Die natürliche Tochter*.

The three preeminent literary figures of what George R. Havens calls the "Age of Ideas" in prerevolutionary France perennially fascinated and inspired Goethe. In her penetrating study of Goethe and Voltaire, Geneviève Bianquis notes a multiplicity of analogies between the two; despite Goethe's criticism in his autobiography, she finds that no man of letters was "more present to Goethe, at all times, than Voltaire." She asserts, furthermore, that Faust in old age, with his ultimately philanthropic drive, mirrors his author's veneration for the Patriarch of Ferney.[53] Goethe told Eckermann (January 3, 1830) that his account in *Dichtung und Wahrheit* failed to indicate adequately his momentous obligation of earlier years to "Voltaire und seine grossen Zeitgenossen." [54] By these "great contemporaries" he must have meant primarily Diderot and Rousseau. His commendations of Diderot (last in 1831) and his translations from the latter's works sufficiently attest his esteem. Goethe has been styled "the first great discoverer of Diderot" in Europe of the nineteenth century by Norman L. Torrey,[55] who suspects an influence on the German poet too fundamental for ordinary analysis.[56] Of all contemporaries of Diderot, says Dieckmann, Goethe showed the most thorough, unprejudiced understanding of Diderot's greatness; he alone accepted him in his entirety.[57] It was also in the year 1831 that Goethe characterized Rousseau as one "revered in the highest sense" (W.A. II, 6:110).

Goethe avoided all partisanship regarding the famous "querelle des philosophes" of 1757,[58] about which debate is "extremely delicate" even in our day, according to Torrey.[59] George Brereton observes that it is two hundred years too late to take sides in that controversy.[60] We might assume that Goethe felt no interest in the quarrel, were it not for his comments on some of the minor participants.

Loiseau thinks that Goethe probably heard of Voltaire's being arrested when the latter stopped in Frankfurt in 1753.[61] But since Goethe was only four at the time, his mention of that incident in the outline of *Dichtung und Wahrheit* (W.A. I, 26:349) is more likely due to reflection long afterward. In any case, statements in his letters and diaries show that from Leipzig on Goethe was occupied with Voltaire's works; the reviews contributed to the *Frankfurter gelehrten Anzeigen* in the years 1772 and 1773 (W.A. I, 37:197) indicate acquaintance with Voltaire's correspondence. *Saul*, which Goethe read in his boyhood, so aroused his "childishly fanatic zeal" (according to his recollection in *Dichtung und Wahrheit*) that he would no doubt have "throttled" the author, had he been able to lay hands on him (W.A. I, 28:103). As early as 1767 he translated the madrigal which Voltaire had addressed to Princess Ulrike of Prussia (W.A. I, 37:47). Goethe mentions the pamphlet *Sur la tolérance* favorably in his autobiography (W.A. I, 28:140). He was conversant with a large part of the writings themselves, as well as with a number of works on Voltaire (W.A. I, 38:85). Of the plays, Goethe translated and adapted *Mahomet* for the Weimar stage in 1799 and *Tancrède* in 1800. *Zaïre*, which he had seen while a student at Leipzig, was produced by Goethe at Weimar in 1810.

In *Dichtung und Wahrheit* (W.A. I, 28:58–62) Goethe discusses the growing antipathy toward French literature on the part of himself and his friends at Strassburg, and he mentions the fact that many French tragedies had disappeared from the theater. He adds that Voltaire could not miss the opportunity to edit Corneille's works in order to show how imperfect his predecessor had been, although Voltaire himself was not generally considered his equal. Hereupon Goethe declares: "And this same Voltaire, the wonder of his age, was now himself aged like the literature which he had animated and dominated throughout nearly a century" (W.A. I, 28:58). Goethe adds that the increasing influence of society upon French writers caused literature to become the plaything of the aristocracy (W.A. I, 28:59).

Elsewhere he lists many qualities demanded of a great writer—especially by the French. He finds that Voltaire meets all of them, except perhaps "essential depth" and "finish in execution." Goethe states that "Voltaire's wish and effort had been directed from his youth up toward an active, social life, toward politics, toward gain on a large scale, toward relationship with the lords of the earth." Voltaire's prominence was so great, Goethe continues, that he not only captured the minds of his countrymen, but received homage from rulers and even popes (W.A. I, 28:61–62).

Goethe does not refer to any further altercations between Voltaire and Rousseau during the quarrel that defined the two main currents of eighteenth-century thought—the Encyclopedic, basically scientific and social, and the Rousseauistic, which stressed Romantic individualism.[62] When Goethe, in his autobiography, opposes Rousseau and Diderot to Voltaire, he is speaking of literary currents, not personal prejudices.[63] In his notes to *Le Neveu de Rameau*, Goethe translates Rousseau's characterization of Rameau as the best available (W.A. I, 45:201–206). At the same time, he describes Voltaire (in his most detailed appraisal of the latter) as one of those in whom nations are fortunate enough to see the sum total of their merits expressed: just as Louis XIV is the French king, so Voltaire appears as the greatest and most characteristic writer of France (W.A. I, 45:215–216).

Goethe observes the same neutrality concerning the break in the fifteen-year friendship between Rousseau and Diderot. He repeatedly names them together impartially, as when he lists the *Devin du village* and the *Père de famille* among the French plays he saw during the occupation of Frankfurt (W.A. I, 26:148). A frequently cited passage in *Dichtung und Wahrheit* describes the two authors as engaged "in quiet preparation for the coming upheavals" (W.A. I, 28:65), while a variant credits them both with furthering Goethe's intellectual development (W.A. I, 28:360). Diderot's appeal to Goethe and his associates, as stated in *Dichtung und Wahrheit*, was comparable to that of Rousseau. Though regretting the "rabble" of Diderot's "children of nature" which has "thriven all too well on the German Parnassus," Goethe admits that "Diderot was closely enough related to us, since in everything for which the French find fault with him he is a true German" (W.A. I, 28: 64–65). For the *Frankfurter gelehrten Anzeigen* (1772) Goethe wrote a brief announcement of Diderot's stories, which had just appeared in Zurich in German translation as *Moralische Erzählungen*—remarkably enough, as Goethe indicated, in the same volume with Gessner's *Idyllen* (W.A. I, 37:284). The next reference to Diderot is a diary notation for April 3, 1780, telling of his reading *Jacques le fataliste* straight through in five and a half hours, enjoying, "like Bel of Babel," the devouring of "such a huge meal." He elaborates this in a letter to Merck on April 7. The mention of a "manuscript sneaking around" refers to the then current installments of the *Correspondance littéraire*. On August 15, 1780, Goethe asked Charlotte von Stein to pass *Jacques le fataliste* on to Herder. In 1781 *La Religieuse* was circulated in the same manner.

Goethe sent Diderot's *Bijoux indiscrets* to Schiller on July 25, 1794, and in his letter of December 15, 1795, he suggested *La Religieuse* would be a good publication for *Die Horen*. Most of Goethe's references to Diderot, however, concern the works which he translated: *Essais sur la peinture* and *Le Neveu de Rameau*. After sending Schiller a copy of the

Essais, Goethe wrote: "... It is a splendid book and it appeals almost more to the poet than to the plastic artist, although it often inspires the latter with a mighty torch" (December 17, 1796). He adds that it would be worth one's trouble to translate it with a commentary.

Goethe published his translation of the first two essays in *Die Propyläen* in 1799, under the title *Diderots Versuch über die Malerei, mit Anmerkungen begleitet* (W.A. I., 45:322). In his "Confession of the Translator" Goethe emphasizes his independence of judgment with respect to Diderot as follows: "I converse with him anew; I criticize him when he departs from the way which I consider the right one; I rejoice when we again coincide; I grow angry at his paradoxes; I take pleasure in the vivacity of his views as a whole; his eloquent presentation charms me; the quarrel becomes vehement, and I of course have the last word, since I am dealing with a deceased opponent" (W.A. I., 45:349). Goethe essentially disagrees with Diderot in the first essay (W.A. I., 45:282), but acknowledges that he is more in accord with Diderot in the second.

Goethe's translation (from a manuscript hitherto unpublished) of Diderot's *Neveu de Rameau*, undertaken at the instance of Schiller in 1804, stimulated many of Goethe's innumerable references to Diderot. In the *Tag-und Jahreshefte* (W.A. I, 35:181) and in *Über Kunst und Altertum* (W.A. I, 41²:14–15, 85–88) Goethe relates the story of the original manuscript's wanderings, its retranslation into French, and the 1823 printing of the author's own text (obtained from his daughter, Madame de Vandeul, by the Paris publisher Brière).

Goethe's admiration for Diderot remained constant. On April 24, 1830, he told Chancellor von Müller that the French would never have another eighteenth century, no matter what they might do, and asked: "Where do they have anything to show that could be compared with Diderot?" To Zelter he wrote (March 9, 1831): "Diderot is Diderot, a unique individual; whoever carps at him and his affairs is a philistine, and there are legions of them."

Goethe's acquaintance with the circumstances of the "philosophers' quarrel" and its aftermath stemmed from numerous and varied sources. Among them are the *Confessions*; Rousseau's letters (as contained in the Geneva edition); the *Correspondance littéraire, philosophique et critique* (partly in its originally circulated manuscript form); the *Mémoires* of Marmontel; those of the Abbé Morellet; Palissot's *Philosophes*; and Madame de Vandeul's *Mémoires pour servir à l'histoire de la vie et des ouvrages de M. de Diderot.* It may seem surprising to those who have scanned even a substantial part of the extensive research on the roles of certain persons concerned in the controversy (e.g., Madame d'Épinay, Madame d'Houdetot, Saint-Lambert, and Thérèse Levasseur) that Goethe left no mention of them whatever. He refers to Holbach (likewise a German) only in connection with the latter's *Système de la nature*, which he judged inadequately, as I have endeavored to show in another study.[64] While Goethe could not be expected to approve of Holbach's atheism, a closer examination of his ideas and principles in general would have revealed to him that the two shared a number of interests.

Especially noteworthy as a source of information concerning this controversy was Goethe's personal association with the German-born Friedrich Melchior Grimm, initially a pupil of Gottsched, whom the young student Goethe had visited in Leipzig.

A diary entry records Goethe's disappointment over his first encounter with Grimm (near Gotha, October 8, 1777): "I felt so fervently . . . that I had nothing to say to the man who is going from St. Petersburg to Paris." Four years later, however, Goethe looks forward to a second meeting. On October 1, 1781 he writes Charlotte von Stein concerning an invitation from the Prince of Gotha: ". . . Grimm is over there, and I shall probably go the day after tomorrow. Acquaintance with this 'ami des philosophes et des grands' will certainly be epoch-making in my case . . . . Through his eyes, like a Swedenborgian spirit, I intend to see a broader horizon." On October 9 Goethe informs Charlotte: "I am finally learning to make use of the world. Acquaintance with the *friend* has brought me the advantages I foresaw; not one was lacking, and it is very valuable to me to know him, too, and to judge him rightly and properly."

What Grimm may have told him about the dispute is nowhere divulged, but Goethe apparently maintained an open-minded attitude. About eight months later he wrote the above-mentioned letter to Karl August praising both Rousseau and Diderot, and in another letter to Frau von Stein he enthusiastically acclaimed Rousseau's *Confessions* (First Part), then just off the press. The French Revolution brought Goethe and Grimm together again in the year 1792. In the *Campagne in Frankreich* Goethe tells of finding Grimm among the emigrés thronging into Düsseldorf (W.A. I, 33:202). The two talked over old times, but we cannot know whether the "quarrel" was among the subjects discussed. (Certainly, the events of the moment offered sufficient conversational material!) The diary entry of August 29, 1801 states that he visited Grimm at Gotha. The *Tag- und Jahreshefte* for that year (written in 1824) relate that among the regular dinner-guests of the Prince was Goethe's old acquaintance, whom he characterizes as "a man well-versed in the social graces and an agreeable fellow guest," who, "nevertheless, could not always hide an inward bitterness at the loss he had suffered."

Except for a greeting in a letter to Silvius von Franckenberg (November 4, 1801), there is no further word of communication with Grimm, whose death in 1807 Goethe nowhere mentions. In *Dichtung und Wahrheit* he states that Grimm enjoyed the reputation among the French of being one of the few foreigners who had completely mastered their language (W.A. I, 28:53), and that he had often been helpful to Germans in Paris (W.A. I, 29:168).

While preparing the literary criticisms incorporated in his autobiography, Goethe reread the *Correspondance littéraire*, as is shown by near-daily diary entries during the period of October 10–21, 1812. He wrote to Knebel on October 17: "... It will always remain a most important work, a rich document of a unique era. Everyone can acquire something therefrom, and yet it is not unjust to say: one finds out a great deal through it, but one learns nothing from it." Goethe added that he was thinking of compiling a "dictionnaire détractif" of the numerous terms of censure in that journal. (Some of these were directed at Rousseau.) When he later published such a series, the Brussels paper *Vrai libéral* (February 4, 1819) charged him with having overstressed the negative element. In reply, Goethe disclosed, as "the secret behind the communication of the word-lists," that he, through favor of high-ranking persons, had regularly read the *Correspondance* as it appeared in manuscript. He viewed the circulation of Diderot's most famous works as the most important function of the journal (W.A. I, 41^1:145–146). Not wishing that his allegation regarding detractory terms should remain attached to Grimm alone, Goethe promised a general discussion of the matter (W.A. I, 41^1:145–146), which he evidently never wrote. The only subsequent allusions to Grimm and the *Correspondance littéraire* are incidental to reiterated praise of Diderot in 1830 and 1831, respectively, to von Müller and Zelter emphasizing the uniqueness of that writer and the exceeding popularity of his prose tales when they were first circulated.

Goethe's personal contact with Grimm appears, then, to have been congenial, though somewhat casual. While he esteemed Grimm within limits, he manifestly did not regard him as the distinguished critic he was destined to become in the opinion of Sainte-Beuve and Edmond Scherer.[65] As René Wellek reminds us, even the importance of Grimm as an intermediary between Germany and France has been exaggerated.[66] Too often, also, the fact has been overlooked that Rousseau's works were much more favorably reviewed in the *Correspondance littéraire* by Meister than by Grimm.[67] Perhaps Goethe was aware of that circumstance. In any event, however much he may have learned from conversations with Grimm about the leading "philosophes," there is no evidence that he veered from his neutral attitude toward their dissensions.

While a student at Leipzig, Goethe quoted stanzas from Marmontel's *Charmes de l'étude, Epître aux Poètes* in a French letter to his sister Cornelia (May 11, 1767). In 1772 he wrote a rather negative evaluation of a German version of *Bélisaire* for the *Frankfurter gelehrten Anzeigen* (W.A. I, 38:341). With manifest approval Goethe translated Madame de Staël's *Essai sur les fictions* (in 1796), in which she hails the *Contes moraux* as outstanding (W.A. I, 40:234). *Dichtung und Wahrheit* contains appreciative comments on the operetta *Zemire et Azor*, set to music by Grétry (W.A. I, 29:43), as does *Über Kunst und Altertum* (W.A. I, 41¹:114). Apparently, Goethe took little notice of Marmontel the literary critic, who had vigorously rejected *La Nouvelle Héloïse* ("ce mélange de vice et de vertu").[68] He was chiefly interested in the *Mémoires d'un père pour servir à l'instruction de ses enfants*, which was published just before he began his annotation of *Rameaus Neffe* in 1805. Goethe wrote Schiller (January 14): "I take pleasure in sending the Life of Marmontel; it will entertain you very agreeably for a few days . . . ." He then asked Schiller to record the pages referring to the financier Bouret for the notes, in which Goethe, apropos of a reference to Madame de Tencin, praises Marmontel's excellent contribution through the *Mémoires* to a knowledge of mankind, especially the French (W.A. I, 45:214). In a letter to Johannes von Müller (January 25) Goethe said that Müller surely must have enjoyed reading the book. He also promised Heinrich Carl Eichstädt (January 26) a review of it for the *Jenaische Allgemeine Literaturzeitung*. That same month Henriette von Knebel sent her brother an enthusiastic letter about the *Mémoires*, saying in part: "Marmontel, who was by nature finely jovial and sociable, sees Rousseau in quite an unfortunate light. Goethe . . . spoke quite cleverly about it. He said it was true that the friends who were in close association with Rousseau often fared badly, but that Marmontel was too small a person not to take a one-sided view."[69] Here we encounter not only Goethe's sharpest criticism of Marmontel, but also a second instance of his defending Rousseau within a year's time (the other occasion was in a conversation with Mme de Staël in 1804). He esteemed Marmontel as a writer of reminiscences, but disapproved of his attitude toward Jean-Jacques.

With few exceptions, Goethe's comments on Palissot relate to Rousseau or Diderot. His discussion of *Les Philosophes* (which he had seen performed as a boy in Frankfurt) is his longest pronouncement concerning Palissot, whose *Cercle* and *Petites lettres contre les grands philosophes* he also read (W.A. I, 41²:79). For his notes to *Rameaus Neffe* Goethe consulted the *Mémoires pour servir à l'histoire de notre littérature*. Regarding the translation of Diderot's dialogue he told Schiller (December 21, 1804) that its explosive character and the fact that Palissot was still living made caution necessary.[70]

In *Les Philosophes*, says Goethe, Palissot "sinned against Rousseau" and likewise mocked Diderot (W.A. I., 45:187). Goethe concludes his sharp criticism of Palissot (too long for complete quotation)[71] with the following comments:

. . . No one belongs as a human being to the world. Let each one make these fine demands on himself; whatever is wanting, let him set it right with God and his heart and convince his neighbors of what is good and true in him. On the other hand, he belongs to the world in the capacity for which nature particularly formed him, as a man of power, activity, intellect, and talent. All excellence is efficacious for an infinite circle, and the world should gratefully accept that, not imagining that it is in any other sense authorized to sit in judgment.

(W.A. I., 41²:77–78)

The passage ends with the notation: "Written and printed in the year 1805. Again and once more approved, 1823" (W.A. I, 41²:80). Hence after eighteen years Goethe repeats his criticism of Palissot, "one of the mediocre natures," who dared subject Rousseau and Diderot to ridicule. It is true that Goethe's last comments on Palissot in the notes to *Rameaus Neffe* are conciliatory; for example: "We are far from considering Palissot the villain he is represented as being in the dialogue." There is even the suggestion that Palissot, having bravely weathered the Revolution, might jest in his critical writings about his adversaries' caricature of him (W.A. I, 45:213). Yet Goethe never withdrew his censure of Palissot.

These quotations demonstrate that Goethe, who in his last years still rendered the highest praise to Voltaire, Diderot, and Rousseau, preserved consistent neutrality concerning their disagreements. Although we can only conjecture what Goethe may have heard Grimm say concerning the quarrel, he unequivocally took Rousseau's part against the strictures of a lesser figure, Marmontel. Finally, he directed one of the most forceful reprimands in all his literary criticism at Palissot for belittling Diderot as well as Rousseau, two geniuses equally worthy of esteem. Far from taking sides in their disputes, he ultimately revered the great "philosophes" as a complementary trio, each of whom Goethe described as "extraordinary." Although the French authors of smaller stature with whose works Goethe was acquainted form a veritable catalog, the three literary giants remained for him the focal point of belles-lettres in eighteenth-century France.

Goethe fully realized and readily acknowledged his indebtedness to French literature and culture. In turn, he had gradually attained an eminence in France beyond that of being simply "the author of *Werther*," as is proved by Théophile Gautier's plaudit accorded him a generation after his death: "His sovereign fancy journeyed through all times and all lands. Successively, he was Homer, Hesiod, Hafiz, . . . Shakespeare, Calderón, Beaumarchais, *Jean-Jacques Rousseau* (my italics), and even Cuvier, and yet at the same time he always remained Goethe." [72]

II

Jean-Jacques
according to Goethe

Goethe made numerous statements concerning Rousseau during his lifetime. Despite the obvious significance of these comments for the proper understanding of his relationship to Rousseau, they have not been treated in their entirety: that task is attempted here. This chapter includes all references to Rousseau in Goethe's works, letters, diaries, and conversations, some in shortened form. The material appears in chronological order, except for quotations from *Dichtung und Wahrheit* referring to earlier periods of his life.

Most of Goethe's allusions to his first awareness of Rousseau occur in the distant retrospect of his autobiography, written more than half a century afterward. The earliest instance is the controversy which arose after the Lisbon earthquake of November 1, 1755, when "the God-fearing were not wanting in reflections, nor the philosophers in grounds for consolation, nor the clergy in warning sermons." It was all the more difficult, he continues, for the young mind to resist those impressions, "since the wise and Scripture-learned themselves could not agree as to how one should regard such a phenomenon" (W.A. I, 26:42–43).

Any doubt as to the identity of the "philosophers" is dispelled by the variant, "Voltaire and Rousseau concerning this natural occurrence" (W.A. I, 26:349). Goethe's comment, however, seems to reflect his later reading of Rousseau's *Lettre sur la Providence*,[1] sent on August 18, 1756 to Voltaire as a refutation of the latter's *Poème sur le Désastre de Lisbonne*.[2] For even the first, unauthorized publication of the letter by Formey in Berlin did not occur until 1759, when it attracted only slight attention; it finally appeared in authorized editions of Rousseau's works in 1763-64.[3] Voltaire's poem itself caused widespread debate throughout Christendom as soon as it was published and circulated. Whatever Goethe's own general recollection of the reaction in the Frankfurt of his boyhood may have been, discussions of the earthquake apparently made a deep impression on him. In a letter to Goethe dated November 24, 1810, Bettina Brentano records his mother's recollection of his comment after hearing a sermon defending God's wisdom toward the victims: "Perhaps all may be even much simpler than the preacher thinks. God must well know that no harm can come to the immortal soul through an ill fate."[4] This remark might well have met with Rousseau's approval.

Chronologically, Goethe's earliest references to Rousseau are contained in his Leipzig correspondence of 1767, and both concern his amorous associations in that city. In his epistle of October 12–14 to his sister Cornelia he tells of playing the tutor to his girl friends (a Rousseau-like pose) and then adds that he has almost entirely given up Konstanze Breitkopf, who has read too much. Cornelia should not laugh, either, at these seemingly paradoxical theses, for they are "the noblest verities," founded upon the most venerable truth, "Plus que les mœurs se raffinent, plus les hommes se dépravent." His letter of November 10 to Behrisch describes his state of alternating despair and hope in his love for Käthchen Schönkopf. In obvious allusion to *La Nouvelle Héloïse*, Goethe appends the words: "So will it be tomorrow, the day after tomorrow, and evermore." Then, after his return to Frankfurt, Goethe wrote to Adam Friedrich Oeser (February 14, 1769): ". . . *Émile* will remain *Émile*, even if the pastor at Berlin were to go mad, and no abbé will detract from Origenes."[5]

Goethe's Strassburg dissertation for the licentiate (1771) is reminiscent of the *Contrat social*, since in that treatise he examines the relationship of religion and the State and concludes that the legislator has not only the right, but the duty to impose a form of worship. Lack of mention of Rousseau makes the question of direct influence conjectural. At that time, however, Goethe read Rousseau's *Lettre à Christophe de Beaumont, archevêque de Paris* and copied four extracts from it into his *Ephemerides*, including: "Posterity will see even in his errors only the wrongs of a friend of virtue" (W.A. I, 37:98). Thus one can at least say that Goethe was concerned with Rousseau's ideas on religion and morality while writing his dissertation.

There is a similarity of thought between Goethe's *Brief des Pastors zu *** an den neuen Pastor zu ****, "from the French" (1773), pleading for religious toleration and freedom from dogmatism and rationalism, and Rousseau's *Profession de foi du vicaire savoyard*. Attention has been called repeatedly to the parallelism of two passages, the first by Rousseau, the second by Goethe who alludes directly to the French work:

> We have set aside all human authority, and without it I could not see how one man can convince another thereof by preaching an unreasonable doctrine to him. . . . O hardened heart, grace has no meaning to you. . . . That is not my fault; for, according to you, one must already have received grace in order to know how to ask for it.
>
> (O.C., 9:83; 86)

> I do not know whether one can prove the divinity of the Bible to anyone who does not feel it. . . . For when you have finished, and someone answers you like the Vicar of Savoy: "It is not my fault that I feel no grace in my heart," then you are vanquished and can answer nothing, unless you want to engage in prolixities about the freedom of the will and predestination.
>
> (W.A. I, 37:160–161)[6]

On leaving Wetzlar (September 11, 1772), Goethe sent Charlotte Buff the following message: ". . . For you know all; you know how happy I was during these days. And I am going—to the dearest, best people, but why away from you? That is the case, and it is my fate that to today I cannot add tomorrow and the day after tomorrow—a thing which indeed I often did in jest." Here, as five years previously when in love with Käthchen, Goethe identifies his situation with that of Saint-Preux. Goethe's next mention of Rousseau stems from that same year of 1772. In a review of B. Münter's *Bekehrungsgeschichte des vormaligen Grafen J. F. von Struensee* for the *Frankfurter Gelehrten Anzeigen*, he numbers Rousseau among those philosophers whom he considers preferable to Pascal. "We simply must say it," he avers, "because we have long had it at heart: Voltaire, Hume, Lamettrie, Helvétius, Rousseau, and their entire school have not done nearly as much harm to morality as the stern, sickly Pascal and his school" (W.A. I, 37:256).

In a letter of January 19, 1773 to Sophie von La Roche, Goethe makes his first extant reference to *Pygmalion*, which he mentions more often than any other writing of Rousseau. Characterizing that play as "an excellent work," containing "so much truth and goodness of feeling" as well as "so much frankness in expression," he asks to keep Sophie's copy a while longer, since it "must be read aloud to all whose sensibility I esteem."

Werther was already in circulation when Goethe again referred to Rousseau, also in a letter to Frau von La Roche (December 23, 1774). A copy of that novel, he told her, had just come back to him with these words written on the fly-leaf: "Tais-toi, Jean-Jacques, ils ne te comprendront point!"—"That," Goethe added, "had the strangest effect on me, because this passage in Émile was always very remarkable to me."

Goethe revisited Leipzig in 1776. His letter of March 25 to Charlotte von Stein tells of his call on the Schönkopf couple and their daughter Käthchen, long since the wife of Dr. Kanne (to whom she had become engaged even before the student Goethe returned to Frankfurt). Old friendship was renewed, he relates, then he quotes Rousseau: " 'Mais—ce n'est plus Julie!' " Here again he repeats his identification with the hero of La Nouvelle Héloïse through a quotation fully as familiar to Charlotte as to Goethe.

In view of this relatively small total of recorded utterances concerning Rousseau from Goethe's "Sturm und Drang" years, the period of his early enthusiasm for the Genevan, one is surprised at Loiseau's statement that Rousseau's name recurs less often thereafter in Goethe's writing, and "in less exalted terms."[7] Actually, there are more frequent references to Rousseau by Goethe in the succeeding decade. Perhaps Loiseau attaches undue importance in that regard to the Triumph der Empfindsamkeit (1777), where Andrason insists, until halted by a vision, that both La Nouvelle Héloïse and Werther be consigned to the flames (W.A. I, 16: 56–57). Aron remarks that if Satyros is a renunciation of Rousseau (as Loiseau believes), then the Triumph der Empfindsamkeit could be styled with equal justice "a renunciation of Goethe."[8]

Rousseau died July 2, 1778, at Ermenonville. However Goethe may have expressed himself orally, there is no written record of his mentioning Rousseau's death. Goethe's homage took the form of a pilgrimage to the Island of St. Pierre the following year, during his second Swiss journey, in company with Duke Karl August. On October 9, 1779, he wrote from Lauterbrunnen to Charlotte von Stein about their visit: "Early on the fifth we sailed on the cantonal boat from Biel to the island in the Lake of

Bienne to which Rousseau went when he was driven away from Geneva. The island belongs to the Hospital at Bern, and the steward and his wife, who run the inn themselves, are still the very same ones who waited on Rousseau." Goethe wrote his name on the wall of the room that the famous man had occupied. "It was Werther's visit to Julie," says Edmond Jaloux.[9]

Writing to Merck on October 17, Goethe mentions "a half-stormy, fine day on the lake, on the way to Rousseau's island, just then in the midst of the vintage." He adds that he "ate enough grapes for three years." Even this passing remark perhaps indicates a realization that the spot belongs to the memory of Rousseau, for Goethe may have recalled Rousseau's description of the vintage-time at Clarens (O.C., 9:316–324). His real tribute to Jean-Jacques, however, finds expression in another letter (October 23) to Charlotte: "We went to Vevey; I could not keep back the tears when I looked across to Meillerie and the Dent de Jamant and had before me all the scenes that the eternally lonely Rousseau peopled with animated beings." This excursion appears climactic in a series of days each of which was so fine that it seemed "more beautiful than the preceding one."

Virtually without exception Goethe's statements concerning Rousseau in his correspondence during the years immediately following reveal his continued interest and esteem. Indeed, the tone is even more complimentary to Rousseau than during his so-called enthusiasm of the 1770's. Thus on August 4, 1780, he sends Frau von Stein an enclosure with a note saying, "Here is a letter by Rousseau." A year later (August 11, 1781) he writes his mother, "The *Devin du village* arrived yesterday. . . ." and two days afterward he addresses himself to the musician Kayser concerning Rousseau's *Consolations des misères de ma vie ou Recueil d'airs, romances et duos*: "I suspect that you are not yet acquainted with the collection of Rousseau's songs that came out after his death; therefore I am writing by today's mail to the bookseller Bauer at Strassburg to send it to you at once, and I rejoice in advance at your delight in this inestimable legacy. Mamsell Schröter, who has played and sung most of them, insists that there are defects of harmony in them." Goethe further says that he thinks the latter may be errors in printing and that he wishes to have Kayser's expert judgment in this matter, in order to ensure an accurate transcription. In a postscript he asks Kayser to "thank Frau Schulthess for the *Devin*."

Because of Goethe's simultaneous preoccupation with that opera and with Rousseau's collection of melodies, Wilhelm Bode places Rousseau beside Gluck in importance for Goethe's musical interests at that time.[10] Corona Schröter's singing of the songs is also confirmed by diary entries for August 12 and 15; under the latter date he comments, "I was delighted." On August 26 he sends Charlotte von Stein the brief message, "The songs are being transcribed." About the beginning of September he invites her to an informal dinner, on which occasion she can hear them sung by Corona Schröter to the harp accompaniment of Georg August Zahn, the court musician. On September 10 he pens the following postscript to Kayser, expressive of true enthusiasm: "When this letter was already sealed, I received yours concerning Rousseau's songs. I can imagine that they gave you great pleasure. I have had the parts written out, and so I have already heard most of them a few times. One never tires of them, and I admire, along with their simplicity, the great diversity and the pure feeling, where everything is in its proper setting. How I long to get a letter from you when you have heard and seen so much more!"

Writing from Gotha on December 8, 1781, Goethe tells Frau von Stein of the warm reception accorded him the day before and of the presents handed out by St. Nicholas. "From the Duchess," he says, "I have a pair of handsome cuffs, and from the chief lady-in-waiting a snuff-box with Rousseau's picture." He closes his missive of February 19, 1782, to Charlotte with the request, "Send me the volume of Rousseau and a token of your favor." In another letter of that year (May 9) to Charlotte, Goethe sounds his warmest praise of Jean-Jacques the writer: "Mama has presented me with the fine new Geneva edition of Rousseau; the *Confessions* are included. Even the few pages at which I have looked are like shining stars; imagine several volumes like that! What a heavenful! What a gift to mankind a noble human being is!" A further note to Frau von Stein (June 5) relates how nicely her son Fritz read aloud to Goethe from the *Confessions* the previous evening and how he "seemed to understand nearly everything." On July 13, 1782, Luise von Göchhausen wrote to Knebel: "Goethe came just as I was about to seal this letter, and he tells me, among other things, that you have written some very good comments on Rousseau's *Confessions*."[11]

A few weeks earlier (June 16) Goethe had called Duke Karl August's attention to Jean-Jacques the botanist: "In Rousseau's works there are quite charming letters on botany, in which he presents this branch of science to a lady in the most comprehensible and graceful manner. It is really a model of how one should give instruction, and a supplement to *Émile*. I therefore take occasion to recommend anew the beautiful realm of flowers to my fair lady friends." The same day on which Goethe commends the *Lettres sur la botanique* from both the aesthetic and the pedagogical angle was a very restful one for him, he tells Charlotte, "such as I have not enjoyed for a long time." In this connection he mentions his drawing and "Rousseau's music."

Goethe's high regard for the Genevan's *Correspondance* is evident in his letter of August 26, 1782, to Charlotte, where he remarks on "Rousseau's letters, a precious part of his literary legacy." Then, after citing the unusual intellectual accomplishments and social graces of the Prince of Saxe-Gotha, he continues, "I am sending you a pleasing essay on Rousseau by him." One finds an even stronger expression of admiration for Rousseau in a letter of July 9, 1784 (likewise to Frau von Stein): "I have taken a few quiet moments to read in Rousseau. . . . How wonderful and gratifying it is to find the soul of one now departed and the innermost sentiments of his heart lying open upon this or that table!"

Goethe's diary entry for October 7, 1786, during his first visit to Venice, contains the following significant reference: "This evening I arranged for the splendid singing of the boatmen who sing Tasso and Ariosto to their melody. By moonlight I got into a gondola, with one singer in front and the other at the back; they began their song and sang alternately, verse after verse. The melody, which we know through Rousseau, is of a type between a chorale and a recitative . . . ." Goethe refers to a number from the *Consolations des misères de ma vie*, which, as we have seen, he loved from first acquaintance on. He then describes in great detail the melody and the mode of singing it. Only minor changes were made in that passage for the *Italienische Reise*, which was not published until 1816–17, although based largely on the letters and diary of his stay in Italy (W.A. III, 1:279–281). The same work contains the following reflection of sympathetic understanding, written on March 17, 1787, at Naples and retained without essential alteration thirty years afterward: "Sometimes I recall Rousseau and his hypochondriac wretchedness, and yet I can understand how such a finely organized mentality could be disarranged. If I did not feel such interest in the things of nature, and if I did not see that in the apparent confusion a hundred observations can be compared and classified . . . , I should often consider myself mad" (W.A.

I, 31:58). When Goethe returned to Venice in 1790, he must have thought once again of Rousseau's sojourn there, for one of the *Venezianische Epigramme* (W.A. I, 1:328, No. 92) presents yet another variation of Saint-Preux' wish for the continuance of a happy present:

Sage, wie lebst du? Ich lebe! und wären hundert und hundert Jahre dem Menschen gegönnt, wünscht' ich mir morgen wie heut.

In 1796 Goethe translated Madame de Staël's *Essai sur les fictions* and published it under the German title of *Versuch über die Dichtungen*, in the *Jenaische allgemeine Literaturzeitung*. The essay is especially noteworthy for its enthusiastic praise of Rousseau, exemplified by the following lines (preceded by a complimentary allusion to *Werther* and other well-known novels):

There is in the world one work, *La Nouvelle Héloïse*, whose greatest merit consists in the eloquence of its passion; and although the object is often moral, nevertheless we really gain thereby only the impression of the omnipotence of the heart. This kind of novel cannot be put into any class. In a century there is one soul, one genius who can attain to that; there can be no genre in that case, nor can any ultimate aim be seen. . . . Readers who receive such a talent with enthusiasm number only a few. . . . Leave this enjoyment to souls on fire and full of feeling! . . . They would think they were all alone in the world, and they would soon curse their nature which separates them from all men, if passionate and melancholy works did not . . . bring them a few rays of the happiness that flees from them in the midst of the world. In these joys of solitude they find recreation from the vain efforts of deluded hope, and when the world moves away from the unhappy being, then an eloquent and tender work of literature remains with him like a true friend who knows him well. Yes, the book that dispels grief for a single day deserves our thanks; usually it serves the best people, for it is true that there are griefs which originate from faults of character, but how many come from a superiority of mind or from a sensibility of the heart! . . .

(W.A. I, 37:123–129)[12]

In reading this laudatory passage we must constantly remind ourselves that it is Goethe's translation rather than his own production, for it gives the impression of being a labor of love.[13] I believe that Goethe was sufficiently in agreement with the quotation that he, as a translator in the fullest sense, appropriated it, gave it an original touch and let it be his appreciative judgment of *La Nouvelle Héloïse*—presumably for the same reason that he gave to Eckermann for using an adaptation of Ophelia's song from *Hamlet* in *Faust*.[14] Viewed in this light, it is, in my opinion, one of Goethe's most important pronouncements on Rousseau and his chief acknowledgment of a novel which he has been accused of passing over in silence.[15]

Two years later (1798), as previously mentioned, Goethe translated Diderot's first two *Essais sur la peinture* as *Versuch über die Malerei*. Diderot defends Rousseau and his play *Pygmalion*, striking a theme also treated by Lessing in the *Laokoon* (which Goethe admired). Diderot says:

> One may well pardon the poet if, in order to create an interesting situation in fancy, he imagines his sculptor as being really in love with a statue produced by himself; if he invents for him eager desires for the same; and if he finally lets it come to life in his arms. Indeed, that makes an indecent little story that is very nice to listen to; for the plastic artist it remains an unworthy legend. . . . Had Pygmalion been able to feel desire for his statue, he would have been a bungler, incapable of producing a figure that would have deserved to be esteemed as a work of art or of nature.
>
> (W.A. I, 45:263)

It seems probable to me that Goethe agreed with Diderot's praise of *Pygmalion*, although he expressed disagreement with a number of statements in the work he was translating (see, for example, W.A. I, 45:282).

Diary entries for April 27 and May 1, 1798 both read, "In the evening *Pygmalion* . . . ," the reference being to a presentation of Georg Benda's musical adaptation of Rousseau's play, with Iffland playing the title role. That production is also simultaneously the subject of several letters to Schiller (then at Jena). Although Rousseau's name does not occur in these, Goethe's discussions constitute an indirect reference to Jean-Jacques. On April 25 of that year Goethe writes Schiller that he is curious about the coming performance of the play, which he has seen several times. Calling it "a very curious undertaking," he characterizes Iffland as "much too clever" to choose anything without being sure of a desired effect. He then promises to send Schiller news of the outcome. Accordingly, in a brief note of April 27, Goethe expresses himself as being infinitely pleased with Iffland's acting and not at all disturbed by the limitations of the latter's talent to which so many take exception. His next letter to Schiller (April 28) contains the following verdict: "Yesterday there was an exceedingly interesting presentation. *Pygmalion* demands the highest theatrical dignity and depth. . . . What he (Iffland) achieved cannot be uttered in words." Schiller, although dubious about the choice of *Pygmalion* and about Iffland, voices his regret (May 1) at having to miss the performances. In regard to the controversial aspects, Goethe says in his letter of May 2 to Schiller: "I believe we shall soon be in agreement, for one can speak of this monodrama only insofar as one assumes the manner of the French tragic theater and the rhetorical treatment of a tragic, or in this case a sentimental, subject to be permissible. If one rejects the latter entirely, then *Pygmalion* will be rejected along with it; but if it is accepted, with its worth or worthlessness, then here also there is room for praise or censure." Thus, even though Goethe had evolved a mature, critical understanding of drama and of the theater, we find him still fascinated by a poetic creation which had aroused his enthusiasm a quarter of a century earlier. Furthermore, he is ready to defend it against Schiller's objections.

Two short passages in *Die natürliche Tochter* (1803) are interpreted by Michel Bréal as referring to Rousseau, in the guise of the Princess Eugenie's preceptor.[16] The first reads:

> Schon ihren ersten Weg geleiteten
> Ein ausgebildet Weib, ein weiser Mann.
> (W.A. I., 10:252)

The second states:

> Ihr alter, erster hochgeliebter Freund
> Und Lehrer wohnt, von dieser Stadt entfernt,
> Verschränkt in Trübsinn, Krankheit, Menschenhass.
> (W.A. I., 10:312)

"Enmeshed in melancholy, illness, misanthropy"—here, if Bréal's interpretation is correct, Goethe pays Rousseau the unusual tribute of mention in a major creative work. (One is reminded of the later eulogy of Byron as Euphorion in *Faust II*.)

The next mention of Rousseau in the letters, also addressed to Schiller (January 23, 1804), concerns Madame de Staël, who was then visiting in Weimar. Apropos of the *Correspondance originale et inédite de J.-J. Rousseau avec Mme La Tour de Franqueville et M. du Peyrou*, which had lately been reviewed in the *Jenaische allgemeine Literaturzeitung*, Goethe writes: "There is truly nothing new under the sun! And did not our excellent lady traveler assure me this morning, with the greatest naïveté, that she intended to have printed all my words of which she could gain possession? This news about Rousseau's letters is really playing a malicious prank on the lady in my case. One sees oneself and the grotesque striving of French femininity in an adamantine mirror."

In the *Tag- und Jahreshefte* (written in the years 1819–1825), Goethe explains his attitude more fully. Not only does he show strong displeasure at what he considers a betrayal of Rousseau's confidence, but he likewise makes common cause with the latter, as it were, in the face of Madame de Staël's admitted intention. He then continues:

> Now although I had no cause at all for dissembling toward her . . . , nevertheless, an external circumstance arose just at this point which made me momentarily shy. I received a French book that had just appeared, containing the correspondence of some women with Rousseau. They had really quite mystified the unapproachable, timid man, by managing first to gain his interest through small matters and then to entice him into an exchange of letters with them, which, after they had enjoyed the joke enough, they let be collected and printed.
>
> I made known my disapproval of this to Madame de Staël, who took the matter lightly, in fact, seemed to approve of it, and gave me clearly to understand that she thought to proceed in about the same way with us. Nothing further was needed to cause me to be attentive and cautious and to become somewhat non-communicative.
>
> (W.A. I, 35:169)

Despite subsequent defenses of Madame La Tour de Franqueville, notably by Sainte-Beuve (who unfavorably contrasts Rousseau's treatment of her with Goethe's acceptance of Bettina Brentano's publication of their correspondence),[17] Goethe sincerely believed that Rousseau had been the victim of an unwarranted imposition. It is equally clear that the depth of his sympathy stemmed from a fear that Madame de Staël would take similar liberties with him. (His use of the phrase "with us" presumably refers to Schiller, perhaps also to Wieland.)

In his outline of a review (for the *Schriften zur Kunst*, 1788–1790) of "a small number of French satirical engravings on copper plate," Goethe describes without comment the one in which Rousseau's works are about to be stepped on by a donkey already trampling upon those of Descartes and Racine (W.A. I, 47:360). However, he could not take lightly the satirization of Jean-Jacques by the dramatist Palissot in the latter's play *Les Philosophes*. In the notes to his translation of Diderot's *Le Neveu de Rameau* Goethe echoes and amplifies Diderot's own criticism of Palissot, calling him "one of the mediocre natures," incapable of appreciating what is "extraordinary," as exemplified by Rousseau (W.A. I, 45:186). Further on Goethe adds: "As if it were not enough that Palissot paraded his literary confrères before the court and city (of Paris), he also introduced a caricature of Rousseau, who at that time had made himself known in an admittedly paradoxical, but nevertheless worthy manner. Whatever among the peculiarities of this extraordinary man might strike men of the world as strange was represented here, by no means wittily and jovially, but awkwardly and with ill-will" (W.A. I, 45:188). In a subsequent note (specifically concerned with "*Les Philosophes,* a comedy by Palissot") he particularly stresses the following scene: ". . . Finally there appears a clown of a servant on all fours, with a head of lettuce, to ridicule the natural state depicted as desirable by Rousseau" (W.A. I, 45:192). Later we shall find him repeating this, with slightly different wording, in *Dichtung und Wahrheit;* apparently, Palissot's clumsy mockery of Rousseau was his most persistent memory of *Les Philosophes.*

A passage in another of the *Anmerkungen zu "Rameaus Neffe"* reads: "One must recognize in M. Rameau a very great talent, much ardor, a head for euphony, a great knowledge of harmonic inversions and of all means which produce effect; one must concede to him the art of appropriating the ideas of others, of changing their nature, of ornamenting and embellishing them, and of giving a manifold turn to his own. He had, on the other hand, less facility in inventing new ones, more cleverness than productivity, more knowledge than genius, or at least a genius stifled by too much knowledge, but always force, gracefulness, and very often a beautiful song" (W.A. I, 45:204). This sounds like one of Goethe's own characterizations from *Dichtung und Wahrheit.* Actually, it is a paragraph from his translation of Rousseau's *Extrait d'une lettre à M. Grimm sur les ouvrages de M. Rameau.*[18] Goethe prefaces his five-page quotation with the remark: "The following opinion of Rousseau concerning Rameau's merits exactly coincides with Diderot's assertions and will help facilitate a survey of the chief question for our readers" (W.A. I, 45:201). Except the sentence just quoted and the dates and places of the French musician's birth and death, the entire note on Rameau consists of Rousseau's letter, with which Goethe, on his own testimony, is fully in accord. On April 23, 1805, he sent his manuscript to Schiller for critical examination; in reply, Schiller praised the inclusion of the passage from Rousseau (April 24).

In preparing these notes Goethe made some use of Marmontel's *Mémoires*, which he had been reading in connection with his translation of Diderot's play. His opinion of Marmontel in relation to Rousseau is preserved in a letter of late January, 1805, from Henriette von Knebel to her brother Karl, quoted in the previous chapter (pp. 29–30). It is worthy of note that he regularly sided with Rousseau against petty criticism, including Marmontel's caviling.

In a diary notation for August 30, 1806, Goethe mentions his returning an essay on Rousseau by the Göttingen physicist Werneburg to its author. Judging by Goethe's comments in several letters (e.g., to Eichstädt, December 1, 1803, where he refers to him as "a good but strange fellow"), his general opinion of Werneburg's articles and reviews was not very high, and this essay, too, probably did not impress him favorably.

From 1809 on Goethe was periodically engaged in writing the memoirs of his boyhood and youth; the first three parts appeared during the years 1811–1814. Hence *Dichtung und Wahrheit* is thoroughly a product of the poet's mature reflection as a sexagenarian, attempting to resurrect the ideas and impressions of the early decades of his life. If one counts the variants, there are no less than sixteen allusions to Rousseau in that work, according to the Weimar edition. The references to him in connection with the Lisbon earthquake and the performance of the *Devin du village* at Frankfurt are quoted above. A preliminary outline of Goethe's autobiography contains the statement: "1761 . . . *Nouvelle Héloïse* appears; I read it later" (W.A. I, 26:352).

In *Dichtung und Wahrheit* Goethe also relates his love affair with Gretchen to *La Nouvelle Héloïse*. It was on the eve of the election of the emperor, he tells us, when he explained to an admiring Gretchen just what was to take place and how it would proceed, making illustrative drawings on the table. At the proper time they separated for the night, and in especially good spirits. Goethe then comments:

> For with a young couple more or less harmoniously formed by nature, nothing can make for a finer union than if the girl is eager to learn and the boy is fond of teaching. . . . She sees in him the creator of her spiritual existence, and he in her a creature who owes her perfection neither to nature, nor to chance, nor to any one-sided volition, but to a mutual will; and this reciprocal effect is so sweet that we must not wonder, if, since the time of the old and the new *Abelard* (my italics), the most powerful passions, and as much happiness as unhappiness, have arisen from such a communion of two beings.
>
> (W.A. I, 26:297–298)

44

Whether or not Goethe had read the novel at the time of his association with Gretchen, he still esteemed it sufficiently in later life to connect it significantly with his boyhood romance.

One mention of Rousseau is incidental to Goethe's account of the visit paid him in Leipzig by his future brother-in-law, Johann Georg Schlosser, who became private secretary to Friedrich Eugen, a brother of Duke Karl Eugen of Württemberg. Confusing the former with his elder brother, Ludwig Eugen, Goethe states: "It is this prince . . . , who, in order to get advice regarding the training of children, wrote to Rousseau, whose well-known answer begins with the questionable phrase: 'Si j'avais le malheur d'être né prince' " (W.A. I, 37:83).[19]

Perhaps most frequently misinterpreted is the passage in *Dichtung und Wahrheit* where Goethe explains his decline in health while a student at Leipzig. Loiseau, for example, thinks that Goethe's illness was due to foolish practices which Rousseau's *Émile* caused him to commit, in an effort to harden his physique.[20] What he actually says is: "My natural disposition, supported by the adequate strength of youth, fluctuated between the extremes of unrestrained gaiety and melancholy discomfort. Moreover, the epoch of bathing in cold water, which was unconditionally recommended, had then begun. One was to sleep on a hard bed, only lightly covered, whereby all usual perspiration was suppressed. These and other follies in consequence of misunderstood suggestions of Rousseau, would bring us, we were promised, nearer to nature and rescue us from the corruption of morals" (W.A. I, 27:186). Goethe blames his bad state of health not on Rousseau's regimen of cold baths and hard beds, but on his own *misunderstanding* of those precepts.

In a variant relating to Book Seven of *Dichtung und Wahrheit* Goethe notes that "a sort of idyllic bent" came into being through such poets as the Swiss writers Haller, Gessner, and Bodmer, and that the tendency toward a simple enjoyment of nature and of one's individuality on the part of the young was repressed by pedantic instruction at school, conventual attitudes, the higher ranks of society, Philistinism, and considerations of livelihood. Then, referring to the struggle against that repression, Goethe asks when such motifs first appear in novels. After mentioning his own *Werther* and Johann Martin Miller's *Siegwart*, he raises the question of earlier occurrences. Finally, in obvious answer, he adds "Rousseau's prize essay against civilization" (W.A. I, 27:389).

While relating his experiences in Strassburg (Book Eleven), Goethe endeavors to recall the opinions of French literature held by him and his student friends around 1770: "We did not fail to recognize the fact that the great and splendid French world offered us many an advantage and gain: for Rousseau had truly appealed to us. Yet, when we contemplated his life and destiny, he after all had to take his greatest reward for all that he had accomplished in being allowed to live unacknowledged and forgotten in Paris" (W.A. I, 28:63–64). This, once more, bespeaks both admiration and sympathy for Rousseau.

Goethe then characterizes Diderot as being "a true German" in everything for which the French criticize him, adding: "Thus it was he also who, like Rousseau, spread a disgust with the life of society—a quiet introduction to those enormous changes in the world in which all existing order seemed to perish.

"It is more proper for us, however, to put these observations aside for the time being and to note what influence these two men exerted upon art. Even here they were pointing, even here they were urging us toward nature" (W.A. I, 28:65). Here, some four decades later, we find an expression of grateful acknowledgment to Rousseau and Diderot for having shown Goethe the way to the natural in artistic production.

As already noted, while writing *Dichtung und Wahrheit*, Goethe renewed acquaintance with Grimm's *Correspondance littéraire, philosophique et critique*, which had just belatedly appeared in print, but which he had read extensively in manuscript form many years earlier, when it was being circulated among German provincial courts. In his letter to Knebel of October 17, 1812 containing his summary of that work (quoted in part above), Goethe makes this further criticism: "There is little that is edifying to the spirit. Voltaire is in the process of vanishing; Rousseau is in obscurity; Buffon enjoys no real esteem. . . ." So the sexagenarian Goethe finds no satisfaction in a trend away from three erstwhile leading figures in French intellectual life, one of whom is Rousseau. Deference to those same three (along with two others) is likewise shown in the following lines of January 6, 1813 addressed to Fritz Jacobi: "Yet the mass of important men in the last century was so great that, even if one does not wish to go beyond this epoch, there is certainly always a great harvest to be reaped. I miss, for example, Voltaire, Rousseau, Buffon, Helvétius, Montesquieu. . . ." This comment likewise places Jean-Jacques in esteemed company and offers renewed indication that Goethe continued to revere Rousseau while he was working on *Dichtung und Wahrheit*. In this work he also resumes his discussion of *Pygmalion*, which had once again engaged his particular attention at the time of its production at Weimar in 1811, as shown by six diary notations within the period from January 22 to February 2. With obvious reference to that latest experience of the play, Goethe writes his most frequently quoted criticism of it:

> I also wish to mention a work small in scope, but remarkably epoch-making: it is Rousseau's *Pygmalion*. Much could be said about it, for this strange production likewise wavers between nature and art. . . . We see an artist who has otherwise achieved the highest perfection, and who still does not find satisfaction in having represented his idea artistically, apart from himself, and conferred a higher life upon it; no, it is to be brought down to him, into earthly life. He would destroy the highest thing that mind and deed have produced, through the most common act of sensuality.
>
> (W.A. I, 28:67)

To be sure, Goethe utters dissatisfaction with *Pygmalion*, but his expression of regret at the author's attempt to blend art with nature is a matter of disagreement rather than a denial of Rousseau's genius. In a variant to that passage, Goethe describes *Pygmalion* as a "curious phenomenon," in which an artist reflects upon himself and his work. He then refers to the mingling of the sensual with the artistic and of prose with music, to a "re-iterated melodrama," and to an "awakening naturalism" in art. Especially significant is the closing, "further benefitted and prepared by Rousseau and Diderot" (W.A. I, 28:360). With this observation the mature Goethe accords recognition to the importance of that pair for him as formative influences. His intention—on his own admission never adequately carried out—to depict the developmental role played by Rousseau and others during his Strassburg period is announced in a letter to Zelter (December 3, 1812):

> I must likewise concur in what you say about Rousseau's *Pygmalion*. Of course this production is most remarkable as a symptom of the chief malady of that time, where state and custom, art and talent, along with a nameless essence . . . called nature, were to be stirred . . . into one porridge. I hope my next volume will demonstrate this operation: for was I not also seized by this epidemic, and was it not beneficially responsible for the development of my essential nature, which is now conceivable to me in no other way?

Pygmalion, then, is emblematic of a tendency which Goethe has long since outgrown, but which he considered indispensable for his evolution as a poet. His words suggest a feeling of gratitude to Rousseau. Goethe has been criticized for alleged failure to acknowledge his "indebtedness" to *La Nouvelle Héloïse* in connection with *Werther*, especially his reference in Book Thirteen of *Dichtung und Wahrheit* only to English literary manifestations of the spirit underlying his own novel.[21] In Book Twelve, however, he has this to say about his Wetzlar days with Lotte Buff: "And so one ordinary day followed another, and all seemed to be festive days; the whole calendar should have been printed in red. He will understand me who remembers what was prophesied by the happily unhappy friend of the 'New Heloise': 'And sitting at the feet of his beloved, he will break hemp, and he will wish to break hemp, today, tomorrow, and the day after tomorrow, yea, his whole life long' " (W.A. I, 28:155).[22] Here, while quoting Rousseau, Goethe repeats essentially the message quoted previously to Lotte herself at the time of his departure from Wetzlar in 1772. How that identical thought, in ever varying form, keeps on recurring throughout his life is further shown by a letter to Sulpiz Boisserée (October 22, 1826) in which he states that he does not devote sleepless hours to vague, general thoughts, but considers just what is to be done the next day. He then begins it in the morning and carries it out as far as possible. "And so," he adds, "I perhaps do more and complete sensibly, in the days allotted to me, what one neglects at a time when one has the right to believe or imagine there will be tomorrow and always tomorrow."

An almost reverent attitude is evidenced by an allusion in *Dichtung und Wahrheit* to Leuchsenring's collection of correspondence of noted persons. Excerpts of general significance were read and discussed at gatherings of a Frankfurt circle to which Goethe himself belonged in the early 1770's. "The letters of a Julie Bondeli," he relates, "were very highly prized; she was famous as a woman of sense and merit, and as a friend of Rousseau. Whoever had stood in any sort of relationship to this extraordinary man enjoyed a share in the glory that emanated from him, and in his name a silent community was spread far and wide" (W.A. I, 28:179). Thus Goethe again uses the adjective *extraordinary* ("ausserordentlich") to characterize Jean-Jacques, four decades after the time in question.

Goethe's friendship with Friedrich Maximilian Klinger, whose play *Sturm und Drang* gave to that whole literary movement its well-known appellation, largely belongs to the pre-Weimar period. Although the characterization of Klinger occurs in *Dichtung und Wahrheit* and was therefore written some forty years later, it deserves attention at this point on account of the pronouncement concerning *Émile*. Goethe portrays Klinger in a most advantageous light, describing him as a talented artist with a prepossessing personality, in fact, as a young man who, apart from his material struggles, appears in many respects comparable to himself. He continues:

Rousseau's works were bound to appeal particularly to such a youth. *Émile* was his principal and fundamental book, and those sentiments bore all the more fruit with him since they were exerting a general effect upon the entire cultured world; indeed, more in him than in others. For he, too, was a child of nature; he also had begun at the bottom; that which others were supposed to reject he had never possessed; conditions from which they were expected to emancipate themselves had never oppressed him; and so he could be considered one of the purest disciples of that gospel of nature, and in consideration of his earnest striving and his conduct as a man and son, could very well proclaim; "All is good as it comes from the hands of nature!"—But adverse experience also forced upon him the conclusion: "All is corrupted in the hands of man!" He did not have to struggle with himself, but outside himself, with the world of traditional custom, from whose fetters the Citizen of Geneva thought to deliver us. . . .

(W.A. I, 28:254)

It is significant that the mature Goethe, while praising Klinger above all other companions of "Sturm und Drang" days, should place such emphasis on the latter's preoccupation with Rousseau. There is no question here of a Werther-like Lenz (whom Goethe unfavorably contrasts with Klinger), going aground on the very extremes often supposed to have been fostered by the works of Jean-Jacques. Goethe makes it clear that Klinger was the sort of person who could understand and appreciate Rousseau's true value (even as Charlotte von Stein said Goethe did). If we bear in mind the frequent inclination of Goethe's autobiography toward a higher subjectivity, then his depiction of Klinger in relation to Rousseau can be applied in many respects to himself.

As previously stated, Goethe's *Italienische Reise*, which he put into final form in 1816–1817, retains his contemporaneous references to Rousseau in the diaries and letters recording his sojourn in Italy three decades before. On November 14, 1816, he wrote Zelter that a melody sung by the Venetian gondoliers "was in a volume of compositions of Rousseau's songs which came out about thirty years ago; like a thousand other things, it got lost, else I would send it." Goethe therefore retained the admiration for the *Consolations des misères de ma vie* which, as we have seen, he

49

expressed so enthusiastically to another composer, Kayser, in the 1780's.

The *Campagne in Frankreich*, which recounts events of 1792, but which Goethe edited for publication in 1821–1822, contains this comment about his visit with Fritz Jacobi and the latter's associates at Pempelfort: "Rousseau's views concerning conditions of nature were likewise not unknown to this circle, which excluded nothing, therefore not even me, although it really only tolerated me" (W.A. I, 33:194–195). The same autobiographical work records his acquaintance with the Princess Gallitzin (at Münster), whom he characterizes as follows: "Upon closer consideration, one could only regard the state of mind of the princess as loving ("liebevoll"): she early attained to the feeling that the world gives us nothing; that one must withdraw into oneself; that one must be concerned, in an inner, restricted circle, with questions of time and eternity. She had grasped both; the highest temporal excellence she found in what was natural, and here one may recall maxims of Rousseau about bourgeois life and the bringing up of children. There was a desire to return, in all things, to what was simple and true" (W.A. I, 33:231). Goethe's loving depiction of the princess as a "schöne Seele" (beautiful soul) because of her devotion to the same precepts held by Rousseau implies his own agreement with these maxims.

During the summer of 1824 Goethe was intensively occupied with Rousseau's *Botanique* and *Lettres relatives à la Botanique*. He discussed the *Botanique* with Friedrich von Müller on June 13, and diary entries for June 18 and 28, July 31, and August 1 and 2 refer to that text, in the edition illustrated with copper plates by Redouté. In a letter of June 25 to Karl August, Goethe remarks that "among so much else, the pictorial clarification of the botanical pleasures of Rousseau's youth (sic) is most welcome; I am thinking of going through his essay on them again soon; the memory of it still hovers before me from my earliest years." It was to Karl August that he had originally written with enthusiasm about the letters on botany, forty-two years before. The passages from *Dichtung und Wahrheit* quoted above and the correspondence suggest that his recollection of the essay in question is just one of numerous memories of his first acquaintance with Rousseau's writings.

Goethe is concerned with the man as well as with the botanist, as is evident from the rough draft of another letter to Karl August, dated August 1, 1824, in which he tells of his recent closer examination of the Rousseau-Redouté work, whereupon he "considered with admiring regret how hard such an excellent man toiled in these fields fifty years ago." Here is a further example of Goethe's attributing "excellence" to Rousseau. The following day (August 2) he wrote in his diary that he had "reflected upon Rousseau's *Botany* along with other matters pertaining to morphology." As we shall see, Goethe meditated increasingly upon that work.

Though fewer in number, the contemporaneous allusions to Rousseau not relating to botany deserve attention. For instance, Eckermann records a conversation on December 9, 1824, concerning a great flood at St. Petersburg, during which Goethe "laughed approvingly about a statement of Rousseau, who had supposedly said that one could not prevent an earthquake by building a town near an erupting volcano. 'Nature goes her way,' said he (Goethe), 'and what seems to us an exception is according to rule.' "

A rereading of *La Nouvelle Héloïse* is listed in Goethe's diary as part of the "Agenda" for January 14, 1826. Chancellor von Müller tells of speaking to Goethe on June 24 of that year about the assertion made by the *Journal des Débats* that a certain melody in Weber's opera *Der Freischütz* contained motifs borrowed from Rousseau's music. Thereupon Goethe expressed lively disapproval of all such brooding ("Nachgrübeln") about parallel passages. He said that of course everything written, argued, or spoken had already existed, but how could there be any reading, conversation, or living together, if one always objected, "why, I have read that before in Aristotle, Homer, and the like." Von Müller remarks in conclusion that Goethe was "quite negative, ironical, and contradictory" in his attitude.

One of the *Aufsätze zur Literatur*, likewise from 1826, deals with the French edition of Goethe's dramatic works issued by Albert Stapfer and reviewed in *Le Globe* (Nos. 55–64). Goethe translated the critique, in which the reviewer states:

> The role of Tasso seems to me wholly suited for an admirable representation of the perplexities of an imagination which, a prey to itself, is inflamed, encouraged, reduced to despair at a single word, clings to a memory, is enraptured over a dream, makes an event out of every excitement, a torture out of every bit of unrest; which, in short suffers, enjoys, and lives in a strange, unreal world that has, nevertheless, its tempests, its joys, and griefs. Just so is Jean-Jacques revealed in his *Rêveries*, and the poet had long been like that, and it seems to me that he himself speaks from the mouth of Tasso, and through this harmonious poetry one hears echoes of Werther.
>
> (W.A. I, 41^2:188)

Not only does this translation, set forth without any qualifying comment, imply Goethe's probable agreement, but one also senses a tacit acknowledgment of the suggested relationship between himself and the author of the *Rêveries du promeneur solitaire.*

The German edition of Carlyle's *Life of Schiller*, published in 1828, contains a preface by Goethe in which he remarks in connection with a picture of Carlyle's house: "Cultured minds, sensitive natures, who strive toward a distant good . . . can scarcely overcome the wish to see brought before their eyes the portraits of honored and beloved persons far away, and then the pictures of their homes . . . . Is not . . . Rousseau's place of refuge a locale never portrayed enough for his admirers?" (W.A. I, 42^1:190). After expressing a similar importance for Craigenputtock, Goethe quotes Carlyle's praise that ". . . Rousseau would have liked it there almost as well as on his Island of St. Pierre. Indeed, I find that most of my city friends impute to me a motive similar to his in coming hither, and predict no good from it" (W.A. I, 42^1:192). The entire context indicates Goethe's admiration for Rousseau and a vivid recollection of his own visit to that island sanctuary nearly half a century earlier.

After reading Gérard de Nerval's French translation of *Faust I*, Goethe told Eckermann (January 3, 1830):

Strange thoughts run through my mind when I reflect that this book even now is important in a language in which Voltaire held sway fifty years ago. You cannot imagine what goes on in my mind about this, and you have no conception of the significance that Voltaire and his great contemporaries had in my youth and how they dominated the whole moral and ethical world. It is not clearly evident from my autobiography what an influence these men had on my youth, and what an effort it cost me to defend myself against them and to stand upon my own feet in a truer relationship to nature.

Voltaire's "great contemporaries" would unquestionably include Rousseau (as explained in the preceding chapter). Goethe's words to Eckermann on March 14, 1830 bear out this inference still further: "A German author, a German martyr! . . . And I myself can scarcely complain; the others all fared no better, most of them even worse, and in England and France exactly as in our country. What did Molière not have to suffer! and . . . Rousseau and Voltaire! Byron was driven out of England by malicious tongues. . . ." Even as late as 1830, then, Goethe's esteem for Rousseau remains undiminished. Not even these utterances, however, can be considered Goethe's final tribute to Rousseau. For that let us return to his renewed absorption in Rousseau's botanical writings from 1824 until the last year of his life. As early as 1817 Goethe had undertaken to write a history of his study of botany; it is one of the numerous treatises eventually assembled under the heading *Zur Morphologie*. In its revised and expanded form, the *Geschichte meines botanischen Studiums* dates from 1831 and thus can be regarded as Goethe's ultimate verdict on Rousseau. Especially during the year 1830 he prepared himself before writing the history. The records of the Weimar Library show that in May of that year he borrowed not only *La Botanique* but also the complete works of Rousseau (in a one-volume edition of 1826).[23] Likewise, numerous diary entries for May, 1830 bear witness to this preparatory reading. In a note of May 19, Goethe inquires whether Riemer can do him the special favor of finding "the passage in the *Confessions* where Rousseau recalls his botanical wanderings and studies." Five days later (May 24) he writes again to Riemer, asking: "Where is there some detailed information about Rousseau's *Botaniste sans maître*? In his works there is nothing about it in evidence; I suppose that it concerns the letters that he wrote to Mlle Delessert in the years 1771–72. . . ." The diary tells of their reading the appropriate pages of the *Confessions* together on May 28. On October 14 Goethe sent Soret the section of the *Geschichte meines botanischen Studiums* dealing with Rousseau as a botanist, requesting that Soret make a new translation (into French) of "the whole passage." Finally, on January 3, 1831, Goethe again borrowed *La Botanique*, with the highly-prized Redouté illustrations, and kept it for more than six weeks.

Near the middle of his essay, after naming numerous prominent forerunners as his benefactors in the botanical field and telling of the unusual advantages he enjoyed in acquiring specimens, Goethe turns to another inspirational force contributing to his study: "I became aware of a hermit-like lover of plants who had devoted himself with earnestness and diligence to this subject. Who would not follow Jean-Jacques Rousseau, *a man revered in the highest sense* (my italics), on his lonely wanderings, where . . . with real, straightforward mental vigor he acquaints himself with the quietly charming children of Nature?" (W.A. II, 6:110–111). This is the most unequivocal expression of the mature Goethe's sentiments regarding Rousseau. Goethe then sets forth his idea of how Rousseau's interest in botany arose: "It is not known to me that he had from his earlier years any inclinations toward flowers and plants other than those which really would only intimate sentiment, disposition, or tender recollections; but according to his definite statements he may have first become attentive on the Island of St. Pierre, in the Lake of Bienne, to this realm of Nature in its fullness, after a tempestuous life as an author. . . ." (W.A. II, 6:111).

This last surmise (which concerns the writer as well as the botanist) clearly echoes Goethe's impressions while visiting Rousseau's island refuge in 1779. While tracing the latter's increasing preoccupation with the flora about him, Goethe reminds his readers that while in England Rousseau had looked around rather freely and extensively, and that his relationship with plant lovers and experts, especially with the Duchess of Portland, might have directed his attention more toward a broader field. "A mind like his," Goethe continues, "that feels called upon to prescribe law and order for the nations, surely must have reached the conjecture that in the immeasurable plant kingdom no such great multiplicity of forms could occur unless an underlying law, however deeply hidden it might be, reduced them all to a common unity" (W.A. II, 6:111). Goethe therefore sees Rousseau's view of nature as being essentially in agreement with his own, which Aron appropriately calls "an integral part of Goethe's *Weltanschauung*," permeating his later poetry also.[24] Yet Goethe indicates that Rousseau's insights concerning nature are implied rather than expressed because of the latter's reticence, in spite of his deep absorption in the realm of plants and his feeling that "a certain methodical progress throughout the whole is possible." Adding that it will "always be profitable to hear how he expresses himself about it," Goethe translates the following excerpt from Rousseau:

As far as I am concerned, I am a pupil and am not well-grounded in this study. In botanizing I think rather of diverting and amusing than of informing myself, and with my hesitant observations I cannot conceive the presumptive thought of instructing others in what I do not know myself.

Yet I confess that the difficulties I encountered in the study of plants led me to some ideas as to how means might probably be found to facilitate the same and to make it useful to others . . . by knowing how to follow the thread of a system of plants by a more progressive method, less far removed from the senses, than did Tournefort and all his successors, not excepting even Linnaeus. Perhaps my idea is not capable of being carried out; we shall talk about it when I have the honor of seeing you again.

(W.A. II, 6:111–112)[25]

The above passage relates not only to the botanist but also to the teacher. Goethe remarks that Rousseau wrote these lines at the beginning of the year 1770, and that the matter occupied him continuously from then on, until in August, 1771, "upon friendly inducement he takes upon himself the obligation to instruct others; in fact, to recite to some women what he knows and perceives, not by any means for playful entertainment, but in order to give them a thorough introduction to the science." How well, in Goethe's opinion, Rousseau served the cause of instruction and that of botanical lore may readily be seen from the concluding paragraph:

Here he succeeds in reducing his knowledge to the primary elements demonstrable to the senses; he displayed the plant parts individually and taught how to distinguish and name them. Scarcely, however, did he restore the whole flower from the parts and designate them . . . partly through trivial names, and in part faithfully introduce the Linnaean terminology . . . when he immediately gives a broader view of them as a whole . . . ; and by making the differences perceptible in this way in an increasing multiplicity and interrelationship, he leads us gradually toward a complete and gratifying survey. For since he has to talk to women, he understands how . . . to call attention to the use, advantage, and harmful effects, and to do this all the more skilfully and easily, since, taking all examples for his teaching from the surrounding country, he speaks only of the native flora and makes no claims concerning the exotic plants . . . .

(W.A. II, 6:112–113)

Goethe then praises the 1822 edition of *La Botanique de Rousseau*, whose colored illustrations were taken from the drawings of the "excellent Redouté, representing all those plants of which he (Rousseau) had spoken." Goethe notes with pleasure that "only plants are shown which he could see directly upon his walks." Referring to Rousseau's method of selection for the obvious purpose of classification by families, Goethe remarks that the discourse made all the greater impression upon him since he himself was also inclined at that time toward such observations. Just as young students adhere most readily to young teachers, he continues, so the dilettante may gladly learn from the dilettante. He admits that this would be a dubious procedure, had experience not shown that dilettantes contribute much to the advantage of science. Rousseau's profound interest in the plant world is confirmed by the *Fragmens* [sic] *pour un Dictionnaire des termes d'usage en Botanique*. Goethe concludes: "Let this much be said here, in order to indicate in some degree what we owed him in that epoch of our studies. Even as he, who was free of all national inflexibility, relied upon Linnaeus' results, which in any case were progressive, so may we for our part observe that it is a great advantage when we enter a scientific field new to us and find it in a crisis and an extraordinary man busy accomplishing something worthwhile . . ." (W.A. II, 6:113–115).[26]

The last volume of the scientific writings includes several pages of "Paralipomena" dealing with Rousseau's botanical studies and their importance for Goethe. While these passages (dating from 1830) for the most part duplicate the thoughts contained in the final version, there are some exceptions worthy of notice. He says: "Rousseau's nature and striving here also concerned what was closest to him. Each region where he tarried became his enclosed scene of action. He had an aversion toward all greenhouses and their strange, captive inhabitants, and indeed justly in the natural sense, for every foreign creature transports the person of pure feeling to foreign places and changes for the moment his inmost being . . ." (W.A. II, 13:47). Goethe also states that Rousseau's comment about the misfortune of botany to be associated with medicine could be excused, in view of the fact that in his time there was still a dispute as to whether botany could be an independent discipline (W.A. II, 13:50). On one page we read of Rousseau's "pure, genuine straightforwardness" and his "powerful mind, completely equal to everything to which he chose to apply himself," on the next page about the "memory of an extraordinary mind" (W.A. II, 13:45–46).

Thus Goethe sees Rousseau working in the direction that he himself was destined to follow. Goethe's persistent use of the word "striving" in connection with Rousseau reminds us of *Faust*, which he was then laboring to complete. His description of the course of his botanical study manifestly commends not merely Rousseau the botanist, as some have asserted in times past, but rather the whole man, in the totality of his ideas and perceptions. Any lingering doubt of his veneration for the "Promeneur solitaire" should be dispelled by this homage from the octogenarian Goethe. Such eulogy more than compensates for earlier inadequacies of acknowledgment (if one regards them as such), and it places Rousseau undeniably among those to whom Goethe attributed a role of lasting inspiration for his own intellectual and artistic evolution. At the end of his life, even as long years before, he still considered Rousseau an "extraordinary" man—exceptional in the most exalted sense of the term.

III

Literary Echoes
from Four Decades

Goethe's own statements show that his interest in Rousseau continued
unabated until his death in 1832. This chapter summarizes the often-
treated effect of Rousseau upon Goethe's early production and that of
his middle years, covering works from the late 1760's to 1806, the year in
which he finished *Faust I*. In some instances the alleged influence of
Rousseau is demonstrable, in others his inspiration seems probable, and in
still others striking parallels testify to a kinship of spirit, even where direct
influence cannot be proved. The subsequent chapters will study in some
detail analogies and similarities between Rousseau's writings and Goethe's
principal works of his later years.

As previously stated, the letters of the Leipzig student indicate some
acquaintance with Rousseau's writings. Benrubi suggests that a spirit of
revolt against social distinctions which he discovers in Goethe's correspondence with Cornelia should be attributed to Rousseau.[1] In the opinion of
Loiseau, certain "somber touches" of the *Leipziger Lieder* derive from
Jean-Jacques, whom he sees as a check on Goethe's lapses into Rococo artificiality.[2] Although Goethe's early play *Die Mitschuldigen* was not actually written until after his return to Frankfurt, it reflects in part some of
his Leipzig experiences. Richard M. Meyer likens the rather sordid milieu
of that drama and the characters to certain descriptions in Rousseau's

Confessions. Meyer holds that the latter work served as a model for the novelistic technique which Goethe employed in his detailed execution of love-scenes in the drama and for the clear, sententious treatment of the psychological development.[3]

The first of Goethe's works to evoke general mention of Rousseau is *Götz von Berlichingen*, with its powerful "Sturm und Drang" championing of natural rights and protest against conventionality and artificiality of the social structure. Édouard Rod, who calls Götz "an elder brother of Karl Moor" (in Schiller's play *Die Räuber*), maintains that, despite Goethe's effort to lend him a Renaissance coloring, he remains a man of the late eighteenth century "who has read the *Contrat social* and *Émile*."[4] Whereas Loiseau would ascribe any so-called Rousseauesque traits in Götz to other sources, such as the influence of Diderot, the Encyclopedists, or even Voltaire himself,[5] Christian Gauss[6] asserts that Goethe followed the line indicated by Rousseau in Saint-Preux' letter to Julie, where he says that subjects treated dramatically should concern the lives of those who make up the audience; namely, that at Bern, Zurich, and The Hague the ancient tyranny of the House of Austria should be represented, and that the Roman tragedies of Corneille are irrelevant to the people of Paris (O.C., 8:362).

Several vivid contrasts in the play echo Rousseau's advocacy of the simple, natural life and "the good old ways" over so-called refined society. Götz' little son Karl can recite parrot-like that "Jaxthausen is a village and castle on the Jaxt which has belonged in property and heritage to the Lords of Berlichingen for two hundred years," but he cannot answer when his father asks to whom it now belongs (W.A. I, 8:27). Karl has been sheltered by his gentle Aunt Maria, who wants him to become "a pious Christian knight" (W.A. I, 8:21). Georg, on the other hand, is a manly youth with all the vigor of the unspoiled "Volk" who wishes to become a "Reiter" like his patron saint (W.A. I, 8:27).

Brother Martin reflects this same Rousseauesque sentiment when he complains to Götz about the unnatural state in which he is compelled to exist, bound by the triple oath of poverty, chastity, and obedience and denied the chance to be a human being. "What," he asks, "are the hardships of your life compared with the miseries of a station which condemns the best urges, through which we come into being, grow, and thrive, from the mistaken desire of moving nearer to God? . . . Happy is he who has a virtuous wife! he will therefore live twice as long. I know no women, and yet woman was the crown of creation!" Götz sympathizes inwardly (W.A. I, 8:14–16).

The simple rugged life at Götz' castle points up the corrupt luxury of the court of the Bishop of Bamberg. Even before we first glimpse the episcopal court, we hear Götz tell Weislingen, whom he has taken prisoner, how different it all might have been had he followed Götz' advice and plea to accompany him to Brabant. "Then the unlucky court held you fast, and the lolling around and flirting with women. I always told you, when you were associating with the vain, disgusting slatterns and told them about unhappy marriages, seduced girls, the rough skin of a third one, or whatever else they like to hear about, I said, 'You're becoming a rascal, Adelbert' " (W.A. I, 8:30).

The ignorance and unscrupulousness of the ecclesiastics at the court stand in marked contrast to the sincerity and simplicity of Brother Martin. The Bishop himself and the Abbot of Fulda have to be informed by Olearius about Justinian and the *Corpus Juris* (W.A. I, 8:36). Liebetraut sings a light, flirtatious love song at the court, whereas Georg at Jaxthausen sings a folk song.

Weislingen loves both Götz' sister Maria and Adelheid von Walldorf. Maria leads a virtuous life at Jaxthausen, the beautiful and ambitious Adelheid embodies the decadent court life. In rejecting his promise to Maria and Götz' friendship for Adelheid and the false attraction of the court, Weislingen brings about his own destruction. Maria, however, weds Franz von Sickingen, who, like Götz, is an upright man and a defender of the vanishing feudal order.

In the ninth of the *Lettres écrites de la Montagne*, Second Part, Rousseau contrasts the laws of England with those of Geneva, stressing the greater liberty allowed by the former (O.C., 6:438–446). Goethe, whose admiration for the practicality of the English and their institutions is well known, told Eckermann (March 12, 1828) that Englishmen were fortunate in their personal freedom, which they enjoyed to a larger extent than the Germans. Rousseau and Goethe are both praising the Germanic law, which had continued to develop in England after it had yielded to Roman jurisprudence in Germany and elsewhere on the Continent.

Goethe's emphasis on the time-honored Germanic law as opposed to the newly-introduced Roman law is of special import in connection with his preference for the simple life over that of the court. William Witte calls attention to the relative neglect of Goethe's legal training by his biographers, quoting one of the *Maximen und Reflexionen* to the effect that all laws are attempts to approximate the intentions of the moral world order in the course of the world and of life (W.A. I, 42^2:215); in this light, the positive law is often lacking, Witte continues, as in the wedding scene in *Götz von Berlichingen*, where Götz himself urges some peasants who had been wronged to protest and to seek amends for it. He thus supports a principle of natural law which holds that the validity of any legal ruling depends solely on its just operation.[7]

Witte also reminds us that despite the praise of the Roman law by the learned jurist Olearius, it is the secret tribunal, the "Femgericht," which finally brings Adelheid to justice, taking action when the regularly instituted courts fail in their function. Although without official constitutional standing, it is representative of the "innate sense of justice" in the common man, and its verdict rests on the "natural instinct" mentioned by the *Corpus Iuris Canonici* in its definition of "ius naturale" (p. 89).[8] Both Goethe and Rousseau attribute that inborn feeling of what is right to the "plain people," those close to nature. Between the writing of the original version, *Geschichte Gottfriedens von Berlichingen dramatisiert* (1771), and the publication (1773) of the revision, Goethe had experienced the outdated and hopelessly inefficient "Reichskammergericht" at Wetzlar. The chaotic state of that supreme court must have seemed to Goethe a concrete example of the situation he had intuitively depicted in the first version of the play.

Götz von Berlichingen likewise embodies the first of Goethe's broadsides against the moribund First German Empire, the last gasps of which he was to witness.[9] Maximilian, revered even by Götz, is portrayed as a man who tries, but who is unable to control the anarchic situation of the realm. It is Weislingen who advises the Emperor to take stern measures against Sickingen, Selbitz, and Berlichingen. Having already expressed his impatience at the obstinacy of the princes and at the complaints of two Nürnberg merchants that they have been robbed by Götz, Maximilian exclaims, ". . . When a merchant loses a sack of pepper, one is expected to call the whole Empire under arms; and when there are quarrels of great concern to the Imperial Majesty and the Empire so that it affects kingdom, principality, dukedom, and other matters, then no human being can bring you together" (W.A. I, 8:81–82). In his last speech Götz predicts the "times of deceit" which lie ahead (W.A. I, 8:169), words prophetic of the ruinous age which the seventeenth century was to be for

Germany after the external pomp of the reign of Emperor Charles V.

As Albert Fuchs appropriately states, the young Goethe's national fervor was transformed into a preoccupation with the real situation of his country. In *Götz*, says Fuchs, he has inscribed a national thought which was to have a future flowering. His is a patriotism without injustice or brutality. This same humanism leads from the discourses and dreams of Götz, besieged at Jaxthausen, to the services which Goethe himself rendered to the Duchy of Saxe-Weimar.[10]

Goethe's fondness for Rousseau's *Pygmalion*, so abundantly evidenced by his letters and diaries, is also shown by his repeated use of the theme of that "Scène lyrique" in which Pygmalion, enamored of his statue of Galathée, prays to Venus, ". . . Goddess of Beauty, spare Nature the affront that such a perfect model should be the image of what is not." To his delighted amazement, he sees the figure move and come down from the pedestal (O.C., 11:317–326). In *Künstlers Erdewallen* (1774) the artist is in love with his painting of Venus Urania (W.A. I, 16:143–144). Also in *Künstlers Apotheose* (first outline 1774) the Muse converses with the deceased and now transfigured artist about the picture of her that he painted in his lifetime (W.A. I, 16:159–161). In the dramatic fragment *Prometheus* (1774), however, there is a scene wherein the hero shows the goddess Minerva some statues which he thereupon calls to life. Stopping at the sculptured figure of a woman, he addresses her:

> Und du Pandora,
> Heiliges Gefäss der Gaben alle,
> Die ergötzlich sind
> Unter dem weiten Himmel,
> . . . .
> Das All in All—meine Pandora!
> (W.A. I, 39:202)

Künstlers Morgenlied (1774), according to Fuchs, illustrates how contact with a great work of art engenders a creative life. It gives one strength and courage to lead a strong and natural life, even if it runs counter to propriety and convention. Here, then, "Homer rejoins Rousseau" (p. 447).

In the *Tag- und Jahreshefte* for 1807 Goethe states that Prometheus was for him "an ever-present and animated fixed idea" (W.A. I, 36:27). Edith Braemer says that Goethe came into constant contact with the Prometheus theme.[11] This personification of defiance, which recurs so frequently in world literature, occupies a position of central importance in Goethe's "Sturm und Drang" productions, extending far beyond the dramatic fragment *Prometheus* and the ode of the same title. It is reflected again and again, Braemer asserts, in his poems and especially in his plays of that era, e.g., in the *Urfaust* and *Egmont* (pp. 118–120). Our present concern, however, is the relationship of the unfinished *Prometheus* to Rousseau.

The similarity between Prometheus' calling the statues to life and Pygmalion's animating Galathée in Rousseau's lyrical playlet has been pointed out. Just as striking is Goethe's depiction of primitive man's first steps toward cultural development in Rousseauesque terms.

A valley at the foot of Mount Olympus is the setting for the episode in which Prometheus defies Zeus:

> *Sieh nieder, Zeus,*
> *Auf meine Welt: sie lebt!*
> *Ich habe sie geformt nach meinem Bilde,*
> *Ein Geschlecht, das mir gleich sei,*
> *Zu leiden, zu weinen, zu geniessen und zu freuen sich*
> *Und dein nicht zu achten*
> *Wie ich!*
>
> (ll. 243–249)

Then, as the stage direction informs us, one sees the human race, already spread out through the entire valley. Some have been climbing trees to break off fruits, some are bathing in the water, and others are racing on the meadow, while maidens are plucking flowers and weaving garlands. This "liebliche Uridylle," as Richard M. Meyer describes it,[12] is interrupted when a man with some young trees that he has cut down steps up to Prometheus and tells him that he has brought them, as required. Prometheus asks how he got the trees out of the ground, and the man points to the sharp stone that he used. Hereupon Prometheus shows him how to make of trees and turf a shelter impenetrable to the elements. The man thanks Prometheus and inquires whether all his brethren may dwell in his hut, but Prometheus replies emphatically:

> *Nein!*
> *Du hast sie dir gebaut und sie ist dein.*
> *Du kannst sie teilen*
> *Mit wem du willt.*
> *Wer wohnen will, der bau' sich selber eine.*
>
> (ll. 274–278)

Immediately afterward two men appear, quarreling about goats. The first man tells the second that he shall not take a single one, for "Sie sind mir mein" (l. 281); he captured them alive with great difficulty and guarded them throughout the night. The second man claims that he himself killed a goat the day before and divided it with his brethren. He asks the first man for one of the goats, adding that the latter needs only one today, and that they can catch more tomorrow. Upon the refusal of the would-be owner, the second man knocks him down and escapes with one of the goats, to the great indignation of the victim, who complains bitterly to Prometheus.

At this point, mankind has reached the stage of development which Rousseau characterizes in the first sentence of the second part of his *Discours sur l'Inégalité parmi les hommes*: "The first man who, having enclosed a piece of land, dared say: *This is mine*, and found some people simple enough to believe him was the true founder of civil society" (O.C., 1:270). These parallels would certainly appear to be more than mere coincidence.

Goethe's farce *Satyros oder der vergötterte Waldteufel*, dating from 1773, has caused much controversy among critics, especially regarding its connection with Rousseau. For instance, Loiseau says that it has been very reasonably interpreted as a reaction to Rousseau's doctrines and their consequences.[13] As if echoing Loiseau, Barnes labels *Satyros* as a satirization of the Genevan's views.[14] The most satisfactory interpretation of the little drama is that of Hans M. Wolff.[15] Unlike Loiseau and Barnes, Wolff sees in the play not so much a satire on the ideas of Rousseau but a criticism of the pretentiousness and excesses of the adherents of "Sturm und Drang." He bases his conclusion on the text itself, especially Satyros' long speech at the end of the third act in which he incites the mob to return to a "natural" life. His harangue is divided into three parts, each of which has its particular significance. The first section, according to Wolff (p. 170), refers unmistakably to the first two treatises of Rousseau:

> Habt eures Ursprungs vergessen,
> Euch zu Sklaven versessen,
> Euch in Häuser gemauert,
> Euch in Sitten vertrauert,
> Kennt die goldnen Zeiten
> Nur als Märchen, von weiten.
> (ll. 123–128)

63

By developing an artificial civilization, mankind has lost contact with nature and has given up the pure happiness of original existence.

With the mob moaning its agreement, Satyros continues:

> Da eure Väter neugeboren
> Vom Boden aufsprangen,
> In Wonnetaumel verloren,
> Willkommelied sangen,
> An mitgeborner Gattin Brust,
> Der rings aufkeimenden Natur,
> Ohne Neid gen Himmel blickten,
> Sich zu Göttern entzückten.
> Und ihr—wo ist sie hin, die Lust
> An sich selbst? Siechlinge, verbannet nur!
>
> (ll. 130–139)

This part differs from the beginning of the speech, Wolff says, in that here the contrast between the old era and the new rests not on the moral superiority but on the poetic superiority of the primitive state (p. 171). The natural world depicted by Satyros is that of Hamann and Herder rather than that of Rousseau, Wolff tells us, and the ideas contained in this part of the speech are those of "Sturm und Drang" (p. 171).

Only in the third section does the satirical significance of the oration become apparent, as Satyros converts the "Volk" to a foolish cult of nature:

> Selig, wer fühlen kann,
> Was sei: Gott sein! Mann!
> Seinem Busen vertraut,
> Entäussert bis auf die Haut
> Sich alles fremden Schmucks
> Und nun, ledig des Drucks
> Gehäufter Kleinigkeiten, frei,
> Wie Wolken, fühlt, was Leben sei!
> Stehn auf seinen Füssen,
> Der Erde geniessen,
> Nicht kränklich erwählen,
> Mit Bereiten sich quälen;
> Der Baum wird zum Zelte,
> Zum Teppich das Gras,
> Und rohe Kastanien
> Ein herrlicher Frass!
>
> (ll. 141–156)

Satyros' plea for an immediate return to a natural existence so inflames the crowd that they shout their approval, even yearning for the promised raw chestnuts: "Rohe Kastanien! O hätten wir's schon!" (l. 157). This "paradise" is patently ludicrous.

The satire, Wolff declares (p. 170), lies in Satyros' inference that Man can return to the Golden Age depicted by Rousseau and Hamann— something they knew to be impossible. Rousseau had limited his demands to a more rigid organization of society, and Hamann had confined his requirements to a renewed recognition of feeling in the aesthetic field. Satyros knows nothing of these limitations, nor of the irreconcilable contradiction between Rousseau's ethical man and Hamann's poetic man (p. 172). Satyros is the demagogue who uses the slogans and dynamics of "Sturm und Drang" to bend the mob to his will, but he ignores completely the disastrous results his power will have upon the people. Wolff suggests that Goethe is questioning the morality of genius; with all due admiration for heroism such as that of Götz and for Promethean Titanism, such egocentric lawlessness precludes any possibility of order in the world (p. 175). Wolff concludes that it is highly significant that as early as 1773 Goethe should see the conflict between the ethics of genius and the need of ordinary people for an external order. Satyros, he says, represents a step away from "Sturm und Drang" and toward "Humanität" (p. 176).

Obviously, if one accepts Wolff's conclusions, there remains no room whatever for the notion that in Satyros Goethe satirizes the ideas of Rousseau. Instead, we find the young Goethe already beginning to reflect upon the ultimate effect of brilliant heaven-stormers upon the world and to direct his thought gradually toward constructive endeavor in behalf of mankind, even as Jean-Jacques had earlier progressed from the impetuosity of the First and Second Discourses to the profound lessons of law and social order for mankind found in his more mature works.

The scholarly controversy over the nature of Rousseau's role in Satyros is minor compared with that which has surrounded the relationship between Die Leiden des jungen Werther and La Nouvelle Héloïse. Since the appearance of Goethe's novel in 1774, opinions concerning Rousseau's influence have ranged between the extremes of direct imitation and no relationship at all.[16] Until recently the issue was clouded by the mistaken assumption that Goethe's enthusiasm for Rousseau had cooled and by excessive attempts to interpret both novels biographically.[17]

Comparisons between the two novels began to appear almost at once. For example, on April 13, 1775 Johann Rudolf Frey, a Swiss lieutenant-colonel in the French service, wrote to Isaak Iselin, then clerk of the city council of Basel and a figure of some reputation in the literary world, asking whether his friend had read *Werther*:

Yesterday I devoured the First Part and have just finished the Second. Neither Richardson nor Jean-Jacques Rousseau affected me more strongly than the author of this novel (if it is one). . . . Certainly, I have also noticed a few flaws here and there, but they are easily excused by divine beauties. One could even object that this work was copied after *La Nouvelle Héloïse; Werther* does indeed remind one very much of Saint-Preux and Lotte of Julie, while Albert has nothing in common with Wolmar. However, you will have to confess that here everything is much more probable, much more in accord with the nature of things than in Rousseau's novel, details of which are delightful and often sublime, but the plot of which is absurd.[18]

The enthusiastic reception of *Werther* in France, impressively documented by Fernand Baldensperger,[19] commonly included its identification with *La Nouvelle Héloïse*. Such contemporaries of Goethe as Julie von Bondeli, Frey, Iselin, and Madame de Staël made this connection, as did later Sainte-Beuve, Émile Montégut,[20] and Pierre Leroux (an able translator of *Werther*). Not only did Goethe's chief fame in France continue to rest on *Werther* through more than half a century, but that work was regularly mentioned together with *La Nouvelle Héloïse* as a prototype for such novels as Constant's *Adolphe* and Chateaubriand's *René*. As late as 1905 Joachim Merlant refers to "two great names [which] now obtrude themselves upon the history of the autobiographical novel: Rousseau and Goethe."[21]

Erich Schmidt's monograph *Richardson, Rousseau und Goethe* appeared in 1875 and dominated scholarship on the Goethe-Rousseau question in both France and Germany for decades. After discussing in the second part the origin of *La Nouvelle Héloïse*, its reception, and its widespread effect on German writers of that period, Schmidt then offers a fairly detailed comparative analysis of *Werther* and Rousseau's novel. At the outset Schmidt discusses the content and composition, pronouncing *Werther* the more artistically executed work because it lacks the long digressions found in *La Nouvelle Héloïse*. Episodes in Goethe's novel are compared with those of Rousseau's narrative, whose tendentious character is stressed. Schmidt deals with the two love stories, finding a great similarity between Saint-Preux and Werther, although Goethe's hero wins praise for being the more consistent.[22] Understandably, the subject of suicide occupies a conspicuous place (p. 229). Lastly, there is a consideration of stylistic matters, while supplements present data on "models and descendants" of the two romances (pp. 230–317).

In his important survey of the German novel during Goethe's era, Hans Heinrich Borcherdt calls attention to the fact that only eight years lie between the appearance of Wieland's *Agathon* (1766) and the publication of Goethe's *Werther* (1774). The one he describes as a "crystal-clear" novel of self-development characteristic of the "Aufklärung," the other as a "passion-filled" psychological novel of "Sturm und Drang." Rousseau played an important role in the intellectual revolution which transpired between those two dates, Borcherdt continues, and with *La Nouvelle Héloïse* the history of the novel in modern times begins.[23] Yet Wieland himself had derived inspiration from Jean-Jacques, and the immense popularity in Germany of Rousseau's novel and then of *Werther* had been prepared in part by Gellert, Gessner, Klopstock, and other German writers,[24] and in part by the English novelist Samuel Richardson (whose significance for Rousseau is treated in the first part of Erich Schmidt's book).

German critics continued to magnify the points of similarity between the two novels until well into our century. Even Friedrich Gundolf retained the view that *La Nouvelle Héloïse* was the "technical model" for *Werther*, although he suggested that Goethe would probably have chosen the form of the lyrical "Briefroman" without Rousseau's example.[25] In 1921, however, Hans Gose cautioned against exaggerating the likenesses and ignoring certain fundamental differences.[26] Other scholars turned away from the oversimplified Schmidt interpretation of *Werther* as a sentimental novel in the Richardson-Rousseau tradition.[27] The psychological aspects were treated by Max and Helene Herrmann around the turn of the century,[28] a generation later by Ernst Feise (with only slight reference to Rousseau),[29] and toward mid-century by Robert T. Clark. The latter's analysis of the schematic framework of the novel indicates that its psychology can be systematized according to ideas of Herder which were familiar to Goethe.[30]

There is no denying the resemblances between *La Nouvelle Héloïse* and *Werther*. The heroes in both experience passionate but hopeless love, as the beloved weds another. There is in both a reverence for "God-

Nature," a fondness for people in humble walks of life and especially for children, depiction of the joys and sorrows of country or village folk, and the contrasting of their simple existence with the corrupt or pampered ways of life frequently found in upper classes of society. Both Saint-Preux and Werther are given to cultivating the "reality of the imaginary," to use Marc Eigeldinger's expression,[31] and, like Faust, they insist upon the primacy of feeling.

The divergences are also numerous. Rousseau uses six main characters, Goethe three. The letters which the author allegedly edits are all written by Werther himself, rather than by several persons, as in Rousseau's novel. *La Nouvelle Héloïse* contains only letters, with any comments appearing in footnotes, while the author of *Werther* at times allows narration to intervene. Long digressions on such subjects as English gardens, dueling, marriage, social circles, and the theater in Paris are replaced in *Werther* by actual episodes, such as those of the jealous peasant, the insane man, and the slight endured by Werther in an aristocratic milieu. The leading figures in Goethe's novel are all of the middle class, while Saint-Preux is the only one in Rousseau's narrative who is not of the lesser nobility.

Loiseau finds the action itself profoundly different despite apparent likeness of situations. Rousseau shows us at the outset the passion of Saint-Preux already at its height. The sole obstacle in the way of the two lovers, their different social levels, proves insuperable.[32] Julie marries within her class, Saint-Preux continues to love her, but he is resigned to renunciation. No further action is possible, and the novel ends lamely with the opportune death of Julie. By contrast, Loiseau points out, Goethe allows us to witness "by eminently pathetic gradation" the birth, slow growth, and explosion of Werther's tragic love. Renunciation is impossible for a man like Werther, and his suicide is both psychologically motivated and highly dramatic. Loiseau adds (with his anti-Rousseau penchant) that the characters in *Werther* are more natural and life-like than those in *La Nouvelle Héloïse*. He particularly contrasts Julie with Lotte in this regard (p. 328).

Julie von Bondeli penned the oft-quoted statement: "Werther is a Saint-Preux, more ardent, gloomier, and still more eccentric."[33] Yet there is a fundamental difference in that Saint-Preux does not commit suicide, for all his talk of it, but eventually recovers his equilibrium. Werther, on the contrary, is a pathological case. It is a commonplace that he would have killed himself sooner or later, even without his disappointment over

Lotte. As Wilhelm Nowack expresses it, he cannot live, like Saint-Preux, in the house of his beloved when she is married to another.[34]

One tends to forget that most readers of *Werther* are not familiar with the original version of 1774, but only with the revision of a decade later. The variations between the two, which have been set forth in detail by Martin Lauterbach,[35] hardly indicate a turning-away from Rousseau, as the outworn nineteenth-century theory held. In fact, Goethe's addition of the "Bauernbursch" episode indicates that he had moved even closer to the sentiments of Jean-Jacques on social questions and, perhaps, on matters of instinct and the subconscious. (Probably the main reason for its inclusion was, as Hans Reiss suggests, that Goethe wished to accentuate certain features of the character of *Werther*.)[36]

The nature descriptions in *Werther* have continued to inspire comparison with *La Nouvelle Héloïse*, as has been mentioned. In the *Briefe aus der Schweiz*, of which Werther is also the supposed author, there are descriptions of Alpine scenery which could hardly be distinguished, at a casual reading, from those in *La Nouvelle Héloïse* and the *Confessions*. In fact, one French biographer of Goethe styles those letters from (and about) Switzerland a "perpetual commentary" on Rousseau's gospel of nature.[37]

Enthusiasm for nature likewise permeates Goethe's lyric poetry of the early 1770's, from Sesenheim on. Particularly emblematic of the pantheistic feeling of being at one ("Einssein") with nature is *Ganymed*. Arthur Kutscher considers Goethe's and Herder's interest in the "Volkslied" a reflection of Rousseau's assertion that poetry is not the private inheritance of a few highly cultured men, but a gift to the world and the nations.[38] Using many diary quotations, Maurice Bémol traces the inspiration derived from Rousseau through Goethe's lyric creations as far as *Wanderers Nachtlied II* (1780).[39]

As in *Werther*, the problem of the individuality destroyed by conflicting forces appears in *Clavigo*. This, says H. J. Meessen, is the issue which occupies Goethe rather than the matter of a faithless lover who yields to arguments in favor of the prerogative of the exceptional man. Meessen finds it regrettable that *Clavigo* is often dismissed with a brief discussion in which Goethe is chided for returning to the dramatic technique of the French after producing *Götz von Berlichingen*, and which generally quotes Merck's criticism that others could write a play like that.[40] Although Goethe followed the *Mémoires* of Beaumarchais for most of the content of the drama, Georg Grempler relates it to the "Wertherstimmung" and to Rousseau, especially since it was written directly after *Werther*. As Grempler points out, the sentimental mood ("empfindsame Stimmung") in *Werther* rests on the antithesis between "Natur und Kultur" and in *Clavigo* on the contrast between the simple middle-class existence and the corrupt world of the court. He particularly attributes the "sentimental feeling" of the titular hero to the effect of Rousseau's works (*Émile* as well as *La Nouvelle Héloïse*) upon Goethe.[41]

Goethe's next completed drama, *Stella, Schauspiel für Liebende*, published in January, 1776, at once caused a controversy. The theme of bigamy shocked the theater-going public, as well as many readers, to such an extent that Goethe finally revised it in 1805 as a "Trauerspiel" in which Fernando shoots himself instead of living happily with both Stella and his wife Cäcilie. The original version is the important one, forming the transition between *Werther* and *Faust* and introducing a new note in that it deals with the situation of a man whom erotic love precipitates into a conflict between that love and freedom, which he soon gives up for a new passion. In *Faust*, to which, Meessen declares, *Stella* forms the pendant, the conflict is between love and "freedom for boundless experience."[42]

Here, too, a Rousseauesque element is present. The play, it has been said, deals solely with love, and the dilemma of the sentimental, vacillating hero is not resolved by suicide, as in the case of Werther, or by renunciation, like that of Saint-Preux or even of Eduard in *Die Wahlverwandtschaften*. Instead, a "ménage à trois" is happily arranged, composed in this instance of a man and two women—the opposite of the sometime affair of Mme de Warens with Jean-Jacques and Claude Anet.

Goethe tells us in *Dichtung und Wahrheit* that the opera *Erwin und Elmire* was inspired by the poetic romance that Goldsmith inserted in *The Vicar of Wakefield*, and which, he declares, "had delighted us" (presumably himself and Lili Schönemann) "in our best time, when we did not suspect that something similar lay ahead of us" (W.A. I, 29:160). Although Goethe does not make reference to Rousseau in this instance, the plot and other features of his "Singspiel" strikingly resemble the *Devin du village*, which he saw performed by the French players at Frankfurt as a boy. In the *Italienische Reise* Goethe himself calls attention to the kinship of *Erwin und Elmire* with the French operettas (W.A. I, 32:79–80); although he does not mention Rousseau specifically in that passage, the *Devin* is undoubtedly among those to which he refers.[43] The "Singspiel"

Claudine von Villabella was also inspired by the *Devin du village*.[44]

The above-mentioned "Singspiele" and monodramas, Goethe's liking for the *Consolations des misères de ma vie*, and the fondness of both Goethe and Rousseau for Italian (or Italianate) opera all suggest a far-reaching correspondence of opinion concerning music. Aron, referring to Goethe's plan for a *Tonlehre* as a companion-piece to his *Farbenlehre*, finds essential agreement between Goethe's statements about music and Rousseau's discussion of false analogy between colors and sounds in the *Essai sur l'origine des langues*.[45] Finally, Goethe's acknowledged appropriation of Rousseau's letter to Grimm concerning Rameau for the notes to his translation of Diderot's dialogue further indicates a similarity of viewpoint.

Egmont figures prominently among the works of Goethe listed by Kayser (H.A. 4:596) as following in the wake of Rousseau's *Pygmalion*. He refers mainly to the widely discussed operatic ending, but one thinks also of the songs sung by Klärchen. The musical potentialities of the play were sufficient to make it attract even Beethoven's genius. The play is noted for its folk scenes in Brussels, namely, in four of the five acts: first, the "Armbrustschiessen" (W.A. I, 8:173–183); then the opening scene of the second act, on the square, where Egmont appears with his retinue (W.A. I, 8:210); next, at the beginning of the fourth act, the scene "Strasse," in which the burghers of Brussels are excitedly discussing Alba's order prohibiting conversation on the street by even two or three people (W.A. I, 8:244–252); and, lastly, Klärchen's valiant effort to marshal the aid of the citizenry for freeing Egmont (W.A. I, 8:274–280). These scenes exhibit a Rousseau-like character, in that a few well-defined individuals stand out as representatives of the lower middle class—"Kleinbürger" similar to those of Frankfurt in Goethe's boyhood. Compare Rousseau's vivid depiction (in the *Confessions*) of persons from the humbler walks of life with whom he came into contact, such as Madame Basile, at Turin (C.G., p. 66), Claude Anet (C.G., pp. 164–165), or the peasant who fed the wandering Jean-Jacques (C.G., pp. 150–151).

The conflict of opposites representing "Gefühl" and "Verstand," common to Rousseau and Goethe, is especially evident in this drama, whose hero takes a stand on the side of "Gefühl" which associates him with Klärchen—a "Mädchen aus dem Volk" *par excellence*—and with his middle-class compatriots, in contrast to the adherents of "Verstand," like Oranien and Alba. Egmont acts from intuition, or from those "natural sentiments," which, according to the Vicar of Savoy in Émile, are to be distinguished from "acquired ideas," since we feel before we gain knowledge. The Vicar characterizes love of good, hatred of evil, and acts of conscience (all of which are characteristic of Egmont) as born of feeling rather than of judgment (C.G., p. 353).

There are also certain points of tangency between Rousseau's La Nouvelle Héloïse and Goethe's Iphigenie. The psychological complexity in both strikes a new note. R. M. Browning points out that Iphigenie's doctrine of humanity does not preclude her own self-interest; it is only when she admits her personal motives to Thoas that her humane goal is achieved. The harmonizing of the double motives, personal and idealistic, lends the play a certain modernity.[46] Lester G. Crocker sees the psychological aspect of La Nouvelle Héloïse as its true greatness. Rousseau introduces his readers also to a complex world of double motives, where the mixture of the conscious and the unconscious in the human soul is depicted. This psychological realism explains the renewed interest in Rousseau's novel in the twentieth century.[47]

Vermeil sees a distinct similarity between Julie and Iphigenie. While Iphigenie experiences no fall through passion, she is descended from the Tantalids and does bear the weight of the evil fatality afflicting her race. Hers too is a soul at the same time serene and passionate. Although she exerts a beneficent influence, she feels a distaste for this easy practice of virtue. Her life is "an anticipated death"—a nostalgia like that of Julie after her marriage. Iphigenie's revelation of the secret of her origin to Thoas reminds Vermeil of Julie's acknowledgment of her fall. Both are not able to live without perfect self-esteem, for they possess and reflect the divine image.[48] Iphigenie cures Orestes, even as Julie cures Saint-Preux. The latter, says Vermeil, has his Pylades in the person of Milord Éduoard. Finally, in beseeching the gods, "Rettet euer Bild in meiner Seele" (l. 1717), she utters a thought akin to the following words of Julie (who also guards her integrity and preserves the divine image): "Enter again into the depths of thy soul; there thou wilt see that eternal image of the truly good, which our passions unceasingly sully, without being able to efface it." Vermeil asks also whether Julie is not the first personification of the Eternal Womanly celebrated in Faust (p. 64).

Various other aspects of Goethe's play remind one of Rousseau. Above all, the "reine Menschlichkeit" which Iphigenie so peerlessly represents is in conformity with Rousseau's immediate concern for his fellow men and with his fondly cherished ideal of an eventually higher humanity. The classical setting and the almost Greek simplicity of the play offer a strong contrast to the seventeenth-century "Roman" dramas of Corneille and others, which Rousseau felt had little meaning for the theater-going public of Paris in his day (O.C., 8:362). He, who had experienced the bitterness of exile, could have readily understood her longing:

> Und an dem Ufer steh' ich lange Tage,
> Das Land der Griechen mit der Seele suchend.
> (ll. 11–12)

Goethe himself admitted that he had put much of his own life and situation in Weimar into *Torquato Tasso* (1790),[49] but he also received stimulation from Rousseau. For instance, Rousseau's *Consolations des misères de ma vie*, which contains the Tasso verses sung alternately by the Venetian gondoliers, had prepared Goethe for full appreciation of their skill when he first visited Venice in 1786. Several decades later Goethe translated the preface to Stapfer's French edition of *Tasso*, in which Rousseau and Werther are linked with the Italian poet, a further apparent corroboration of Goethe's association of Rousseau with Tasso.

Paola Ambri Berselli traces the allusions to Tasso in *La Nouvelle Héloïse*, including him with Petrarch and Metastasio as the poets of Italy who exerted the greatest charm upon Rousseau.[50] His predilection for Tasso could hardly have been lost upon Goethe. Before his Italian journey and his attendant occupation with the subject of Tasso, he had read the *Confessions* (First Part) and was therefore readily able to associate in his mind the two writers and their individual complexities. James Sime suggests that Goethe probably thought of Tasso, too, when he wrote his well-known words about Rousseau's hypochondria and his own similar, if less extreme, tendency.[51]

Various passages in Goethe's drama seem to apply as appropriately to Rousseau as to Tasso. When Duke Alfons complains of Tasso's "old failing" of seeking solitude rather than society (ll. 243–244), one thinks immediately of Diderot and the others who criticized Jean-Jacques for the same propensity.

Above all, the conversation between Tasso and the Princess Leonore about the Golden Age has been associated with Rousseau. Eigeldinger states that Rousseau's creative work invites us to consider the Golden Age not as an idle fancy, but as an intimate reality which we must discover

73

through ourselves in order to confer upon it a spiritual duration (p. 161).
The Princess echoes this idea when she says:

> Mein Freund, die goldne Zeit ist wohl vorbei:
> Allein die Guten bringen sie zurück;
> Und soll ich dir gestehen, wie ich denke:
> Die goldne Zeit, womit der Dichter uns
> Zu schmeicheln pflegt, die schöne Zeit, sie war,
> So scheint es mir, so wenig als sie ist;
> Und war sie je, so war sie nur gewiss,
> Wie sie uns immer wieder werden kann.
>
> (ll. 995–1002)

In his discussion of Goethe's mainly fragmentary dramatic efforts to deal with the French Revolution, Brunet maintains that *Der Grosskophta* shows Goethe to be "a disciple of Rousseau and a friend of truth." As illustrations of the congruence of their ideas he lists the depiction of the greed and lack of principle of the "entire mass of rogues or naive persons" in that play, the thirst for wealth and the unscrupulous self-interest portrayed in *Die natürliche Tochter*, the vices of the nobility in *Die Aufgeregten* and *Das Mädchen von Oberkirch*, and the class distinctions accentuated in the latter work.[52]

Brunet states that preventing these evils is the task of a good administration. Opportune reforms should be made before men's minds have had time to turn to thoughts of revolt. This principle triumphs in the *Bürgergeneral* and in *Die Aufgeregten*, another incidence of Goethe's sharing Rousseau's ideas (p. 48). Brunet remarks that benevolent, charitable nobles like Wolmar, or Lothario and Nathalie, never provoke revolutionary violence (p. 51). He goes on to say that by depicting in *Der Bürgergeneral* a great nobleman animated by paternal sentiments toward his subjects and by lending to the countess in *Die Aufgeregten* such a desire for justice Goethe wished to demonstrate "that there was a solution to the problem of classes and that revolutions could be prevented by wisdom on the part of those governing." His love of order leads him to detest all excesses: those of despotism, like Rousseau, and, again like Rousseau, those of the brutalized and stupid mob, given over to unbridled license as soon as their chains are shaken off (p. 52).

Attention has been called (in chapter two) to the unusual distinction which Goethe conferred upon Rousseau by mentioning him in *Die natürliche Tochter* in the role of Eugenie's former preceptor. Even without

that complimentary gesture there would repeatedly be occasion for recalling the principles and maxims of Jean-Jacques. In this, the last of
Goethe's works centering around the French Revolution, the unhappy
conditions of the realm are depicted in a manner reminiscent of those
which Rousseau describes in his Second Discourse as conducive to "Despotism's gradually raising its frightful head" (C.G., p. 90). One may assume that disregard of his social and political theories has caused, at least
in part, the bitterness and growing misanthropy of the "wise man" who
was once the Princess's teacher, just as in actuality policies contrary to
Rousseau's doctrines brought on the catastrophe only a little more than
a decade after his death.

Goethe never came nearer to creating real villains than in this drama,
which according to Ernst Jockers has been treated as a "stepchild" by
Goethe scholarship in general. Jockers sees in this play the "Verbürger-
lichung des Adels," or the process of converting the nobility to citizens[53]
—a concept suggestive of Rousseau's "civil state" as outlined in the eighth
chapter of Book One of the Contrat social (C.G., pp. 246–247). The
sacrifice of Eugenie as an individual, whether for reasons of state or for
the advantage of unscrupulous persons, is as much against Rousseau's
precepts as the general injustices causing the debacle. "Man," Julie insists, "is a being too noble to have to serve simply as an instrument for
others, and people ought not to use him for what suits them without considering also what suits him in relation to himself" (O.C., 8:214). Thus,
in the crucial epoch of the Revolution, Goethe remains in accord with the
Citizen of Geneva.[54]

Wilhelm Meisters Lehrjahre (completed 1796) was rarely connected
to Rousseau during the era of Erich Schmidt and his followers. Recent
decades have brought an increasing realization of his importance for that
novel, whether in its original and fragmentary form, Wilhelm Meisters
theatralische Sendung, to which Hugo von Hofmannsthal accords such
high praise,[55] or as the finished Lehrjahre. Rousseau's ideas are probably
more in evidence in the mature work than in the Sendung, though sometimes less tangible as such than in the Wanderjahre (final version 1829).

Madeleine B. Ellis regards La Nouvelle Héloïse as a synthesis of its
author's thought,[56] and much the same could be maintained regarding
the Lehrjahre for the period of its completion. Not only are both to a large
extent novels of education, but each presents a Weltbild. This is true of
Wilhelm Meister to a greater degree than of Werther because of its length

and scope, although the earlier novel is artistically more satisfying and touches briefly upon a vast segment of human experience. But along with La Nouvelle Héloïse and Émile, according to Melitta Gerhard, the impact of Rousseau's Confessions was so decisive that that work, as a great example of the new evaluation of the inner life, became indirectly a forerunner of the "Entwicklungsroman."[57] The Lehrjahre, then, encompasses numerous features of all three of Rousseau's works. Among the Rousseau-like characteristics which Benrubi discovers in the Lehrjahre is the fundamental fact that Goethe does not present to his readers a man already made, and still less a perfect man, but rather makes them witness the inner development of a man solely concerned with realizing the vocation for which he feels he was born. In the same manner as Rousseau, says Benrubi, Goethe abhors any form of education which aims only at training a child for a trade or profession instead of first making a man of him.[58] Henri Lichtenberger considers "this education for liberty" ultimately based on Rousseau's faith in the holiness of nature and the original goodness of Man.[59] Ronald Gray sees this novel as the first of a long line of narratives deriving in part from Émile, and in part from the picaresque novel and its descendants in the eighteenth century dealing with the theme of self-development. Therefore Gray designates it as the first "Bildungsroman" of importance.[60]

We are dealing, then, with the education of an individual for life. The training of children finds more specific treatment in Wilhelm Meisters Wanderjahre (discussed later in chapter six). There, says Benrubi, Goethe remains in accord with Rousseau when he repeats what he has already stressed in the Lehrjahre, namely that the secret of true education is in developing the faculties with which children are endowed.[61]

As Vermeil points out, Wilhelm begins with a sentimental crisis that causes him also to think of suicide; then he triumphs by elevating his entire personality in the trials that destiny brings to him—an idea common to Rousseau and Goethe. Meister, like Saint-Preux, is cured of his "absorbing sentimentality" and of his dilettantism and arrives at a knowledge of mankind as well as self-mastery. Vermeil stresses the importance for both authors of travel for that process,[62] as does also Rodolfo Mondolfo.[63]

The naturalness and spontaneity of the actors with whom Wilhelm associates make them appeal to him as individuals. His favorable impression of them is just the opposite of what Saint-Preux describes in his letter to Julie concerning the theatrical performances he has attended in Paris

(C.G., pp. 227–228). As an example of that naturalness W. H. Bruford cites the confession of Madame Melina before the magistrate (whose reaction to it is less favorable than that of Wilhelm).[64] Bruford considers this novel both a mirror of society and a far-reaching criticism thereof. He links it with Werther, Tasso, and Faust by the contrast in all four works between the inner and the outer world. The hero, Bruford continues, learns during his apprenticeship to adjust his dreams to the reality of actual life (p. 28). Here Wilhelm follows the example of Saint-Preux, who likewise comes to terms with a more realistic mode of existence than that envisioned in his erstwhile dreams.

Furthermore, the women and girls whom Wilhelm meets remind one not infrequently of those encountered in the autobiographies of both writers. For instance, Philine appears as real and convincing as the girls depicted in the pages of the Confessions and Dichtung und Wahrheit.

Nor is the mystic, transcendent element lacking. The supposed revival of Julie, with the resultant belief among the servants and peasants that she is not dead, is repeated in the Lehrjahre upon the passing of Sperata (W.A. I, 23:280–283), who is a forerunner in this respect of Ottilie in Die Wahlverwandtschaften. In short, these and other instances suggest that an avid reader of Rousseau could feel at home in Goethe's Wilhelm Meister.

With the exception of Werther none of Goethe's writings has been mentioned in connection with Rousseau as often as Faust, especially the First Part, which falls chronologically within the confines of this chapter. Specific phases of the Second Part which seem to bear some relation to Jean-Jacques are treated in later chapters.

Particularly the Faust of "Sturm und Drang," as he appears in the Urfaust, has been linked repeatedly with Rousseau. For instance, Benrubi asks whether there is anything more Rousseauistic than the pessimism of Faust regarding civilization, as expressed in the opening monologue. On the basis of "terrible personal experiences," Faust declares that the accumulation of knowledge, or rather the progress of civilization, does not constitute the true happiness of the human race. He is weary of a civilization that furnishes him no inward satisfaction. He has a horror of verbalism and pedantry. Like Rousseau, he feels that life comes before all action. Instead of living nature, in which God created Man, Faust sees skeletons around him. He, too, is tormented by the desire for a return to nature, in which he sees the source of all true life.[65]

According to George Santayana, Faust's magic arts are the sacrament of initiation into his new religion, that of nature. His turning to nature in its wild aspects is seen as more characteristic of the era of Goethe than of that of his hero.[66]

Like Werther, Faust feels tempted to commit suicide, but like Saint-Preux, he is dissuaded. On his Easter walk with Wagner, in the scene "Vor dem Tor" (which offers an unrivaled folk-pageant), he beholds people of all classes enjoying a festive day in the open with a carefree abandon equal to that of the vintagers at Clarens (*La Nouvelle Héloïse*, C.G., pp. 559–564). Their joy in being alive and "resurrected," as Faust describes them, receives a Rousseau-like expression from him:

> *Hier ist des Volkes wahrer Himmel,*
> *Zufrieden jauchzet gross und klein:*
> *Hier bin ich Mensch, hier darf ich's sein!*
> (ll. 938–940)

Just as Rousseau's Vicar of Savoy aspires to the moment when, delivered from bodily shackles, he will be himself, without contradiction or division, and will need only himself to be happy (*Émile*, C.G., p. 358), so Faust, while on that same Easter outing, longs to soar aloft, following the now setting sun in its course. After lamenting, in conversation with the rationalistic Wagner, the presence of two conflicting souls within his breast, Faust calls upon whatever airy spirits may hold sway between earth and sky:

> *So steiget nieder aus dem goldnen Duft*
> *Und führt mich weg zu neuem, buntem Leben!*
> (ll. 1120–1121)

From the "Volk," so abundantly and variously represented in this scene of holiday merrymaking, comes Gretchen, Goethe's most charming and appealing creation of femininity—even before her redeeming mission in behalf of Faust becomes evident. His reply to Gretchen's troubled inquiry about his religious beliefs has been compared to the Vicar's profession of faith. The latter expresses the inability of Man to comprehend the Supreme Intelligence who governs the world, who formed the universe and all that exists, and who has made and ordered everything (*Émile*, C.G., pp. 346–347). Similarly, Faust asks who may name, or dare proclaim belief or unbelief in, the One thus characterized:

Der Allumfasser,
Der Allerhalter,
Fasst und erhält er nicht
Dich, mich, sich selbst?
Wölbt sich der Himmel nicht da droben?
Liegt die Erde nicht hierunten fest?
Und steigen freundlich blickend
Ewige Sterne nicht herauf?

(ll. 3438–3445)

Benrubi views the whole course of the action of *Faust* as exemplifying a community of ideas on the part of Rousseau and Goethe. Having broken definitely with civilization, Faust seeks happiness in the satisfaction of his egoistic needs, only to experience much greater deception and bitterness than in the case of his accumulation of knowledge: not only does he feel his own wretchedness, but likewise that of those whom he has selfishly plunged into unhappiness. Yet Faust's pessimism with respect to civilization and egoistic enjoyments is not an absolute one. His discontent, just as in Rousseau's instance, is the necessary consequence of a higher ideal of human destination that he vaguely feels within himself. Referring to the conclusion of Part Two, Benrubi states that Goethe's *Faust* may be called "the finest illustration of Rousseau's faith in the original goodness of Man."[67] Certainly, Faust's sympathy with the sum total of human misery as a result of Gretchen's plight at the end of Part One resembles Rousseau's general concern for mankind.

An external parallelism that was early observed is the similarity of situation between ll. 2687–2728 of *Faust* and Part I, Letter 54, of *La Nouvelle Héloïse*, in that each hero tarries alone in the bedchamber of his beloved. Both Saint-Preux and Faust call the room a sanctuary, and the place heightens the feeling of love on the part of each.[68]

Especially significant is the correspondence between the "Pact Scene" in *Faust* and a passage in the Fifth Promenade of the *Rêveries*. There is both a general likeness of situation and a noteworthy resemblance of phraseology. Faust defies the Devil to bring him to the point of such enjoyment as will make him say to the passing moment: "Stay, thou art so fair!"[69] The *Promeneur*, after speaking at some length on the changeability and transitoriness of everything on earth, remarks: ". . . I scarcely believe there is such a thing as enduring happiness. Even in our supreme enjoyments there is indeed hardly a moment where the heart really says to us: *I would that this moment might last forever!* (*Je voudrais que cet instant durât toujours!*)." And Rousseau himself italicized these words.

The foregoing résumé embraces the four decades extending from Goethe's student days at Leipzig to his completion of *Faust I* in 1806. It summarizes numerous studies which seek to establish a literary relationship between Goethe and Rousseau. Some theories are convincing, others are tenuous (for example, Vermeil's comparison of Iphigenie to Julie might be regarded as contrived), but in their totality they suggest that Rousseau exerted a strong inspirational effect upon Goethe. From this survey of what others have demonstrated or postulated for Goethe's early and middle years as a starting-point, we shall proceed to compare several of his mature works with Rousseau's chief writings. The comparisons which follow constitute in the main the original research of this book.

IV

Memories
and Memoirs

Like Rousseau, Goethe preferred biography to history. His extensive acquaintance with autobiographical writings started with Augustine's *Confessiones*, although his closer preoccupation with famous men began with the Renaissance. His interest in Benvenuto Cellini's autobiography caused him to translate it, and he admired the memoirs of the Milanese physician Girolamo Cardano. Like Rousseau, he was fascinated by Montaigne's self-analysis. Most important of all, a sixteenth-century German knight's account (an *apologia*) of his tempestuous career inspired Goethe to dramatize it as *Götz von Berlichingen*, which in 1773 first brought him national renown.

Yet it was three autobiographies from Goethe's own time which touched him most intimately. Two originated within Goethe's circle of friends. In 1777 he actively encouraged Johann Heinrich Jung (called Jung-Stilling) to publish his novel-like memoirs, *Heinrich Stillings Jugend*. Karl Philipp Moritz' *Anton Reiser*, a fictionalized narration of his youthful struggles, dates from the years 1785–1790 (therefore, in part, from the period of his close association with Goethe in Italy). The third work, Rousseau's *Confessions*, largely determined the unsparingly self-revelatory character of *Anton Reiser*, according to Rudolf Lehmann, who considers Moritz a century ahead of his time in the psychological aspects of his novel.[1] Marcel Raymond also discusses Rousseau's relationship to *Anton Reiser*, for here, he says, the "curious hero" encounters "rather metaphysical adventures." Walking between dreaming and waking, between reality and unreality, he "attends the dissection of his life." Asking himself the meaning of his existence, he arrives at the idea "that, before any other step, it was necessary for him to seek himself in the series of his memories of the past. *He felt that existence had no firm support except in the uninterrupted chain of memories.*" Such recollections are feelings or sentiments which help the soul progressively identify itself. It is in this very way, Raymond says, "that Rousseau also tries to find again the chain of his "secret affections.""[2]

In 1782 Goethe compared the recently published First Part of Rousseau's *Confessions*, which he had just read, to "shining stars." Despite such expressions of admiration, the "Goethephilologie" of the late nineteenth and early twentieth centuries generally discounted any deeper significance of Rousseau's autobiography for Goethe. Nearly a century ago Gustav von Loeper asserted that without the *Confessions* Goethe would hardly have attempted the recital of his own life.[3] At the beginning of our own century Richard M. Meyer held that Rousseau was just as important for Goethe's memoirs as for *Werther*.[4] But most scholars echoed Karl Alt (1898)[5] and Kurt Jahn (1908),[6] who, in their well-known commentaries on *Dichtung und Wahrheit* rejected even the possibility that the *Confessions* served as a "model" or even as a stimulus.

Except in an article of anonymous authorship in the *Edinburgh Review*,[7] one notes a decided penchant during the succeeding decades for pointing out contrasts rather than likenesses between the two works. Martin Sommerfeld, for instance, finds that Rousseau wrote without the proper "distance" between the narrator and the reader on the one hand, and between the teller and the hero of the tale on the other. The polemical character of the Second Part causes the author to appear as an advocate rather than as a confessor.[8] Although he discovers a similarity in character presentation, Arthur Franz also sees a basic contrast. Goethe presents his environment and determines the thoroughness and delicacy of his portraits in *Dichtung und Wahrheit* according to the degree to which the persons mentioned affected him, whereas Rousseau emphasizes himself and his feelings and portrays by preference those individuals on whom he made the greatest impression.[9] Ewald A. Boucke, while somewhat grudgingly admitting the general import of the *Confessions* for

Goethe, denies any close resemblance to Rousseau's book in design, style, or technique, except in the idyl of Sesenheim. There, he says, "Goethe also succeeded in dreaming his way back to those blissful days," after the manner of Rousseau, by the "chaîne des sentiments." [10] Loiseau declares that there was no need of the example of the Confessions to inspire Goethe's autobiography, that an abyss separates his objective portrayal of intellectual and moral development from the "so often malignant, illusory, and sophistic pro domo of Rousseau." [11] Moreover, the very studies most indicative of community of interest between Goethe and Rousseau, such as those of Benrubi and Aron, are only slightly concerned with Dichtung und Wahrheit itself.

More recent commentators on the Goethe-Rousseau relationship express a noncommittal or negative view. Ernst Beutler, like many before him, regards the Confessions as pathological. [12] Although most discussions are brief, Roy Pascal devotes a sixteen-page essay to what he terms a search for the "significant differences" between the two authors. [13] Pascal also proceeds from the time-honored assumption that although the youthful Goethe owed much to Rousseau, his later attitude became one of coolness, even hostility. Pascal regards Rousseau's autobiography as thoroughly confessional in character: "a confession of faith as well as a confession of sin." Dichtung und Wahrheit, on the contrary, shows a "serene and vigorous reflection" by the sexagenarian Goethe on his development as a poet and is less of a confession than most of his major works (p. 149). Goethe, Pascal maintains, is often too conscientious about biographical detail; Rousseau evokes only a "brightly-lit" past and shows profound insight into his temperament and those who affected him for good or ill, while his depictions of his world in general are vague by comparison with the milieu reproduced in Dichtung und Wahrheit (p. 151). Pascal points out a fundamental antithesis in Rousseau's belief that accident determined the course of his life, as opposed to Goethe's emphasis on the "necessity governing his development." Rousseau's disgust with social life contrasts with traditionalism in the political thought and behavior of Goethe. Rousseau sees freedom as a personal, psychological principle, whereas Goethe believes that life is purification of self, a finding of "new values," whose worth he learned from other persons. The determined nonconformism of Rousseau is the converse of Goethe's "accommodation" to social and moral proprieties (p. 156).

One of the most striking differences listed by Pascal lies in attitudes toward sex. The nonconformist Rousseau reaches deeply "into the case of irrational instinct" and employs an excessive frankness in the *Confessions*, while *Dichtung und Wahrheit* conspicuously lacks "evidence of normal or abnormal sex life, except in the sublimated form of love." Pascal considers it beyond doubt that the boy Goethe passed through the "sexual experiences common to youngsters" and suggests that they were probably of an unusual liveliness; his suppression of that element, which Rousseau felt constrained to present to the reader, is part of the "whole intention" of his autobiographical work (p. 157). Finally, Pascal maintains that both Rousseau and Goethe see the world of imagination as opposed to that of normal society, but differently; for Rousseau imagination becomes a refuge from normal existence in which Goethe is all the more able to play his part because of the emotive release afforded him by his imaginative province, born of and reflecting the actual world. Somehow Pascal still concludes that however opposite the autobiographical approaches of the two authors are, they nevertheless appear as complementary rather than antagonistic to each other (p. 161).

It is obvious that Pascal's viewpoint is conditioned by two extreme tendencies stemming from the positivistic era: the one sees Rousseau as an utterly subjective paranoiac or, at best (to quote Gustav Roethe), as a "great man with an impure soul,"[14] the other envisions a Goethe of supposedly "Olympian" serenity (as noted previously), objective alike in his depictions of environment and revelations of self. Actually, if the *Confessions* can be taken as a "confession of faith," then *Dichtung und Wahrheit* will qualify equally well in that respect; in fact, Friedrich Hiebel characterizes Goethe's account of his youth as confessional in the most comprehensive sense.[15] The allegedly greater exactness of detail is to be attributed to the external help which Goethe received and to his extensive reference to works contemporaneous with his early years, rather than to any essential difference in conception of the undertaking. Whereas Rousseau cites the loss "into other hands" of all the papers which he had assembled to supplement his memory and to guide him in that enterprise, Goethe writes (October 25, 1810) to Bettina Brentano asking her to record for him all the anecdotes of his childhood which his mother had related to her. He derives the description of the coronation of Joseph II and the attendant festivities largely from books on the subject. Goethe later made similar use of authentic information about the Roman carnival for the *Italienische Reise*. If Pascal judges the milieu reproduced by

Goethe to be less "vague" than that of Rousseau (p. 152), the chief reason lies in just such documentation, which Édouard Rod finds excessive. He misses in *Dichtung und Wahrheit* any trace of the candor, naiveté, and sincerity characteristic of Rousseau. Goethe, he insists, recalls his past for the purpose of explaining his literary works. While Rousseau shows a better recollection of feelings than of ideas, Goethe is often compelled to use his great skill to give a lively expression to certain parts of his auto- biography simply because he has largely forgotten his sentiments of earlier days.[16] Albert Cahen, on the contrary, thinks that Rousseau's autobiography is not sufficiently "composée"; it is too exact, "too much life itself"; the grandeur and the misery are not juxtaposed, but mingled too confusedly.[17]

Even difference of title has been interpreted (for example, by Jahn) as indicative of Goethe's declining interest in Rousseau. Yet Goethe re- ferred on a number of occasions (as, for example, in the above-mentioned letter to Bettina) to his "Bekenntnisse" and only later gave his memoirs their ultimate title. Years afterward he labeled the *Annalen oder Tag- und Jahreshefte* a "supplement to my confessions," meaning not just *Dich- tung und Wahrheit*, but also the accounts of his journeys to Italy and Switzerland as well as the *Campagne in Frankreich, Belagerung von Mainz*, and several shorter travel sketches. Besides, it is in that very narra- tive that he characterizes his literary creations as "fragments of one great confession" (W.A. I, 27:110). The "defensive" quality of the *Confes- sions* has frequently been overemphasized; especially in the First Part, dealing with his early decades, Rousseau sets forth his intellectual and cultural development. In *Dichtung und Wahrheit* Goethe does the same for the first quarter-century of his life.

The two works of course embrace unequal periods of time. While the *Confessions* cover the years 1712–1765, bringing the story of Rousseau's life down to the time when he began the writing of it, *Dichtung und Wahrheit* stops with Goethe's departure for Weimar in the fall of 1775, early in his twenty-seventh year. With his last work, the *Rêveries du promeneur solitaire*, Rousseau made his most significant addition to the *Confessions*. The *Italienische Reise* is the most noteworthy supplemen- tary autobiographical writing by Goethe.

Each author's immense correspondence forms an indispensable phase of the recording of his life history. Next in immediacy are the conversa- tions—much more extensive in Goethe's case, owing to the diligence of

Eckermann, Soret, Chancellor von Müller, and others. In his autobiographical works after *Dichtung und Wahrheit* (except in those parts of the *Italienische Reise* where he closely followed his diary of that journey), Goethe became ever less communicative about his inner life. This is especially true of the *Tag- und Jahreshefte*, written in the years 1819–1825. As if by way of compensation, his literary creations (e.g., *Die Wahlverwandtschaften*) assume an increasingly "confessional" significance.[18]

A well-known instance of fiction in *Dichtung und Wahrheit* occurs at the beginning, where Goethe purports to quote a letter from a "friend" who urges him to preserve his recollections in writing, citing this as one of his reasons for undertaking what he characterizes as always "bedenklich." Several pages further on, he elaborates on his ascribing a dubious character to the writing of one's memoirs in the following, often quoted passage: "For this seems to be the chief task of biography, to present the person amid the conditions of his time and to show how far the sum total worked against him; to what extent it favored him; how he formed from it an opinion of the world and Man; and how, if he is an artist, poet, or writer, he reflected it again externally. For this, however, something scarcely attainable is demanded, namely, that the individual should know himself and his century." Knowledge of self, Goethe explains, refers to how far the aforesaid individual remained the same under all circumstances; knowing one's century means comprehending it as a force which carries the willing as well as the unwilling along with it, determining and shaping them in such a way that anyone born only ten years earlier or later might have become a quite different person with regard to his own development and his effect upon others (W.A. I, 26:7–8).

Thus, even as Rousseau begins by saying that he is forming an enterprise unexampled in the past and never to be reproduced in the future, namely, of showing his fellow humans "a man in all the truth of nature"—himself (O.C., 14:1), so Goethe stresses the unprecedented character of his own undertaking as a scrupulously-minded autobiographer. Each, with his inviolable individuality, announces his intended self-revelation, particularly of the process of his evolution as man and artist in relationship to his surroundings and his contacts with the people about him; each is conscious of having a story to tell that cannot be duplicated—a narrative unique through the imprint of genius. Their expressed objectives, their respective approaches to the problem, and their procedures may differ in various respects, but there remains this fundamental likeness of plan: to bequeath to humanity the inimitable narrative of how its author responded to and acted upon the world of his day.

Now that some of the many claims of divergence between the *Confessions* and *Dichtung und Wahrheit* have been cited, let us observe the resemblances. The external correspondences begin with the two artists' depictions of childhood. "I came into the world," writes Jean-Jacques, "with so few signs of life that they entertained but little hope of preserving me" (O.C., 14:7). "I came into the world," says Johann Wolfgang, "as dead, and only after various efforts was I enabled to see the light" (W.A. I, 26:11). Rousseau informs us that his birth, which cost his mother her life, was the first of his misfortunes (O.C., 14:6). By contrast, Goethe states that his horoscope was propitious (W.A. I, 26:11); he thereby uses a motif employed by Cardano. Then Rousseau relates: "I suffered before I thought; it is the common lot of humanity. I have no knowledge of what passed prior to my sixth year" (O.C., 14:8). Goethe declares: "When we desire to recall what happened to us in the earliest period of youth, it often chances that we confuse what we have heard from others with what we really possess from our own direct experience" (W.A. I, 26:12). Rousseau's father, a Genevan citizen, depended on his earnings as a watchmaker. His son remarks: "My mother's circumstances were more affluent; she was the daughter of one Monsieur Bernard, a minister, and possessed both modesty and beauty; in fact, my father found some difficulty in obtaining her hand" (O.C., 14:5). Goethe's father, a citizen of Frankfurt, was indeed financially independent and in possession of the rather hollow title of Imperial Councilor, but he was the son of a tailor and the grandson of a blacksmith. He, too, elevated his position by a fortunate marriage, namely, to the winsome daughter of Frankfurt's highest official.

Rousseau and Goethe, although subjected as small boys to a certain amount of discipline, nevertheless did not suffer from lack of attention and tenderness. Jean-Jacques, however, states: "I was never permitted, while under the paternal roof, to play in the street with other children; I never had any occasion to contradict or indulge those fantastical humors which are usually attributed to nature, but are in reality the effects of education" (O.C., 14:5). After describing the so-called "garden room" of the house on the Grossen Hirschgraben, where he learned his lessons in the summer and watched thunderstorms and the sunset, Goethe continues: "And when . . . I saw the neighbors wandering through their gardens, caring for their flowers, the children playing, parties of friends enjoying themselves . . . , it early aroused in me a feeling of solitude, and a longing resulting from it, which, conspiring with the seriousness and awe planted in me by nature, exerted its influence at an early age, and showed itself more distinctly in later years" (W.A. I, 26:16).

Each received his first educational stimulus from his father. The elder Rousseau's avowed purpose in spending long nocturnal hours with Jean-Jacques over romances was to improve his son's ability to read (O.C., 14:8). Goethe describes his father as "altogether of a didactic turn," liking to communicate to others what he knew or was able to perform (W.A. I, 26:18). The early reading of both Rousseau and Goethe included Ovid's *Metamorphoses*, Molière's comedies, Fénelon's *Télémaque*, Defoe's *Robinson Crusoe*, and *Lord Anson's Voyage around the World*. Plutarch, whom Rousseau revered most among the first authors he read, was also highly regarded by Goethe. One of the latter's pleasantest memories of French theatricals during the occupation of Frankfurt was that of Rousseau's own *Devin du village* (W.A. I, 26:143).

Rousseau tells of his boyhood infatuation for a certain Mademoiselle Goton, "who," he says, "deigned to play the schoolmistress with me. Our meetings, though absolutely childish, afforded me the height of happiness. . . . While she took the greatest liberties with me, she would never permit any to be taken with her in return, treating me precisely like a child" (O.C., 14:38–39). In like manner Goethe relates that his Gretchen, whose company soon became "an indispensable condition" of his being, insisted on keeping him, a fifteen-year-old boy, at a distance: "She gave her hand to no one, not even to me; she allowed no touch; yet many times she seated herself near me, particularly when I wrote or read aloud, and then, laying her arm familiarly upon my shoulder, she looked over the book or paper. If, however, I ventured to take a similar liberty with her, she withdrew, and did not return very soon" (W.A. I, 26:279).

Jean-Jacques, after leaving the hospice of Lo Spirito Santo at Turin with a few lire in his pocket and then serving as a lackey for a noble family, returned to Madame de Warens bringing little with him except varied experience. His heart beat violently as he approached the home of his protectress, to whom he had written of his glowing prospects in the employ of the Comte de Gouvon: "She looked upon my fortune as already made, if not destroyed by my own negligence. What then would she say upon my arrival?" (O.C., 14:155–156). When the seriously ill Goethe reached Frankfurt after his university days in Leipzig, he seemed to suffer still more in soul than in body: "The nearer I approached my native city, the more I recalled dubiously the circumstances, prospects, and hopes with which I had left home; and it was with a very disheartened feeling that I now returned, as it were, like one shipwrecked" (W.A. I, 27:196).

In the days following his homecoming, Rousseau soon found himself engaged in a sort of informal study of medicine, as he helped his beloved "Maman" pick herbs, compound drugs, and attend to distillations, while pretending, to her great amusement, to be able to distinguish a medical book by its smell. He relates that she made him taste the most nauseous drugs, which he finally felt constrained to take from her dainty fingers, adding: "When shut up in an apartment with all her medical apparatus, anyone who had heard us running and shouting amid peals of laughter would have imagined that we were acting a farce, rather than preparing opiates or elixirs" (O.C., 14:168).

Goethe, while convalescing at home in Frankfurt, carried on studies of alchemy and cabalistic writings with Susanna von Klettenberg and set up some simple chemical apparatus in an attic room (W.A. I, 27:202–208). To be sure, this was a more sedate and circumspect lady than Rousseau's companion; nevertheless, a certain similarity of circumstances obtains. In each case, too, there was the association of a youth with a woman much older than he. Furthermore, Madame de Warens, although at that time a Catholic, had a Pietistic background, traceable (by way of François Magny, translator of German works of that religious movement) to Spener's influence in Swiss circles, and she communicated some of her resultant ideas to Jean-Jacques. In like manner, Fräulein von Klettenberg acquainted Goethe with the beliefs of Pietism. Also, even as Madame de Warens was supposedly for Rousseau the prime inspiration of his conception of the "belle âme" and contributed important characteristics to the heroine of La Nouvelle Héloïse, so Fräulein von Klettenberg served in part as Goethe's model for the "schöne Seele" in his Wilhelm Meister. Rousseau later studied chemistry more systematically, and likewise anatomy. Goethe, who took special interest in chemical and anatomical studies while at Strassburg (W.A. I, 27:408), likewise devoted himself in his mature years more intensively to the latter branch of science.

Recalling his adolescent flirtations with Mesdemoiselles Vulson and Goton, Rousseau comments: "Thus, before my future destiny was determined, did I fool away the most precious moments of my youth" (O.C., 14:41). Similarly, Goethe remarks concerning his Leipzig amusements: "With such harmless fooleries we squandered our precious time" (W.A. I, 27:136). Again and again, then, we encounter instances of similar experience in the adventures and escapades of Rousseau and Goethe during their adolescent and youthful years.

Troubled about the salvation of his soul, the youthful Rousseau resolves to determine once and for all whether he is destined to be saved or not. He throws a stone at a tree; if it hits, salvation will be his, although he confidentially admits being near enough to the tree—a big one—to make sure of his aim (O.C., 14:377–378). Goethe flings his handsome pocketknife into the river to find out whether he is to become an artist: yes, if he sees it fall, no, if the willows hide the sinking knife. The foliage conceals it, but he clearly beholds the water rising as a result of the falling object and laments "the deceptive ambiguity of oracles" (W.A. I, 28:175–176).

Referring to his transitory friendship with Anne-Marie Merceret, whom he had accompanied to her native city of Fribourg, Rousseau states: "I might have married her without difficulty and followed her father's business. My taste for music would have made me love her; I would have settled at Fribourg, a small town, not pretty, but inhabited by very worthy people. I would certainly have missed great pleasures, but I would have lived in peace till my last hour, and I must be allowed to know best what I would have gained by such a step" (O.C., 14:233–234).

Concerning his inner conflict on the occasion of the dissolved engagement to the Frankfurt society belle Lili Schönemann in 1775, Goethe writes: "An affection that is founded on the hope of a mutual possession and a lasting union does not suddenly die away; indeed, it is nourished by the consideration of legitimate wishes and sincere hopes that one cherishes.

"It is in the nature of the matter that in such cases the girl resigns herself more readily than the young man . . . . And how fortuitous is that which gives direction to the choice and decides her who is choosing! I had renounced Lili from conviction, but love rendered this conviction suspect in my eyes" (W.A. I, 29:177–178).

Even as Rousseau could visualize in retrospect the more tranquil yet happier life he might have led with Merceret, so Goethe in his old age told Soret (March 5, 1830): "I was never as near real happiness as in the time of that love for Lili. The obstacles which kept us apart were actually not insurmountable, and still I lost her."

Rousseau says, apropos of the Merceret affair: "Besides, seamstresses,

chambermaids, or milliners have never tempted me; I sighed for ladies!"
(O.C., 14:205). These words have been quoted often with reference to
his subsequent attachment to Thérèse Levasseur. Even though Merceret
was not successful in her efforts to entice Jean-Jacques, he being "too great
a novice to have profited by it" (O.C., 14:222), she is, nevertheless, one
of those who bear witness to the fact that he did not entirely disdain
feminine friends of humble extraction. Nor did Goethe; for Gretchen, in
his account of her, is seen substituting for the waitress on the evening of
their first meeting, and soon thereafter she becomes a milliner, to the displeasure of her admirer, who shares Rousseau's dislike for that occupation.
At Leipzig Goethe transferred his "former inclination for Gretchen" to
Käthchen Schönkopf, an innkeeper's daughter who helped wait on the
guests at table. Not only did she inspire most of Goethe's love songs of
that period, but also the Rococo playlet Die Laune des Verliebten grew
out of her admirer's capricious jealousies (W.A. I, 27:110–112). Such
lower middle-class surroundings as those of Gretchen and the Leipzig
inamorata—and some less respectable environments—gave the impetus to
that other early play Die Mitschuldigen, which (as indicated in the preceding chapter) has been related to the Confessions through its novel-
like execution of scenes and treatment of psychological development.

The depressing reflections of both authors on Paris and Leipzig invite
comparison. Rousseau thus recounts his initial impression of the French
metropolis:

> How much did the first sight of Paris disappoint the idea I had formed of
> it! The exterior decorations I had seen at Turin, the beauty of the streets, the
> symmetry and regularity of the houses had led me to look for something more
> in Paris. . . . On entering the Faubourg Saint-Marceau I saw nothing but dirty,
> ill-smelling little streets, ugly black houses, an air of slovenliness and poverty,
> beggars, carters, menders of old clothes, women criers of tisane, and old hats.
> This struck me so forcibly at first that all I have since seen of real magnificence
> in Paris could never erase this first impression, which has ever given me a
> secret disgust to residing in that capital; and I may say, the whole time I re-
> mained there afterwards was employed only in seeking resources to enable me
> to live far removed from it.
>
> (O.C., 14:245)

Goethe says:

> I had early looked into the strange labyrinths by which civil society is
> undermined. Religion, morals, law, rank, connections, custom—everything

governs only the surface of urban existence. The streets, bordered by splendid houses, are kept neat; and every one behaves himself there properly enough; but indoors it often looks only so much the more disordered; and a smooth exterior, like a thin coat of mortar, plasters over many a rotten wall that collapses overnight and produces an effect all the more frightful, as it breaks into the midst of a condition of repose. How many families had I not seen already, more or less near at hand, either overwhelmed in ruin or kept miserably on the brink of it, through bankruptcies, divorces, seduced daughters, murders, burglaries, and poisonings. . . .

(W.A. I, 27:113)

To Rousseau, living at Les Charmettes seemed all the more delightful because of the contrast to the gloomy, decaying townhouse in which Madame de Warens had hitherto made her home. Goethe found relief from the turmoil of city and university life by escaping to the country, first during his Leipzig years, but especially while at Strassburg, whence on repeated occasions he rode out to Sesenheim and Friederike. He likewise eagerly sought the peaceful surroundings of Wetzlar. At the time of Goethe's engagement to Lili Schönemann, the two were glad of every opportunity to exchange Frankfurt for nearby Offenbach, where, at the home of her relatives, they could live their idyl, away from the city and the constraints of the social circles in which Lili moved.

Rousseau tells us that when he fell in love with Madame d'Houdetot, she was on horseback, dressed in a man's riding-habit (O.C., 15:265). Goethe classes Friederike Brion among those girls who look their best out of doors, in the midst of natural beauty (W.A. I, 28:15). If this is true, as we may well assume, of Rousseau's Julie, it holds equally for a number of Goethe's heroines, such as Iphigenie, Tasso's princess, Dorothea, Nathalie, Werther's Lotte, Ottilie, and Gretchen (as in the garden scenes of Faust).

Both writers display a fondness for describing rustic life, whether in its routine features or in its festive aspects; Rousseau depicts Les Charmettes, Goethe, Sesenheim. Jean-Jacques, being in ill health and persuaded that he had but a short while to live, sought to enjoy his remaining time "without inquietude or concern." He tried, by encouraging Maman's "increasing enthusiasm for the country," to make those days still more pleasant: "Seeking to attach her to her garden, poultry, pigeons, and cows, I amused myself with them; and these little occupations, which employed my time without injuring my tranquility, were more serviceable than a milk diet, or all the remedies bestowed on my poor shattered body, even to effecting the utmost possible re-establishment of it" (O.C., 14:359). Of the harvest season Rousseau then writes: "The vintage and gathering-in of our fruit occupied the remainder of the year; we became more and more attached to a rustic life, and the society of our honest neighbors. We saw the approach of winter with regret and returned to the city as if going into exile" (O.C., 14:360).

During Goethe's vacation days at Friederike's home, he went with her to visit relatives and friends. "On both sides of the Rhine," he relates, ". . . I found those persons dispersed whom I had seen united at Sesenheim, every one a friendly, hospitable host, throwing open kitchen and cellar quite as willingly as gardens and vineyards,—indeed—the whole region" (W.A. I, 28:29–30). Later he adds: "We were . . . just as little interrupted in our cheerful life as Doctor Primrose and his amiable family [Goethe has previously compared the situation to that in Goldsmith's *Vicar of Wakefield*]; for many an unexpected instance of good luck happened both to us and to our friends and neighbors; weddings and christenings, the erection of a building, an inheritance, a prize in the lottery, were reciprocally announced and enjoyed. We shared all joy together, like common property, and knew how to enhance it through esprit and love" (W.A. I, 28:33–34).

Inclination conspired on occasion with circumstance to make wanderers of both Rousseau and Goethe in their younger years. The former reaches his greatest enthusiasm as he describes the last stretch of his walking-trip back to Madame de Warens from that first visit to Paris, confessing as great an unwillingness to end the recounting of those travels as he felt at ceasing to experience them at the time:

My heart beat with joy as I approached my dear Maman, but I went no faster on that account. I love to walk at my ease and stop at leisure; a strolling life is necessary to me. Traveling on foot, in a fine country, with fair weather, with no need for haste, and with the expectation of an agreeable conclusion to my journey, is the manner of living, above all others, most suited to my taste. It is already understood what I mean by a fine country; never could a flat one, though ever so beautiful, appear such in my eyes. I must have torrents, fir-trees, dark woods, mountains to climb or descend, and rugged roads with precipices on either side to alarm me. I experienced this pleasure in all its charm as I approached Chambéri. . . .

(O.C., 14:155–156)

"The wanderer had now at last reached home," Goethe writes of his return from Strassburg. That name, he explains a few pages further, was given to him on account of his wandering about in his home region, adding:

"Frankfurt's geographical site was useful for producing that peace of mind which I felt beneath the open sky, in the valleys, on the heights, in the fields and in the woods . . . I accustomed myself to live on the road, and to wander about like a messenger between the mountains and the plains."

(W.A. I, 28:118–119)

Goethe had already begun his extensive wandering while at Strassburg, making numerous excursions through Upper Alsace, often in mountainous terrain. His description of scenery beheld on his first Alpine journey is reminiscent of that in which Rousseau delighted: ". . . As we kept ascending, we left pine forests in the chasm, through which the Reuss appeared from time to time, foaming over the rocky fall" (W.A. I, 29:120). Further on he continues: "But one felt cheered, though, and elevated by one of the most beautiful, most picturesque, most grandiose waterfalls, which, just at this season overrichly supplied with melted snow, now hidden by clouds, now unveiled, chained us for quite some time to the spot" (W.A. I, 29:122–123).

Familiar to his readers is Rousseau's profound love for his native Switzerland: the scenic grandeur, the freedom-loving people, the quaint, homely customs and, above all, the rugged, provincial sturdiness of the land in contrast to the conditions he observed in France that were leading toward the debacle of 1789. Rousseau, says François Jost, was no less the child of his people than of his epoch; he put his whole Genevan intellect into the Contrat social, and in La Nouvelle Héloïse and the Confessions he "reveals his Swiss heart."[19] Among Jost's repeated references to Goethe one reads that the distances that he covered in his travels were scarcely greater than those traversed by Rousseau (p. 24); also, that the Lion d'Or, in the Haut-Valais, where the latter took lodgings, was subsequently the stopping-place of an impressive list of famous men, headed by Goethe (p. 214). In the opinion of Friedrich Maschek, the Briefe aus der Schweiz are noteworthy for their brilliant descriptions of nature and "Naturschwärmerei" after the manner of Rousseau.[20] The two indeed shared a predilection for Switzerland to a remarkable degree. While still in Alsace, Goethe looked toward the distant Swiss mountains, longing to go there. Of his three journeys to Switzerland, the letters and diaries of which are supplementary to Dichtung und Wahrheit, the second one (1779) is of most interest with respect to Rousseau. In perusing some of the descriptions of Valais or the Lake of Geneva, one hardly knows whether he is reading Goethe or Jean-Jacques. As we have seen, one year after Rousseau's death, Goethe visited the island of his exile, St. Pierre, and wrote to Charlotte von Stein of going to Vevey, describing his emotion at beholding the scenes immortalized by Rousseau in his novel. Even a casual reading of Goethe's letters from Switzerland to friends discloses his fondness for that country.

The boy Rousseau went to Italy, where, amid a multiplicity of adventures, he became acquainted with the people and the language. In Frankfurt the boy Goethe learned Italian from his father amid the atmosphere created by the latter's noteworthy collection of views of Italy as souvenirs of his visit there. Goethe's longing for Italy is well known, and when he at last made his memorable journey (1786–1788), his sojourn in Rome became for him an unrivaled cultural experience. His second, less gratifying stay was mainly at Venice, where Rousseau had been private secretary to the French ambassador during his second residence in Italy.

While the *Confessions* have often been mentioned as a forerunner of *Dichtung und Wahrheit*, relatively little attention was paid to the *Italienische Reise* in this respect prior to René Michéa's searching and detailed study, in which he devotes a chapter to Goethe's interest in Rousseau, citing first the more salient evidences before Italy. Even in his introduction Michéa states that if Goethe studied in Rome, in Naples he lived and observed the way to live, turning, "as a disciple of Rousseau," toward the people.[21] Michéa concedes that Rousseau's name occurs only twice in the *Italienische Reise*, but he attaches much importance to those references. Goethe, he declares, upon hearing the recitative chants of the Venetian gondoliers, recalls Jean-Jacques, who earlier discovered that verses from Tasso were still being sung among the people there in the eighteenth century. The boatmen's singing made an appeal that was then all the stronger because of incipient search for the source of poetry in primitive simplicity. Michéa characterizes these short melodies as "very near to the folksong" and lacking neither grace nor zest (pp. 64–65).

Goethe's other reference to Rousseau is made at Naples, where "in the great, joyous, and turbulent city" the poet reflects upon Rousseau's misanthropy ("Sometimes I think of Rousseau . . ."). While comprehending such a state of mind, says Michéa, Goethe now realizes that one must weigh men "with the big scales of commerce and not with an assay-balance," and in the tumultuous crowd he feels, for the first time, really tranquil and solitary. The noisier the street, the more he recovers his calmness. Michéa sees reminders of Rousseau's Saint-Preux, who disdains social conventions and forms easy, suspicious friendships, for Goethe also has a tender inclination toward the humble among mankind (p. 66).

According to Michéa, Rousseauistic tendencies in the *Italienische Reise* extend far beyond the two cases of direct mention. Even before Sterne, Rousseau revolutionized travel by insisting, in *Émile*, that people should not go like couriers, "but like travelers"; that they should think not merely of the points of departure and arrival, but of the intervening spaces. Quoting Rousseau's passage about the desirability of traveling on foot, like the philosophers of ancient Greece, and of observing the minerals and fossils, the plants and cultivated fields, Michéa calls this the classic page of journeys afoot, corresponding so well to the German "Wanderlust." Goethe, in turn, manifestly conducts his peregrinations in the spirit of Rousseau. Like Jean-Jacques, he gathers plants and collects pebbles, having the whole world for his study. After the manner of Rousseau, he goes among the people. Goethe shares with Jean-Jacques a disapproval of the purely erudite and of those traveling in haste, and sets up a "moral object" of his activity. He resembles the author of *Émile*, in that he has confidence only in his personal experience (pp. 67–68).

Further connections between *Émile* and the *Italienische Reise* are cited by Michéa. Like Rousseau's hero, "full of his Homer," and like his own character, Werther, Goethe shares that enthusiasm while in Italy. Comparisons are also evoked by the respective comments of Rousseau and Goethe regarding monuments to the dead. The former remarks: "Whereas our tombs are covered with eulogies, on those of the Ancients one reads facts." Goethe, viewing the tombs at Verona, utters the thought that the Ancients confined themselves to representing "the simple presence of men" (September 16, 1786). One recalls that page of the *Confessions* where a "Roman Rousseau" is moved to cries of admiration at the sight of the Pont du Gard when reading of "Goethe *civis romanus*" and of his standing at Spoleto or Rome before the ruins of the aqueducts which once supplied the Eternal City with water. All this shows plainly, Michéa continues, that Rousseau and Goethe draw upon the same stock of ideas; since the number of these in circulation at a given epoch is relatively limited, two works of any extent will perforce be in accord on various points. Instead of a borrowing in the narrow, materialistic sense, there are diffuse topics which pass from mouth to mouth and from pen to pen, indicating a community of existence or culture, a kinship of vocabulary, of readings, or of daily contacts (pp. 69–70).

Finally, Michéa notes resemblances between the sentimental course of Goethe's *Italienische Reise* and that of *La Nouvelle Héloïse*. The narrative of travel in Italy passes from the anecdote to personal casuistry, thus following an evolution parallel to that of Rousseau's novel, which proceeds from outer complications toward analysis of feeling. These kindred elements include the problems of love and morality confronting the "friend" of a woman married to another man, his letters to her from distant parts (namely, similarity of tone between the epistles of Saint-Preux to Julie and those of Goethe to Charlotte von Stein), the restorative merit of action and travel to other lands, and the role of anticipation (pp. 71–77).

The two authors' accounts of their respective infatuations for Sophie d'Houdetot and Lotte Buff (taken intrinsically, without regard to connection with *La Nouvelle Héloïse* and *Werther*) invite sundry comparisons. For example, Madame d'Houdetot loved Saint-Lambert, Rousseau's friend; similarly, Lotte was devoted to her fiancé, Kestner, who formed a warm friendship with Goethe. Still, each of these young women was pleased with the adulation of another man. Jean-Jacques thus defines the situation of himself and the Countess:

> I am wrong in calling it an unshared love; what I felt was so in some measure. Love was equal on both sides, but not reciprocal. We were both intoxicated with passion—she for her lover, and I for herself; our sighs and delicious tears were mingled together. Tender confidants of the secrets of each other, there was so great a likeness in our sentiments that it was impossible that they should not find some common point of union.
>
> (O.C., 15:274–275)

Later he recounts how Saint-Lambert sometimes joined them to make it a congenial group of three.

At Wetzlar, the "newcomer," as Goethe styles himself, was

perfectly free from all ties, and careless in the presence of a girl who, already engaged to another, could not interpret the most obliging services as acts of courtship. . . . Indolent and dreamy, because no present time satisfied him, he found what he had lacked in a female friend, who . . . liked him as her companion. . . . Whenever the bridegroom's affairs permitted, he for his part was along with them: they had all three accustomed themselves to one another without intention, and did not know how they had become so mutually indispensable. During that splendid summer they lived through a genuinely German idyl, to which the fertile land furnished the prose, and a pure inclination the poetry.

(W.A. I, 28:154)

In the early 1780's Goethe read Rousseau's words about Madame de Warens: "I had a tender mother, an adored friend; I needed a mistress" (O.C., 15:90). He may have thought of his own friendship with Frau von Stein, which, as previously mentioned, has been interpreted in our century as an affair conducted, from Charlotte's standpoint, in the spirit of La Nouvelle Héloïse—the pattern, as it were, for such a relationship in that age. In each case, the motherly relationship first became strained and then was broken off by flight.

Although Rousseau avers that he never truly loved her, he found in Thérèse Levasseur what he elsewhere depicts as a certain measure of domestic happiness (O.C., 15:91). At the time when Goethe was writing Dichtung und Wahrheit, he could look back over a quarter of a century with his Christiane, and parallels may well have occurred to him as he recalled the Confessions. (We have already seen how acquaintances of Goethe early compared his situation to that of Jean-Jacques.)

Having given up any thought of living again with "Maman" after his return from Venice, Rousseau desired someone in whom he might find his own simplicity and docility of mind and heart. "It was necessary," he explains, "that the happiness of domestic life should repay me for the splendid career I had just renounced. When I was quite alone, there was a void in my heart, which wanted nothing more than another heart to fill it . . . I found in Thérèse the supplement of which I stood in need; through her I lived as happily as I possibly could, according to the course of events" (O.C., 15:91–92). Christiane helped fill a void in Goethe's life when he, having likewise returned from Italy, found friends estranged and Charlotte von Stein in particular cold and unsympathetic. Thus he also soon "repaid" himself with a "little friend," whom chance brought to him on an errand for her brother, even as it had directed Thérèse to the table where Jean-Jacques took his meals.

Rousseau promised Thérèse never to forsake her or to marry her. "This charming intimacy," he relates, "superseded all else" (O.C., 15:92). They continued their liaison for some twenty-three years; then he entered upon a sort of formal marriage with her, although it lacked legality at the time. Goethe considered himself married "in conscience" to Christiane during their eighteen years minus benefit of clergy. The ceremony was finally performed in 1806, after the sacking of Weimar by Napoleon's troops, when Christiane is said to have acted to save Goethe's life and the house with a courage like that attributed to Thérèse when she and Rousseau faced the mob that stoned him at Môtiers.

Especially in the nineteenth century, Rousseau was repeatedly condemned as a veritable apostle of immorality. Yet no one has written such a powerful defense of morals and the sanctity of marriage as La Nouvelle Héloïse, except Goethe himself with his Werther and Die Wahlverwandtschaften (as the next chapter attempts to show). Nonetheless, these novels, like Faust, also brought frequent reproaches, particularly from early readers among the English. Thus Rousseau and Goethe alike experienced widespread misunderstanding of their loftiest intention, and traces of that error regarding both have persisted down to our time.

Neither of the two showed himself sufficiently orthodox to please strict adherents of revealed religion. Hence it helped Rousseau but little that he had affirmed the existence and goodness of God, even against his former friends, the Encyclopedists, or that in Émile he had created such a model of Christian faith and charity as the Vicar of Savoy, whose Profession de foi is reflected, as we have seen, in Goethe's Brief des Pastors . . . (1772). Later called "the Great Pagan," Goethe was as much in disfavor with dogmatists as Rousseau. Once, in a conversation with Rühle von Lilienstern (ca. September, 1810), he protested: "I a pagan? Well, after all, I let Gretchen [in Faust] be executed, and Ottilie [in Die Wahlverwandtschaften] die of hunger. Isn't that Christian enough for the good people? What more Christian thing do they want?"

Goethe's renowned versatility and multiplicity of interests remind one of Rousseau's dozen trades or occupations.[22] Articles on Jean-Jacques as a translator of Seneca[23] and as a chess player[24] are paralleled to a laughable degree by innumerable titles beginning: "Goethe als . . ." or "Goethe und . . . ."[25]

Traces of Rousseau's Genevan accent are said to have marked him as an outlander in Paris until the end of his life, and Alexis François has compiled a detailed glossary of the French-Swiss and Savoyard "provincialisms" occurring in the complete works.[26] Goethe's Frankfurt dialect —much in evidence in the original versions of his pre-Weimar writings— drew laughter from the sophisticated in Leipzig. He not only retained the accent but, even in old age, frequently lapsed into his native speech in familiar conversation.

It can of course be objected that some of the foregoing points of similarity between the *Confessions* and *Dichtung und Wahrheit* (or between the lives of the respective authors) are fortuitous, that others are "allgemein menschlich," or at least generally characteristic of the eighteenth-century scene, and that still others are superficial or, at best, tangential. Still, in their entirety, they seem worthy of consideration, especially since they have been largely disregarded by those who insist upon the opposing or contrastive character of the two works. There remain, however, certain more fundamental comparisons to which we shall now proceed.

Much has been written about the relative extent of "poetry and truth" in both autobiographies. Rousseau scholarship has long since set forth the divergences in the manuscript versions of the *Confessions*, while the editors of the Weimar edition included all variants to the definitive text of *Dichtung und Wahrheit* with the same conscientious thoroughness devoted to the whole body of Goethe's writings. On the basis of the earlier correspondence of each author and other contemporaneous documents, innumerable deviations from fact have been established in both works.

But however great this controversy may be, there is general agreement that both Goethe and Rousseau resorted on occasion to stylization as an aid to memory or as an artistic device. Rousseau's dependence on recollection has been cited repeatedly as an essential difference from Goethe's procedure. Yet if Rousseau lost all the papers he had assembled to guide him, Goethe relied upon Bettina Brentano's memories of his mother's anecdotes for the story of his youth. Both acknowledge remembering little of their earliest childhood; each presents himself in the best possible light. Contrary to documentary evidence, Rousseau claims to have stood out long and stubbornly against embracing Catholicism at Turin (*Confessions*, C.G., pp. 56–59). In like manner, Goethe paints an innocent picture of his involvement in the scandal caused by the "malfeasance in office" of a young man whom he had helped get the appointment through Grandfather Textor's influence (W.A. I, 26:332–337). As mentioned earlier, Goethe's depiction of the coronation of Joseph II as German emperor was based not on memory but on extensive research, as was his description of the Roman carnival in the *Italienische Reise*.

The most significant examples of "poetizing" for both men deal with love, and the studies written on the proportion of truth to fiction in such passages are legion. Goethe doubtless relied as much on memory as Rousseau did in recalling his early loves. If Jean-Jacques stylized various youthful infatuations, such as his love for Suzanne Serre,[27] Goethe did likewise, and probably first of all in the case of his unrequited fondness for a French girl at the time of the occupation of Frankfurt, namely, the melancholy sister of the boy whom he calls Derones (W.A. I, 26:145). A more noteworthy instance is Goethe's account of the episode with Gretchen. We have already seen how he cites the example of "the old Abelard and the new" while instructing the girl about the Imperial coronation. (Her way of hanging on his words is reminiscent of Merceret's imitating Rousseau's speech and repeating his phraseology.)

Whether or not this "Gretchen" was a composite of several young feminine friends of Goethe, as some have suggested, the highly fictionalized aspect of his account extends beyond the reference to Rousseau's novel to identification of the "Roman" of himself and Gretchen with the adventures of the hero and heroine of Prévost's *Histoire du chevalier Des Grieux et de Manon Lescaut* (W.A. I., 26:376–380). Goethe "epitomized" this story, probably one of the first books concerned with the New World that Goethe read[28] (on May 16, 1811, according to his diary); he originally intended it for the conclusion of Book Five of *Dichtung und Wahrheit*. Goethe's reason for finally omitting his summary of *Manon Lescaut*, introduced by a paragraph linking the sad outcome of his love for Gretchen with that novel, has been the subject of varying conjectures. Henry H. H. Remak proposes the plausible explanation that the author left out the lengthy résumé for artistic reasons, and that he withheld his comments on Prévost's work in order not to weaken the effect of the Gretchen adventure upon the reader by revealing its more or less literary origin.[29] Irrespective of the comparison with Manon, however, the story of Goethe and Gretchen shows a double analogy with Rousseau: first, by Goethe's own admission, the relationship to *La Nouvelle Héloïse*; secondly, a novelized treatment which is reminiscent of certain episodes related in the *Confessions*, especially that of Mademoiselle Goton.[30]

There is often a general similarity in detail when we behold the two writers surrounded by admiring members of the opposite sex: Rousseau with Mesdemoiselles Galley and de Graffenried, with Merceret et al., and, later, among Parisian ladies; Goethe with his sister's companions, such as Charitas Meixner and Lisette Runkel, with Konstanze Breitkopf and others (aside from his Käthchen) in Leipzig, with the "sentimental circle" at Darmstadt, and (after the period included in Dichtung und Wahrheit) among the young noblewomen of the Weimar court. Whether the youthful hero of the occasion is Rousseau or Goethe, one always gets the impression of fluttering feminine hearts.

It seems likely that the Confessions at least partly inspired Goethe's depiction of the landscape as a background for his love affairs.[31] One discerns a wealth of kindred motifs in a more or less similar atmosphere. Rousseau's never-to-be-forgotten summer day in the country at Toune in company with Mademoiselle de Graffenried and her prettier companion, Mademoiselle Galley, his idyllic existence (as he recalls it) with Maman at Les Charmettes, his early walks with Thérèse, and, finally, his soul-stirring garden and moonlight scenes with the Countess d' Houdetot find their counterparts in Goethe's Sesenheim romance with Friederike Brion in the setting of a German country parsonage in Alsace, in his moon-lit wanderings with Lili Schönemann, and (at a later time than that embraced by Dichtung und Wahrheit) in his chance encounter with Christiane Vulpius.

Goethe's whole Rousseauesque way of life in the "Gartenhaus" on the fringe of the Weimar Park also invited comparison between the two.[32] Plainly, nature was no more an empty abstraction for Goethe than for Rousseau. Just as Jean-Jacques fondly recalled the happiness, or at least the tranquility he had experienced in the open air, so Goethe could look back over a long life of intimacy with the outdoors. Günter Schulz has established this even for the childhood years at Frankfurt, a period often mistakenly supposed to have been largely barren of contact with the adjacent countryside. According to Schulz, Goethe came under Rousseau's influence regarding a predilection for rural life even during the Leipzig sojourn.[33]

Goethe dramatically ends the Ninth Book with the incident of the curse which the French dancing-master's daughter at Strassburg destines for the girl who next kisses him (W.A. I, 27:289–292). This motif is skillfully introduced into the Friederike affair (in Book Eleven); thus it forms another instance of artistic "anticipation" of a passionate involvement, to which the pendant is his vision of meeting himself on horseback returning for a conciliatory visit (W.A. I, 28:83–84), as he actually did about eight years later. This reminds one of Rousseau's account of his having created the heroine of his novel, Julie d'Étange, in his fancy shortly before he became acquainted with Sophie d'Houdetot (O.C., 15:247–274).

The most striking feature of Goethe's "Stilisierung" of the Friederike episode is of course his reversal of events in order to draw a parallel between the family of Pastor Brion and that of Dr. Primrose in Goldsmith's *Vicar of Wakefield*. As Lawrence M. Price has demonstrated by a convincing chronological reconstruction,[34] Goethe did not hear Herder's reading of that novel until some months after he had become acquainted with the Brions. A shifting of occurrences, in a manner akin to that of Rousseau, is in keeping with the very great importance which Goethe attached to Goldsmith and the latter's fictional work.[35] Such instances can be found repeatedly in *Dichtung und Wahrheit*, especially with reference to "cultural experiences," namely, formative, inspirational stages in his own poetic development.

Thus his brilliant characterization of German literature in his youth, far from being the objective treatment that some have considered it, appears in reality to be as subjective as anything written by Rousseau about his own intellectual and artistic growth. Goethe's depictions of literary figures in this stylized category include his often quoted description of Johann Christian Günther and the account of his visit to Gottsched at Leipzig.[36] Probably the same applies in some degree to the story of his meeting with Herder. That encounter at Strassburg and their subsequent association there are also somewhat reminiscent of the early period of Rousseau's friendship with Diderot (whom Herder had lately met, along with D'Alembert and several lesser Encyclopedists, on his visit to Paris).[37] Correspondences of stylization of the sort indicated more than make up for a host of much-touted "contrasts" alleged to exist between the autobiographies of Rousseau and Goethe by critics who insist that the latter "abandoned" Jean-Jacques upon emerging from the "Geniezeit" in the 1770's.

Moreover, the controversy of fact vs. fiction should not obscure the importance of both works for Goethe and Rousseau as vehicles for self-analysis. Henri Peyre attributes the continued fame of Rousseau the writer through two hundred years in large part to his "struggle for sincerity," in which no like-minded confessors have surpassed him.[38] Despite Rousseau's failure at times to follow his motto, *Vitam impendere vero* (p. 95), Peyre considers that the story of Rousseau's life has never been more truly told than in the *Confessions* (p. 80). Likewise, in spite of Goethe's omissions and inaccuracies, his own assessment of *Dictung und Wahrheit* stands as the most valid pronouncement on that work (to Eckermann, March 30, 1831):

There are [in it] only results of my life, and the individual facts recounted serve merely to confirm a general observation, a higher truth.

This "höhere Wahrheit" is thus the concern of both Rousseau and Goethe; for both narrators it is the complement of "Dichtung" rather than its opposite in a too-literal sense.

Recent commentaries show that the artistry of the *Confessions* has met with proper appreciation only in our time. Madeleine B. Ellis sees Rousseau's autobiography as a work of art.[39] Her illuminating study of Jean-Jacques' narrative of his stay in Venice admirably illustrates how he made use of "allegorical portrayal" of the world about him to reveal his state of mind and the actions it determined at a critical time in his life. His artistic composition, she tells us, is at its best in this fascinating story of his Venetian experience (p. 131).[40] The fidelity with which his literary expression reflects himself is, then, another manifestation of a truth that transcends mere actuality. According to his own too often unheeded statement, Goethe himself appreciated at once the artistry of the *Confessions*. In contradiction to the general attitude of Goethe scholarship around 1900 and even later, Georg Witkowski voiced the opinion that what Goethe most admired about Rousseau was the poetic beauty of his style[41] —that very manner of composition which, Miss Ellis feels, mainly constitutes his genius.[42]

Dichtung und Wahrheit offers a parallel situation. Jürg Fierz emphasizes the surprising fact that it has been so highly regarded as an autobiographical source, but so little valued as a work of art.[43] Fierz remarks further that this one-sided literary criticism of *Dichtung und Wahrheit* has caused it to become merely a catalogue of biographical errors on Goethe's part (p. 12). Thus we see two masterpieces of self-revelation confronted with the same lack of understanding.

Nearly a century ago Sir John Morley made the statement that no great writer of recent ages was so little literary, so little indebted to literature for the most characteristic part of his work as Rousseau, who was formed by life "not in the sense of contact with a great number of active and important persons, but in the rarer sense of free surrender to the plenitude of his own impressions."[44] The statement is just as true of

Goethe. He was unable to write poetry according to any set theory, but sought his own inner esthetics. In the Seventh Book of *Dichtung und Wahrheit*, the one most concerned with his literary antecedents, he declares: "If now I desired a true basis in feeling or reflection for my poems, I was forced to commune with my own self" (W.A. I, 27:109). To Eckermann (February 26, 1824) he uttered the well-known dictum: "Had I not already borne the world within me through anticipation, I would have remained blind with seeing eyes, and all searching and experience would have been nothing more than a wholly lifeless, vain effort."

It is above all, then, the inner life, the inner light which Goethe and Rousseau have in common. Yet Rousseau and Goethe were both spirits driven by restlessness—even from the happiest situations. Rousseau has repeatedly been designated as a "divided soul"[45]; Goethe's Faust is his author's *alter ego* when he complains of the "two souls within his breast" (l. 1112). Rousseau was frequently hesitant, so was Goethe. But at the crucial moment each was true to his *daimon*, or that which is uniquely characteristic of his being. Goethe has defined this concept in the first of his *Urworte. Orphisch*, as well as variously in *Dichtung und Wahrheit*, as for example: "Man may turn whichever way he pleases, and undertake anything whatsoever; he will always return to the path which nature has prescribed for him" (W.A. I, 26:204). Rousseau tells of seeing the beckoning hand of destiny on the road to Vincennes: "All at once I felt myself dazzled by a thousand glittering lights; crowds of vivid ideas thronged into my mind with a force and confusion that threw me into unspeakable agitation. . . . If I could only have written down a quarter of that which I was and felt under that tree, with what clarity I should have brought out all the contradictions of our social system . . . !" (O.C., 16:241).

To his friend "Demoiselle" Delf in Heidelberg, who tries to dissuade him from going to Weimar, Goethe (with a last bit of effective stylization in the closing lines of *Dichtung und Wahrheit*) claims to have shouted the words of his own dramatic personage, Egmont: "Child! child! no more! The sun's coursers of time, as though lashed by invisible spirits, race on with the light car of our destiny, and nothing remains for us but to grasp the reins bravely and now right, now left, to steer the wheels, here from the rock, there from the precipice. Whither the way leads, who knows? Indeed, he scarcely remembers from where he came" (W.A. I, 29:192).[46]

Here, finally, is the greatest and deepest likeness between the two men as revealed in their memoirs—a similarity which comprehends many of the more superficial points of contact outlined above. Each trusted his daemonic urge, daring to stake his future upon the correctness of his natural insight. Likewise, each sensed the unique character of his inborn genius and relied upon it. Believing implicitly in a high destiny as prophets and seers of humanity, they could well defy indifference or hostile criticism or animosity in the present, confident of vindication in the future. And in this belief posterity has borne them out.

V

Of Love
and Marriage

"Hardly any other of Goethe's works," says Martin Sommerfeld, "followed such a strange and contradictory course throughout the nineteenth century . . . as *Die Wahlverwandtschaften*." Like the *Westöstlicher Divan*, this novel, which concerned many of the same perennial problems of humanity treated in *Werther* thirty-five years earlier, did not fully come into its own until our time. It was finally revealed to the poet's nation as a "true and lasting possession."[1] Both the number and the variety of recent studies devoted to *Die Wahlverwandtschaften* testify to the impact of that work upon present-day "Goethekenner." One notes an increasing tendency to relate it to *Werther*. Yet, although Goethe's youthful novel continues to be mentioned frequently in connection with *La Nouvelle Héloïse*, that of the "man of sixty years"[2] is much less often associated with Rousseau, despite identical and additional analogies to the romance of the "two lovers dwelling at the foot of the Alps." In fact, several well-known commentaries and various articles dealing with *Die Wahlverwandtschaften* do not contain a word about Jean-Jacques.[3] There are others, however, which do see *La Nouvelle Héloïse* as foreshadowing certain aspects of what Goethe himself designated as the most thoroughly confessional of his creative writings; among these, only *Werther* outranks *Die Wahlverwandtschaften* as a structurally unified work of fiction.[4]

Probably the earliest recorded suggestion of relationship between *Die Wahlverwandtschaften* and *La Nouvelle Héloïse* occurs in a letter from F. G. Welcker to Wilhelm von Humboldt (December 24, 1823). After seeking to identify Schiller's poem *An Emma* with two passages from *La Nouvelle Héloïse*, Welcker adds: "In *Die Wahlverwandtschaften* there is a beautiful scene borrowed from this rich and great work, the scene in the chapel with Ottilie's corpse."[5] Such observations evidently found but little echo in a generation less conversant with Rousseau's novel than that of the *Werther* era had been. Nevertheless, there was the same eagerness as in the case of *Werther* to establish the degree to which the characters and situations reflected circumstances in the author's life. Goethe's words to Eckermann (February 9, 1829) served rather to mystify than to enlighten the critics: "Nowhere in *Die Wahlverwandtschaften* is there a line which I had not experienced myself, and there is more in it than anyone would be able to take in at a single reading." Again, on February 17, 1830, Eckermann records: "Of his *Wahlverwandtschaften* he said that not a line was contained therein which had not been experienced, but no line *as* it had been experienced."

Perhaps undue emphasis has been placed upon Minna Herzlieb as the inspiration of Goethe's Ottilie.[6] Nineteenth-century source hunters pointed to various other possibilities, including Wieland's novella *Freundschaft und Liebe auf der Probe*. Then Max Morris, after stating that no literary source had yet been determined, laid special stress on a story in *The Thousand and One Nights*.[7] Erich Schmidt himself had called attention to the adultery motif in *La Nouvelle Héloïse* and *Die Wahlverwandtschaften*.[8] Later Friedrich Lienhard, referring to Goethe's visit to the Odilienberg during his Strassburg days, as related in *Dichtung und Wahrheit* (W.A. I, 28:79), maintained that the conclusion of *Die Wahlverwandtschaften* could be explained as a reminiscence of that shrine, but he admitted its occurrence in *La Nouvelle Héloïse*.[9]

In an article on "elective affinity" August Vetter argues convincingly a relationship between the destinies of Goethe and Rousseau.[10] Since he discusses the matter with reference to the characters of *Die Wahlverwandtschaften*, his essay has an important bearing on the question of its literary kinship with *La Nouvelle Héloïse*. Vetter asserts that if the Captain had developed as strong an individuality as that of Eduard, he would have been capable of a deep but different sort of love for Ottilie, whose enigmatic nature belongs to the nocturnal sphere of the feminine soul.

Goethe has hinted at this possibility in the inclination toward Ottilie on the part of the congenial architect and the assistant at the boarding school. The love of this type of person for one of Ottilie's character will always bear the stamp of intellectual leadership, while the wife takes the lead on the sensual side. Such a relationship, Vetter continues, can be designated as "väterlich-tochterhaft." The marriage in the *Wahlver-wandtschaften*, however, shows the opposite characteristics. Charlotte possesses moral superiority over Eduard, whom she thoroughly understands and holds in check. This union is styled "mütterlich-sohnhaft" (p. 104). Vetter's thesis is that Goethe regards only this half (the "day side") of the sex relation as legitimate. He proceeds, namely, from the "Christian solution," and from there he seeks the lost natural relation.

He shares this longing with his age in general, but above all with "its deeply aroused advocate, Rousseau"; the two are also joined by a kindred destiny. The love-life of the Philosopher of Geneva has its culmination in the ecstatic inclination for his latitudinarian "Maman," Mme de Warens, who brings him, a Protestant, back to the Mother-Church. A counterpoint is reached in the liaison with Thérèse Levasseur, a "releasing nature" and the mother of his children (p. 105). Vetter thinks Goethe followed essentially the same path in his relations with Charlotte von Stein and Christiane Vulpius. What Goethe and Rousseau put into practice, Nietzsche later formulated into his idea of the "Zeitehe." The development achieved by Rousseau and Goethe, recommended by Nietzsche, and indicated in the *Wahlverwandtschaften* has its basis "im ritterlichen Minnedienst." Vetter says that in the novel Goethe chooses the inclination of the "son-like" husband who unequivocally determines his course through his marriage to an intellectual and motherly woman. Goethe's narrative gives only a presentiment of the happiness and deficiencies of such a union (p. 108). His own experience at Weimar, which influenced the story and its characters, presents a more sharply defined contrast between these two aspects of a "mütterlich-sohnhaft" relationship than is evident in *Die Wahlverwandtschaften* (pp. 108–109).[11]

According to Aron, a re-examination of *Die Wahlverwandtschaften* should offer conclusive proof that various earlier tales cited as "sources" could be disregarded. The novel might then be considered a work based on the personal experiences of the author, but "formulated as a re-appraisal of the human problems raised in *La Nouvelle Héloïse*." Goethe, he continues, must have been fully conscious of such a correspondence as that of the drowning incidents in both narratives. Moreover, the praise that Goethe accords to the dilettante in *Die Wahlverwandtschaften*, has a parallel in his tribute to Rousseau as a dilettante in botany.[12] Aron does not refer to Vetter's essay.

Although Vetter relates the Eduard-Charlotte situation in *Die Wahlverwandtschaften* to Goethe and Frau von Stein, Hanna Fischer-Lamberg directly links the latter relationship with *La Nouvelle Héloïse*. She suggests the existence of "a perhaps unconscious identification" of these two with the classical pair of lovers in the eighteenth century,[13] describing Charlotte von Stein "not only as Goethe's beloved, but as an important 'Bildungserlebnis' for the poet." Charlotte, Fischer-Lamberg adds, could not free herself from the sentimentality ("Empfindsamkeit") which set in as a reaction to Rationalism (pp. 385–386). This movement combined religious-pietistic feeling with the precepts of English moral philosophy, a "newly-discovered world of feeling," to which Richardson and his imitators first gave literary expression (p. 390). Since feeling formed the central point of this sentimental movement, woman became powerful as "the preferred supporter of feeling." She conquered the moral sphere and, as its uncontested ruler, held sway completely over the "realm of virtue and innocence." The concept of virtue is of special importance if one attempts an estimation of the psyche of that time(p. 387). Body and soul were regarded as antithetical concepts. Sensual love was to be replaced with friendship, which was looked upon as the goal of all relationships between man and woman—even in marriage. Therefore the sentimental judgment of women, who applied the standard of moral feeling of the feminine psyche to all questions, became very significant for men (p. 387). Naming Rousseau, along with Hamann, Herder, and the experience of genius as revealed in Shakespeare as "significant influences" upon the young Goethe and his contemporaries, Fischer-Lamberg states that *La Nouvelle Héloïse* is highly important for the explanation of Goethe's relationship to Frau von Stein (p. 389). It was the custom, she continues, to identify oneself with the characters of novels and with the ideals of virtue and innocence. The concept of the ideal, virtuous woman had taken such a hold on the consciousness of the eighteenth century that Rousseau could not free himself from Richardson and the various English moralists. "Julie," says Fischer-Lamberg, "is the typical representative of the dualistic idea of the erotic which prevailed at that time" (pp. 389–390).[14]

Whatever the degree of Goethe's conscious adaption from *La Nouvelle Héloïse*, there is abundant evidence in *Die Wahlverwandtschaften* of similar circumstances and characters. Except for Saint-Preux, the leading figures in both novels are of the lesser nobility—hence from circles fashionable with eighteenth-century novelists. Both Charlotte and Ottilie have marked traits in common with Julie, as we shall see. Charlotte also resembles Claire d'Orbe in her decided inclination toward reason and practicality. Both novels concern immoral passion.

Julie and Ottilie have a number of common features. In each case the heroine has to suppress her love: Julie as the wife of another, Ottilie as one enamored of a married man. Both seek consolation in looking after children: Julie devotes herself to the care and early training of her own, Ottilie lovingly tends Charlotte's (and Eduard's) child. Julie loses her life as a consequence of saving her young son from drowning, Ottilie voluntarily pays with her life for the forgetfulness of duty whereby Charlotte's baby drowns. These incidents are clearly similar, whether or not Goethe purposely followed Rousseau. Julie expresses many deep reflections in her letters, Ottilie often consigns such thoughts to her diary.

Julie likewise appears reflected in Charlotte. The two women are perhaps equally conscious of marital responsibilities, although Charlotte is sterner and less a creature of feeling. Each is driven by parental authority into a *mariage de convenance*; Charlotte's first matrimonial venture is, to be sure, already past, but the reader learns of a situation much like Julie's alliance with M. de Wolmar. Julie endures her wedded life partly for her children's sake; Charlotte hopes that the birth of a child will draw her and Eduard closer together again. Furthermore, the two wives have in common an almost heroic fortitude in the renunciation of unlawful love. In short, both Ottilie and Charlotte embody characteristics found in Julie. Goethe's essentially motherly friend, Charlotte von Stein, lent even her name to his fictional character, whose resemblance to her is notably closer than to Werther's Lotte.

A kinship between Saint-Preux and Eduard exists in the boundlessly sentimental passion of each as a lover. They also exhibit the same kind of fundamentally benevolent spirit, along with personal attractiveness and various aptitudes. Saint-Preux, however, ultimately achieves a certain mastery over those emotions to which Eduard, like Werther before him, finally succumbs. The more admirable side of Saint-Preux—the tutor and man of learning—finds something of a parallel in the assistant director of the school, who cherishes hopes of making Ottilie his wife and co-worker in that institution. Saint-Preux seeks to escape from despair by extensive travel; Eduard has traveled widely in his younger days and now, driven by his hopeless love for Ottilie, he goes off to the war, in which he distinguishes himself by reckless bravery.

It is Eduard's friend, the Captain, who illustrates Goethe's ideal of "Tüchtigkeit," firmness of decision, and, especially, practical activity. He corresponds in this respect to Julie's description of her husband: "M. de Wolmar is about fifty years of age; his life, unified and regular, and the calmness of his passions have preserved in him such a healthy constitution and such a brisk air that he hardly appears to be forty; and he has nothing belonging to an advanced age except experience and wisdom. His countenance is noble and prepossessing; his approach simple and open; his manners are more courteous than assiduous; he talks little and with great sense, but without affecting either preciseness or aphorisms. He is the same toward everybody, does not seek out or flee from anyone, and never has any other preferences than those of reason" (O.C., 8:543-544).

There is no characterization of the Captain comparable in length to the above passage, but one senses immediately the favorable reaction created by his presence. Despite Eduard's reassuring words about his friend's congenial nature, his knowledge and useful talents, Charlotte has misgivings. Then we learn the following in regard to his arrival: "The Captain came. He had sent a very sensible letter in advance, which set Charlotte completely at rest. So much distinctness about himself, so much clarity about his own situation and about that of his friends made for a cheerful and happy prospect" (W.A. I, 20:28).

The impression that the Captain at once makes upon those around him is thus admirably summed up by André François-Poncet, in terms which would in large part apply to Wolmar also: "The Captain is an *active* man—the word recurs incessantly under Goethe's pen—and of a wholly practical activity. He possesses very extensive knowledge; . . . he has a richness of experience . . . . He is, moreover, marvelously organized for action; his mind is at the same time luminous and penetrating, so that at the first glance he discerns the inmost sense of things and the state of mind of people; he has a strong power of decision; he does not wait, he does not hesitate; as soon as he has perceived the possibility and the utility of an intervention, he intervenes." [15]

Wolmar is pictured as a model manager of his estate. Of the manor Rousseau says: "There all is agreeable and cheerful, there everything betokens abundance and good order; there nothing savors of riches and luxury; there is not a room where one would not be conscious of being in the country, and where one would not find all the comforts of the city" (O.C., 9:70). From the beginning, the Captain supplies the skill and energy lacking in the less practical Eduard. Soon the friend renders himself indispensable, so greatly does he improve upon the administration of the household and lands. Thus the resulting condition is a thriving one reminiscent of Wolmar's ménage and farms (W.A. I, 20:32–35, 41–45).

Many subjects of universal significance are discussed by the characters of both novels. Education occupies an especially prominent part in each, as one might expect. Numerous other questions, social and economic, philosophical, and aesthetic, are debated, often with a striking similarity of ideas. For instance, Rousseau and Goethe are in essential agreement that too great generosity to beggars contributes, in the words of the former, "toward increasing the scoundrels and vagabonds who delight in this slothful trade," instead of disposing of the problem (O.C., 9:217; W.A. I, 20:73).

The two novels disclose a likeness in their descriptions of nature, particularly concerning the quickening effect upon mind and body which hills and mountains exert when one has climbed to their summits. Rousseau depicts the changeableness of nature; Goethe's Ottilie writes in her diary of the "Jahresmärchen," or "tale of the Year's unfolding," of which Spring is the most pleasing chapter. Above all, much of the action in both books takes place in that out-of-doors so dear to the hearts of their respective authors.

Questions of love and marriage form the deepest concern. Julie and Charlotte both recall the happy days of early love, before it was interrupted by a marriage of someone else's choosing. Rousseau's heroine, now married to Wolmar, writes thus to Saint-Preux of that "precious" time when they first met, before she yielded to her father's wishes: ". . . 'Blind Love,' I said, 'was right, we were made for each other, had the human order of things not troubled the relationships of nature' " (O.C., 8:498–499). Similarly, Charlotte says to Eduard: "How fond I am of recalling our earliest relationship! We loved each other deeply in our youth; we were separated: you from me because your father united you with a considerably older woman through his insatiable eagerness for possessions; I from you because I . . . was obliged to give my hand to a man wealthy, not loved, but honored" (W.A. I, 20:9).

Although Saint-Preux eventually learns to tame his passion, he is at the beginning almost raving in the impetuosity of his love for Julie. ". . . I am intoxicated, or rather, insensate. My senses are changed," he writes her, "all my faculties are dimmed by this mortal kiss. . . . Whatever fate a transport of which I am no longer master may announce for me . . . , I can no longer live in the state wherein I find myself, and I feel that it will finally cause me to expire at your feet—or in your arms" (O.C., 8:50).

"In Eduard's state of mind, as in his actions," Goethe relates, "there is no longer any moderation. The consciousness of loving and being loved drives him into the infinite. . . . Ottilie's presence obliterates everything else for him. . . . He can think of nothing else; no conscience speaks to him; everything that was restrained in his nature breaks loose; his whole being streams toward Ottilie" (W.A., I, 20:142–143).

Notwithstanding their missteps, the heroines of both works display a certain moral severity. They demand a pure love emanating from the soul instead of a merely physical one. "It is the union of hearts," Julie tells Saint-Preux, "which makes up their true felicity. You sensual man, will you never know how to love? Recall, oh, do recall that sentiment so calm and so sweet which you once knew and which you described in a tone so touching and so tender!" (O.C., 8:340).

After the assistant teacher at the boarding school has shown his fondness for Ottilie, the latter reveals to Charlotte her wish concerning friendship with the young man: "As good and understanding as my friend is, just so, I hope, there will develop in him the feeling of a pure relationship to me; he will see in me a hallowed person" (W.A. I, 20:378–379).

When Julie realizes that she must give up her love for Saint-Preux, she writes him: "It is time to renounce the errors of youth and to abandon a deceptive hope. I shall never belong to you . . ." (O.C., 8:476).

In the wake of the infant's drowning, Ottilie confesses to Charlotte: "I have strayed from my path, I have broken my precepts . . . ; but as then, so this time, too, in my trance, I have marked my new course. I am resolved . . . I shall never be Eduard's!" (W.A. I, 20:370).

Charlotte, having just consented to a separation from Eduard, now feels constrained to renounce any thought of early marriage to the Captain (who has meanwhile become "the Major"). When, upon taking leave, he asks what he may hope for himself, she replies: "Let me refrain from giving you an answer. We have not deserved, through any fault of ours, to be unhappy; but neither have we merited being happy together" (W.A. I, 20:368).

Julie, who considers marriage without love a crime, declares (in one of her lengthiest epistles to Saint-Preux): "What then! That is not an evil to be lacking in faith, to annihilate, as far as it is in oneself, the force of the vow and of the most inviolable contracts? That is not an evil to force one's own self to become deceitful and lying? That is not an evil to . . . form bonds which make you desire the misfortune and death of another? That is not an evil, a state of which a thousand other crimes are always the fruit? A good thing which produced so many evils would be by that fact alone an evil itself" (O.C., 8:548).

With these words Julie describes a situation like that of the Count and the Baroness, old friends of Eduard and Charlotte. Goethe says that the difficulties of the Count in getting a separation from his wife "made him bitter against everything that concerned matrimony, which he himself nevertheless so eagerly desired with the Baroness" (W.A. I, 20:113).

At dinner, as the conversation turns upon marital troubles, Charlotte expresses regret at hearing that a girlhood friend of hers is about to get a divorce. She remarks that it is unpleasant to learn suddenly that friends whom one imagines as being in fortunate circumstances are facing an uncertain destiny. The Count reminds her that the world of reality is different from a comedy, where the marriage is seen as the last goal: upon its attainment the curtain falls, and one's momentary feeling of satisfaction finds its echo afterward. He then tells of two statutes suggested by a friend which would make trial marriages possible: the first to the effect that each union should be stipulated for a period of five years; the second law would provide that a state of matrimony be considered indissoluble only if either both parties, or at least the one, were married for the third time. In the talk following his disclosure we find the same emphasis as in the case of Rousseau on the evil of forming ties that make the ill-luck and death of another seem desirable. Speaking to Eduard and Charlotte of their previous marriages, the Count says that they turned out well, since death did willingly what the consistories only reluctantly do. When Charlotte observes that they should let the dead rest, he rejoins: "Why? . . . since they can be remembered with due honor. They were modest enough to content themselves with a few years in return for manifold good that they left behind" (W.A. I, 20:115). Repressing a sigh, the Baroness objects that in such cases the best years must be sacrificed. With reference to their earlier marital ventures, the Count tells Eduard and Charlotte that those were marriages of the hateful sort, adding: ". . . Unfortunately, marriages in general have . . . something doltish about them; they spoil the tenderest relationships, and it is actually only a matter of the silly security to which at least the one party attaches some importance . . ." (W.A. I, 20:117–118).

The Count's arguments, like similar reasonings found in Rousseau's novel, are contradicted by both authors. Thus Julie writes Saint-Preux: "It is not only in the interest of the husband and wife, but in that of all men, that the purity of marriage should not be tarnished. Whenever two wedded persons are united by a solemn bond, there begins the silent obligation of the whole human race to respect this holy union and to honor in them the obligation of marriage" (O.C., 8:528).

"Whoever attacks marriage," asserts Mittler, the mediating neighbor of Eduard and Charlotte (referring to the Count and the Baroness), ". . . whoever, through word or deed, undermines this foundation of all moral society, will have to reckon with me. Marriage is the beginning and the pinnacle of all culture. It makes the rough man mild, and the most cultured one has no better opportunity to prove his gentleness. It must be indissoluble: for it brings so much happiness that any individual misfortune is not to be counted at all by comparison" (W.A. I, 20:107).

From Rousseau we learn what renders feminine friendships so lukewarm and so little durable: "It is the interests of love, it is the empire of beauty, it is the jealousy of conquests . . ." (O.C., 8:291). The Baroness quickly divines Ottilie's attachment to Eduard, and Goethe explains her attitude with the words: "Married women, even though among themselves they do not love one another, nevertheless stand quietly in league together, especially against young girls" (W.A. I, 20:120).

Writing to Julie from Paris, Saint-Preux describes the Parisian ladies at considerable length and dwells on the lax attitude in the French capital regarding marriage. "Love itself," he says, "has lost its rights and is no less denatured than matrimony" (O.C., 8:39). The frivolity of social life there, as contrasted with the simple existence, even of the nobility, in Switzerland, finds something of a counterpart in the chapters of *Die Wahlverwandtschaften* devoted to the visit of Charlotte's daughter, Luciane, and her frivolous circle of friends (W.A. I, 20:226–258). As opposed to the genuineness of Ottilie, Luciane is representative of the superficially brilliant and of egocentric affectation. We learn very early that, while they were both at the boarding school, Luciane flaunted her prizes in Ottilie's face when the latter had failed to win any distinctions (W.A. I, 20:61–62).

Like Julie, Charlotte, intent upon carrying out the responsibilities of marriage, demands a great deal of herself as well as of others. What would be possible for her is impossible for Eduard, whose character and temperament she misjudges. Her attempt to save her marriage fails, and after the drowning of the child, she changes her attitude. Although Charlotte was often admired by earlier critics,[16] Hans Reiss points out her inconsistency and shows how Ottilie, on the contrary, is the one who thinks and acts consistently.[17] Upon realizing that fulfillment of her love is in conflict with the sacredness of wedlock, she is unalterably resolved to renounce Eduard and tries to bring him and Charlotte together again (W.A. I, 20:391). Having once formed her resolution, she is as inexorable as Julie, although each continues to love the man she renounces. At the same time, Ottilie too misjudges Eduard; she fails to recognize the fact that he is incapable of such renunciation. This, according to Reiss, is "das tragische Moment" in her sacrifice (p. 169). She follows the example of Julie: both come to regard matrimony as the highest good, which takes precedence over the happiness and desires of love. There is ultimately, however, a difference between their lovers: Saint-Preux (whom Lord Morley so unsparingly condemns)[18] contemplates suicide, but he overcomes the urge with the help of Bomston, while Eduard, although he does not follow Werther's example, succumbs to his lack of the will to live. Gradually Saint-Preux becomes reconciled to the primacy of marriage; Eduard cannot bring himself to acknowledge it.

In both novels one senses a "consciousness of the nearness of death" (to quote Paul Hankamer),[19] and a point is at last reached where passion and conflict are left behind. Not only is Saint-Preux an esteemed and cherished member of the Wolmar household (to which Claire and her daughter also belong), but Julie's father, the Baron d'Étange, now accepts Saint-Preux and even becomes his friend and frequent companion in hunting. The peaceful, harmonious life at Clarens is enlivened on occasion by the visits of Lord Edward Bomston. Nothing seriously disturbs this state of general tranquility until the fateful incident which results in Julie's last illness and death.

A like atmosphere of calmness and serenity prevails among the chief characters of *Die Wahlverwandtschaften*, now reunited, as they are depicted in the next to the last chapter. The Major is present part of the time, and Mittler himself pays regular visits. They renew their evening gatherings, at which Eduard reads aloud, more forcefully and expressively than formerly—apparently, in order to rouse Ottilie from her torpidity. "Every unpleasant, uncomfortable feeling of the intermediate period was extinguished. No one bore any resentment toward another; every sort of bitterness had vanished. The Major accompanied Charlotte's piano-playing with the violin, just as Eduard's flute again coincided with Ottilie's handling of the stringed instrument, as before" (W.A. I, 20:398). This quiet course of life at the manor continues until Ottilie's demise. As at Clarens, there is, so to speak, a "ménage à quatre." In each case, the once all-consuming love affair, now subdued and held within the bounds of propriety, is taken for granted by the other marriage partner: that of Saint-Preux and Julie by Wolmar, that of Eduard and Ottilie by Charlotte.

A general resemblance of circumstances obtains when death comes to the heroines. The faithful old valet of the Baron d'Étange, kneeling at the bedside of the deceased Julie with his gaze fixed upon her lifeless countenance, imagines suddenly that he sees her turn her eyes and look at him, while making a sign with her head. In his excitement, he runs through the house, crying that she is not dead. All who have just made the air resound with their lamentations now shout: "Elle n'est pas morte!" The noise spreads and increases, and the people—"friends of the marvelous," says Rousseau—lend an eager ear to the news (O.C., 8:519–520). In this manner the report of Julie's resurrection originates.

Ottilie's funeral procession is brought to a halt by Nanny, the little girl who waited on her during her last days and, at her lady's behest, ate the food intended for Ottilie. Confined in her parents' house and unable to escape otherwise, Nanny gets to the attic through a passage. As the cortège approaches, she beholds Ottilie, borne along below her, radiant with an unearthly beauty, and beckoning, Nanny thinks, to her. Confused, staggering, and reeling, she plunges to the street. Under pressure from the throng, the pallbearers are forced to set the bier down. Apparently, the child's limbs are shattered by the fall, but as she is being cautiously lifted from the ground, she makes a last effort to reach her mistress. Upon touching Ottilie's robe and folded hands, Nanny first springs to her feet and raises her arms and eyes toward heaven; then she falls reverently upon her knees beside the casket. When she arises, she joyfully shouts that Ottilie, by a look and gesture, has forgiven her, that God has pardoned her, and that she is no longer a murderess among them (W.A. I, 20:409–410). Thus in both cases we encounter the element of the miraculous after the death, a seeming, momentary revival, proclaimed by one person and then, as it were, "witnessed" by a multitude. Also, there is a disposition on the part of those around Julie in her last hours, and especially after the supposed "miracle," to regard her as saintly. This finds a more lasting echo in the attitude and behavior of her family and relatives, particularly as described by Wolmar to Saint-Preux. The apotheosis of Ottilie is prefigured by her likeness painted as an angel-face on the ceiling of the dome (W.A. I, 20:219). After the wondrous healing of Nanny is attributed to her, she assumes all the more the character of a "hallowed person"—to reiterate her words to Charlotte at an earlier time. Because of this belief in her supernatural powers and because of her continuously beautiful appearance in the glass-covered casket, since she has, like Julie, the look of peaceful sleep rather than of death, many seek a cure for their infirmities through a visit to the chapel where she lies (W.A. I, 20:413–414).

Julie and Ottilie both leave their survivors in a confused, uncertain state. Wolmar succeeds only with difficulty in arousing Claire from her distraught condition. They appeal to Saint-Preux to return to Clarens, and we must assume that he will do so and that he will comply with Julie's dying request that he educate her children. One definite prospect is that he will continue single, for Claire, who admits that she has loved him, avows that "a man who was loved by Julie d'Étange and who could resolve to espouse another" would be unworthy in her eyes (O.C., 8:532). Her attitude is therefore in opposition to the wish and request of Julie that Saint-Preux and Claire should marry. There is a similar uncertainty at the conclusion of Die Wahlverwandtschaften. Eduard observes his promise to the expiring Ottilie to live after she is gone more in the letter than in the spirit, and he complains to the Major that genius is necessary for everything, "even martyrdom." Despite the efforts of Charlotte, the friends, and the physician, Eduard withdraws more and more from life, until one day they find him dead, with his mementos of Ottilie spread out before him (W.A. I, 20:415–416). The narrator gives no indication of the future of those who remain: we cannot know whether Charlotte will at last consent to become the Major's wife (as Eduard has asked her to do).

As Hans M. Wolff points out, there is likewise the uncertainty whether Ottilie succumbs to inner tension or voluntarily departs from life. It also remains an open question, he says, whether one should attribute Julie's death to the accident or to lack of the will to live. Wolff finds this parallel enlightening in that each author tries to veil the significance of his heroine's death. In the case of each, death can be comprehended either as the reconciliation of a transgressed law or as the accusation of an all too rigid one.[20]

At the end of her last letter to Saint-Preux, written just before she dies, Julie bids farewell to her "doux ami," being, she says, already in the arms of death. "But," she asks, "would my soul exist without you? without you, what felicity would I enjoy? No, I am not leaving you; I am going to await you. Virtue, which separated us on earth, will unite us in the eternal abode. I die in this sweet expectation: too happy to be buying, at the cost of my life, the right to love you always without transgression, and to be telling you so once more" (O.C., 8:530).

The serene, unruffled bearing of Ottilie in her last days suggests that she, too, contemplates a future existence in which her love for Eduard will no longer be illicit. Just after she is stricken, Eduard returns from a ride. Hearing of her condition, he rushes in, throws himself down at her side, clasps her hand, and silently sheds a flood of tears upon it. Then he asks whether she will not at last speak to him again. Before she answers, he exclaims: "Very well! I'll follow you over there; then we shall speak with other tongues!" (W.A. I, 20:406–407). After Eduard's death Charlotte has him laid beside Ottilie in the vault, where no one else is to be interred. The final paragraph of the book reads: "So the lovers rest side by side. Peace hovers over the place of their repose; happy kindred painted angels look down upon them from the vault, and what a bright moment it will be when they awaken together again" (W.A. I, 20:416).

Thus the two novels, which with equal inexorability uphold the sacredness of marital ties, end on a related note. For both transfigure an overpowering and abiding love which, in conflict with the obligations of marriage, indeed experiences a hapless earthly course, but is destined to flower in the world beyond.[21] In both works we see (before *Selige Sehnsucht* was written) an application of the concept of "Stirb und werde!" which Romain Rolland would trace to Jean-Jacques.[22]

Goethe and Rousseau both knew renunciation in their lives. Six years after writing *Die Wahlverwandtschaften* Goethe again experienced a situation of "elective affinities" that inspired the love songs of his *West-östlicher Divan*. In this, Goethe's greatest purely lyrical creation (of which *Selige Sehnsucht*, mentioned above, probably offers the most frequently quoted lines), Marianne von Willemer participated so effectively that several of her poems were long taken for the poet's own. Such "Angleichung" surpasses Ottilie's adapting herself to Eduard's playing and her appropriating his handwriting. Willemer, whose relationship to his young wife could be called, in Vetter's terminology, "väterlich-tochterhaft," showed an understanding equal to that of Charlotte toward Eduard and Ottilie, or to that of Wolmar toward Saint-Preux and Julie. Goethe renounced, thereby forcing an even harder renunciation upon Marianne.[23] Nevertheless, the attachment continued, in subdued form, until the end of Goethe's life, as we know from their correspondence and occasional exchange of poems.[24] In these verses, as Hans-J. Weitz remarks, the accent rests "auf dem Unverlierbaren."[25] "On what cannot be lost"—this, too, is an attitude with which Jean-Jacques might well have sympathized, no less than with Goethe's wisdom of age expressed in the line: "Es bleibt Idee und Liebe" (W.A. I, 6:83).

To summarize briefly, *Die Wahlverwandtschaften* and *La Nouvelle Héloïse* show many analogous characteristics. Both have a typically eighteenth-century rural setting on estates of members of the lesser nobility. Within similar circles of society, amid corresponding scenes of country life, fundamental human problems are presented in much the same manner in the two novels. Above all, the nearly identical depiction of amorous passion in conflict with marriage offers numerous parallel situations. While insisting upon the inviolability of matrimony, both authors treat the "union of hearts" outside of the wedded state with profound sympathy. Although one cannot determine how far Goethe may have recalled Rousseau's narrative while writing his own mature romance of thwarted love, a deeply internal kinship of the two works is undeniable.

VI

Ideals of Culture

The pedagogical element is discernible in most of Rousseau's writings. In the *Confessions* he devotes much space to relating his own progress in cognition and knowledge, whether it be his early desultory readings and the limited amount of formal instruction which he enjoyed, or his intimate account of the great educational role played by experience. The *Discourses* themselves, like the *Lettre à d'Alembert*, the musical works, and particularly the *Lettres relatives à la botanique*, all reveal the teacher. Even in the most external sense *La Nouvelle Héloïse* is a novel of didactic tendency, and Rousseau dedicated his *Émile* wholly to the cause of education. What does it matter that his venture as instructor to the children of M. Mably at Lyons proved a failure? Through *Émile* he became the teacher and inspirer of the Europe of his age and of the generations to follow. Subsequent educational theorists inevitably took that work as their starting point. From *Émile* dates what Josef Rattner calls the "admirable educational zeal of the eighteenth century, to which modern pedagogy is infinitely indebted." Rattner names Basedow, Wolke, Campe, Salzmann, and Pestalozzi as representative followers of Rousseau in the German-speaking world.[1]

Like Jean-Jacques, Goethe was born with a penchant for teaching. Witness the childhood anecdote of his having prepared lessons to give to the little brother who died, or the schoolmaster-like attitude revealed in letters to his sister Cornelia and in the recounting of his instructing

Gretchen, as related in *Dichtung und Wahrheit*. That work records the mistrust Goethe's father and the latter's contemporaries felt increasingly toward the public schools. In general, tutors did not prove satisfactory, either (W.A. I, 26:189). The deficiencies of the prevailing types of schooling were soon to arouse widespread eagerness for educational reform under the inspiration of Rousseau's writings. After studying under numerous tutors himself and after his university experience, Goethe went to Weimar as preceptor to the youthful Duke Karl August. In that initial capacity, as literary arbiter of the court, as theatrical director, by virtue of his ministerial direction of cultural affairs of the duchy, and as the Sage of Weimar and (in the words of Lord Byron) "the undisputed sovereign of European letters," his entire sojourn of more than half a century there can be viewed as an almost continuous achievement in the interest of culture in the fullest sense. Although his writings did not have as broad an influence pedagogically as those of Rousseau, Goethe was in a position to exercise greater effect directly upon instructional matters. His efficacy, like that of the Genevan, was more through inspiration than through personal activity as a teacher in the usual way. As already mentioned, his guidance of Fritz von Stein was characterized by the boy's mother as being in the spirit of Jean-Jacques. Karl August has been called a pronounced disciple of Rousseau even by some who tended to minimize the importance of the latter for the Duke's mentor himself.[2]

Goethe's ideas on education are especially prominent in both parts of *Wilhelm Meister*, in *Dichtung und Wahrheit* and in *Die Wahlverwandtschaften*. His *Faust* has as its hero a disgruntled pedagogue who, after a well-nigh universal experiencing of the world and of humanity's weal and woe, gains an insight into the ultimate wisdom of life. This chapter will deal mainly with *Wilhelm Meister*.

Opinions vary regarding the pedagogical relationship of the two writers. Rudolf Lehmann argues that Goethe's educational interests had their origin in a direct relationship to the world of children, with equal participation by the artist and the man. Rousseau's aesthetic appreciation of children (whom he compares, as to perfection, to the creations of the plant world) finds emphatic repetition in Goethe's "warmth of perception, joy of contemplation, and fervent human sympathy." Lehmann quotes Werther's letter expressing his love for children and states that these sentiments remained essentially characteristic of Goethe even during his last years.[3] By implication, then, they would extend to *Wilhelm*

Meisters Wanderjahre, which appeared in definitive form in 1829. The monograph by Elisabeth Caspers is the most detailed presentation of corresponding educational views held by Rousseau and Goethe.[4] As Walter Müller points out in his review of her book, she perhaps goes to an extreme in her emphasis on mere similarity of experience where fundamental likenesses are concerned.[5] Oskar Walzel asserts that Goethe, in seeking to give full range to the pupils' personality, agrees fundamentally with Rousseau rather than with Pestalozzi;[6] but the extent of the latter's indebtedness to *Émile* has been repeatedly demonstrated.[7]

According to several commentaries on the *Wanderjahre*, Goethe gave evidence of returning to an earlier point of view, namely, his "Sturm und Drang" penchant for stressing life's variety within its encircling unity. Kurt Jahn, for instance, attributes this tendency to a decrease in inventive originality which caused Goethe to make use of what he found already at hand, especially in matters of detail; even so, Jahn admits a newness of conception and general trend of thought.[8] Ernst L. Stahl rejects the notion of "failing craftsmanship," both on the strength of Goethe's statement that the work was not unified in form but in purpose, and by reason of the labor that he devoted to it. These considerations indicate in Stahl's opinion, a "clear intention" regarding the structure of the novel.[9] August Raabe would relate the question to Goethe's conflict with daemonic forces as characterized in *Dichtung und Wahrheit*. According to Raabe's thesis, the ideals of the poet's later life are expressive of a lofty resolution to let his early struggles and wealth of experience serve the young generation as a guiding force.[10] Goethe's words to Eckermann (September 18, 1823) could well be used, says Raabe, as a motto for the *Wanderjahre*: "But now there is no more time for going astray; we old men were here for that; and what good would all our searching and our erring have done if you younger people, in turn, insisted upon going those same ways? Then we should never make any progress!"

Wilhelm Flitner especially stresses Goethe's views on education as expressed in the *Wanderjahre*, attributing a number of them to Rousseau's influence.[11] According to Flitner, *Émile* was just as determinative for Goethe as *La Nouvelle Héloïse*; the whole generation to which he belonged had grown up on *Émile*, regardless of whether one's attitude was for or against this book. Goethe, who had taken a journey on the Lahn and the Rhine with Basedow in 1774, retained long afterward an interest in the "Philanthropinum," a school which Basedow founded at Dessau, largely in accordance with Rousseau's educational tenets. In Weimar an essential aspect of Goethe's friendship with Herder, Friedrich August Wolf, Wilhelm von Humboldt, and Schiller was the forming of his own ideas on education. Flitner names as the documents of this common endeavor, which was destined to lay a new foundation for German humanistic culture, Herder's *Schulreden* and *Humanitätsbriefe*, Wolf's *Consilia*, Schiller's *Über die ästhetische Erziehung des Menschen*, Humboldt's *Denkschriften*, and Goethe's *Wilhelm Meisters Lehrjahre*. In that middle period of his life, Flitner avers, Goethe remained hostile toward Pestalozzi's educational thinking, which took as its starting-point the problems of society. Later, under the impact of the French Revolution, Goethe dealt in the eighth book of the *Lehrjahre* with the connection between humane education and social crisis (p. 8).

The four chapters describing the Pedagogical Province in the *Wanderjahre* form the core of Flitner's book of selections. He also reunites the two collections of largely didactic aphorisms, "Betrachtungen im Sinne der Wanderer" and "Aus Makariens Archiv," with the *Wanderjahre*, according to Goethe's original order (p. 9).

Flitner cites two contrasting forms of education in the eighteenth century: the middle-class and the aristocratic. While the latter trains one to be a virtuoso, namely well-bred, realistic, universal, and aesthetic, the former appeared pedantic and poor in content to the youth of the "Sturm und Drang" era. It was the wish of the young Goethe and his friends to overcome class constraint and to bring a broad humanistic education to the middle classes (p. 174, note 1).

Although the concept of humanity set forth in the *Lehrjahre* is retained in the *Wanderjahre*, Flitner finds that the latter work develops a manner of education which shows in its methods many antitheses to the pedagogical principles of the *Lehrjahre*. He considers this particularly true of the right choice of a vocation. Whereas in the *Lehrjahre* Wilhelm strives in a Rousseau-like fashion toward becoming a well-rounded man, an individual schooled in pure humanity and versatility, the ideal followed in the *Wanderjahre* shows the influence of Pestalozzi's insistence upon early accommodation of self to a harmonious circle of society (p. 204),[12] a claim which Durkheim makes for Rousseau.[13] The methods, Flitner continues, differ more than the aims, as far as changes of attitude during the intervening years are concerned. The Abbé of the *Lehrjahre*, who represents Goethe's ideal of an educator at that period, teaches a philosophy of life which offers many points of contact with Rousseau and which experienced a conscious further development through the friendship with Schiller. It is the Abbé's theory that every human being possesses an original capability which can be developed into a talent. Man learns only through trial and activity what he is able to accomplish. In order that this talent may be revealed, one must risk treading the paths of error. The right sort of education should enliven the instinctive urge; by this form of testing, everyone can find a talent within himself. According to Flitner, Goethe derived the formula in question directly from *Émile*, even though he maintains that the Abbé's method is strongly opposed in the *Wanderjahre*, and quotes Jarno's words concerning versatility as a preparation for one-sided concentration (W.A. I, 24:50). Nevertheless, Flitner declares that the ideas formulated by Jarno and Lenardo belong to the pedagogical thinking of both Rousseau and Pestalozzi (pp. 211–212). Flitner observes that the contrast between the pedagogy of the Abbé and that of Nathalie corresponds to the difference between Émile's education and that of Sophie, his feminine counterpart (p. 177). Thus, despite the variations to which Flitner calls attention, he repeatedly acknowledges Goethe's essential concurrence with Rousseau. From Flitner's outline we shall proceed to a more detailed comparison of their educational ideas as expressed in representative passages of their works.

"Nature," Julie tells Saint-Preux, "wishes children to be children before being men. If we try to pervert that order, we shall produce precocious fruits which will have neither maturity nor savor, and which will not be long in growing corrupt; we shall have young savants and old children" (O.C., 9:254).[14] Rousseau repeats that thought in *Émile* and gives the following advice: "Treat your pupil in accordance with his age. Put him first in his place and keep him there so well that he will not attempt to leave it" (O.C., 3:121–122). According to Karl Muthesius, Goethe echoes Rousseau's views on children in Werther's well-known words, "On this earth the children are nearest to my heart" (W.A. I, 19:41), and, decades later, in *Dichtung und Wahrheit*, where he describes the constraint endured by children of the upper classes.[15] Muthesius attributes the happy, unrestrained childhood of all three sons of Charlotte von Stein largely to Goethe's fatherly interest in them (pp. 37–38). Charlotte herself realized her friend's accord with the precepts of Jean-Jacques, commenting in her letter of June 2, 1783 to her sister-in-law, Sophie von Schardt, "Goethe is one of the few who know how to grasp Rousseau's inner meaning of education." As Arnold Bork reminds us, long after the break with Goethe she continued to place confidence in him as a guide to Fritz, especially in the matter of her son's entering the Prussian service in 1796.[16] Largely on the strength of the manner in which Goethe taught Charlotte's children, Muthesius regards him as the enunciator and fulfiller of Rousseau's gospel of Nature in Weimar (p. 38). Barker Fairley, however, asserts that in *Dichtung und Wahrheit* Goethe was not interested in "immaturity" except in connection with his own development.[17]

In *Émile* Rousseau proclaimed his reasons for wanting only a vigorous, healthy pupil and his principles for keeping him so, describing briefly the merits of manual labor and bodily exercise for strengthening both temperament and health (O.C., 3:49). Similarly, the leaders of the Pedagogical Province tell Wilhelm that well-born, healthy children have an advantageous start. Nature has given them all that they need, and it is the duty of their teachers to develop these gifts. The emphasis which Rousseau places upon useful physical activity finds an echo in the entire program of the Province (W.A. I, 24:239–240, passim).

Rousseau extolled the rural life in *La Nouvelle Héloïse*. Émile is to be raised in the country, for men are corrupted when they congregate (O.C., 3:56–57).[18] Correspondingly, the boys in the Pedagogical Province form their own world in the freedom of their isolated, hilly region. There are no schoolhouses; as in the case of Émile, the outdoors fulfills that function (W.A. I, 24:232–233, passim). Human intelligence has its limitations, Rousseau asserts, and not only is a man unable to know all things, he cannot even comprehend in its entirety the little that others know. Thus there is a choice in the things that one shall teach as well as in the time for learning them. Of the knowledge within our reach, some is false, some is useless, and some merely nourishes the pride of its possessors (O.C., 3:286). In like manner, Goethe stresses the importance of knowing something worthwhile, rather than merely accumulating knowledge. In one of his maxims on natural science he says: "Hypotheses are lullabies with which the teacher lulls his pupils to sleep. The thoughtful, faithful observer learns more and more to know his limitations. He sees that the farther knowledge is extended, the more problems appear."[19] "Make your pupil attentive to the phenomena of nature," Rousseau advises, "and soon you will render him curious; but, for the sake of nourishing his curiosity, never hasten to satisfy it" (O.C., 3:289–290). Goethe's guidance of Fritz von Stein was carried out in that spirit, and the same can be said of the poet's outlook at a later date, regarding his own life and the concepts expressed in the two *Wilhelm Meister* novels (W.A. I, 23:131; 24:227).

Although Émile's knowledge does not cover a wide range, it is truly his own; he does not know anything merely by halves. Most importantly, he has realized that there is much he does not know but which he may learn some day. His is the universal mind, not by virtue of information, but through the faculty of acquiring it, for he has "an open, intelligent mind, ready for anything, and, as Montaigne would say, if not informed, at least teachable" (O.C., 3:376–377). Goethe expresses a kindred thought in a letter to Friederike Unzelmann (March 14, 1803): "I am well enough acquainted with pedagogical matters in general, and especially with the pedagogy of the theater, to know that everything really depends on a man's realizing what he lacks; the realization of which means he has already acquired it to some extent, because the wish for it is very quickly added to one's perception of what is genuine and useful." Numerous instances both in Goethe's life and works attest to his satisfaction in those who are "teachable," beginning with Gretchen, as depicted in *Dichtung und Wahrheit* (W.A. I, 26:297–298).

A vigorous, full life is advocated by Jean-Jacques: "To live is not merely to breathe, it is to act; it is to make use of our organs, of our senses, of our faculties, of all parts of ourselves which give us the feeling of our existence. The man who has lived the most is not the one who has numbered the most years, but the one who has felt life most intensely" (O.C., 3:19). Rousseau's chief works, *La Nouvelle Héloïse*, *Émile*, and the *Confessions*, are replete with activity. The same may be said of Goethe's works and, above all, of his own life.[20] Both the *Wahlverwandtschaften* and the entire *Wilhelm Meister* emphasize the active life.[21] It is a cardinal principle for the education of the young people in the Pedagogical Province, where its importance is summed up in the song, "Von den Bergen zu den Hügeln" (W.A. I, 24:66–67):

> *Und dein Streben, sei's in Liebe,*
> *Und dein Leben sei die Tat!*

Rousseau in *Émile* (O.C., 3:151–152) and Goethe in the *Wanderjahre* (W.A. I, 25^1:39) both stress proper direction of the pupil's innate urge to be active, which early finds expression in imitation. The country is the ideal setting for Émile's upbringing, Rousseau declares. There, amid natural surroundings and far away from the vices of the city, he is more thoroughly under the control of his tutor, who can direct his impulse for action into a practical channel, such as gardening (O.C., 3:350–351). Just so the boys in the Pedagogical Province, isolated from the outside world, lead an active existence of usefulness, since they are responsible for all manual labor (W.A. I, 24:231–259).

Rousseau and Goethe alike bestow their highest praise upon farming as an occupation. In *Émile* agriculture is termed "the first calling of man, the most honest, the most useful, and consequently the most noble one . . ." (O.C., 3:251). Goethe also elevates the farmer's vocation. When Wilhelm and a companion visit an estate, they assume the imposing but simply clad man who meets them to be a tenant. He introduces himself as the master, however, inviting them to look at his fields and "see how I manage my farm; for certainly to you, as a large landowner, nothing can be of more concern than the noble science, the noble art of agriculture" (W.A. I, 24:209).

Rousseau advises those who lost their heritage of farming or who never had it to learn a trade (O.C., 3:251). The artisan pursues a useful calling while leading the most independent life, he says in *Émile*. While the lord, marquis, or prince is bound by his lot never to be anything else, an artisan is elevated "to man's estate . . . . Remember that it is not by any means a talent that I demand of you: it is a trade, a real trade, a purely mechanical art, where the hands work more than the head, and which does not lead to fortune, but with which one can get along. . . . I absolutely want Emile to learn a trade, an honest calling . . . ," (O.C., 3:351, 355). Similarly, Montan in the *Wanderjahre* emphasizes the importance of mastering one particular trade or profession, since specialization rather than versatility is the vogue. Montan therefore counsels: "Make yourself an expert violinist through practice, and be assured that the conductor will assign you a favored place in the orchestra. . . . It is best to confine oneself to one trade. For the person of least ability it will always be a trade, for the better one an art, and as for the best, when he does one thing, he does all; or to be less paradoxical, in the one thing that he does properly he sees the likeness of all that is rightly done" (W.A. I, 24:50). Rousseau considers carpentry the most desirable trade. It is useful and can be carried on inside. While exercising the body, it demands skill and industry on the part of the workman. And taste and elegance also are necessary for the finished product. Interestingly enough, in the episode of the *Wanderjahre* entitled

"Sankt Joseph der Zweite" the hero tells Wilhelm Meister he was attracted by a painting to the trade once practiced by his namesake (W.A. I,
24:21).

Rousseau and Goethe equally distrust the effect of mechanical and
scientific devices on the human mind. Thus we read in *Émile*:

All the laws of statics and hydrostatics are discovered by experiments that are
rough enough. I do not wish one to go into a laboratory of experimental
physics for any of that: all that display of instruments and machines is dis-
pleasing to me. A scientific air kills knowledge . . . . I prefer that our instruments should not be so perfect and exact, and that we should have clearer ideas
of what they ought to be, and of the operation which should result from them.

(O.C., 3:307–309)

If man does not dull his mind by depending on received knowledge, such
as that from scientific instruments, he will remain more open to discover-
ing new relationships and forming new linkages of ideas (O.C., 3:309).
Goethe's Wilhelm Meister voices a similar attitude. After looking through
a telescope he tells the astronomer he understands the satisfaction afforded scientists by their ability to bring the immense universe as near as
the planet he beheld, but he feels constrained to object:

I have found in life on the average, that these means by which we come to the
aid of our senses do not exert any morally favorable effect on Man. Whoever
looks through spectacles considers himself wiser than he is, for his external
sense is thereby thrown out of balance with his inner competence for judgment . . . . We shall not ban these glasses from the world any more than any
machinery, but it is important for the observer of morals to find out and to
know whence many things about which people complain have crept into
humanity.

(W.A. I, 24:183)

Rousseau admits the advisability of giving a pupil inclined toward
the "speculative sciences" a profession in conformance with that interest.
He could learn, for instance, to make mathematical instruments, spectacles, or telescopes (O.C., 3:362–363). Despite Wilhelm Meister's comment, Goethe in his boyhood eagerly observed the making of various
objects by craftsmen (W.A. I, 26:238). Later, particularly in his early
years at Weimar, he came into contact with a multiplicity of callings, high
and low, because of his numerous and varied administrative duties.

When Émile learns his trade, his teacher will learn it with him, being
convinced that the pupil will learn well only what the two study together

(O.C., 3:363). This reminds one of Goethe's account of how his father (who, of course, was not consciously imitating Rousseau) did not rest content with providing opportunities for his children's education, but on occasion took lessons with them. For example, when a tutor for English was engaged, the elder Goethe joined Wolfgang and Cornelia in an intensive training throughout four weeks (W.A. I, 26:194–195). He did the same with drawing (W.A. I, 26:183–184).

Jean-Jacques maintains that his pupil must work like a peasant and think like a philosopher, in order not to be as indolent as a savage. "The great secret of education," he explains, "is to make physical exertions and those of the mind always serve as a relaxation for each other" (O.C., 3: 366). The same principle is carried out consistently in the Pedagogical Province. A notable instance is the combined activity of the boys' tending herds and practicing their singing (W.A. I, 24:234–235).

Certain related ideas are apparent in the respective plans of the two writers for the musical training of their pupils.[22] For teaching voice Rousseau advises:

In the singing, render his voice exact, even, flexible, and sonorous; his ear sensitive to measure and harmony . . . . I should try to compose some songs expressly for him, interesting for his age and as simple as his ideas . . . . To know music well, it is not sufficient to render it; one must compose it, and the one should be learned with the other . . . . Exercise your little musician first in making quite regular phrases, properly cadenced; then in noting their different conformities by correct punctuation, a thing which is done by the right choice of cadences and caesuras.

(O.C., 3:252)

When Wilhelm inquires about the frequent and melodious singing of the pupils, he receives the following reply:

With us, singing is the first step in education; everything else centers around that and is imparted by means of it. The simplest enjoyment as well as the simplest lesson are enlivened and impressed upon the memory through song . . . . Since we train the children to learn to write sounds which they utter with symbols on the board and then to reproduce them in their throats, according to the inclination of these signs, and furthermore to add the text under them, they exercise hands, ears, and eyes at the same time. . . .

(W.A. I, 24:235)

Rousseau writes that the power which habit exerts comes from the natural indolence of man, and that this tendency increases the more one yields to it. He continues: "The path, once marked out, becomes easier to follow. It can also be noted that the influence of habit on old men and indolent people is very great, but very slight on youth and on lively persons" (O.C., 3:277–278). Montan observes in a similar vein that smoke from charcoal kilns can scarcely be as agreeable to Wilhelm as to himself, accustomed to it from early childhood. He tells of having attempted much in the world and always found that Man's only comfort rests in habit. "We miss even the unpleasant things to which we are accustomed," he says. "I was once afflicted a very long time with a wound which would not heal, and when I finally recovered, it was most disagreeable to me when the surgeon did not come any more" (W.A. I, 24:53).

Both Rousseau and Goethe see the theater as a limited teaching device. In the *Lettre à M. d'Alembert sur les spectacles* Rousseau points out the unavoidable primacy of entertainment in drama: "If the utility can be found, very well; but the principal object is to please, and, provided the people are amused, that object is sufficiently fulfilled. . . . The stage, in general, is a tableau of human passions, the original of which is in people's hearts. But if the painter did not take care to flatter these passions, the spectators would soon be disgusted" (O.C., 2:30–31). On a parallel note, one of the elders of the Pedagogical Province in the *Wanderjahre* rejects Wilhelm's assertion that the theater advances the cause of the other arts, insisting that on the contrary, it ruins them through exploitation. "The actor," he goes on to explain,

will unscrupulously use for his fleeting purposes whatever art and life offer him, and with no slight gain; the painter, on the other hand, who in turn would also like to derive his advantage from the theater, will always find himself at a disadvantage, and the musician too. All the arts seem to me like siblings, most of whom would be inclined to good management, but one of whom, light of heart, had the desire to appropriate and use up the possessions of the entire family. The theater is in this situation; it has an ambiguous origin which it can never wholly deny, either as art, or as a profession, or as dilettantism.

(W.A. I, 25^1:20)

Since books are a necessity even in his educational schema, Jean-Jacques cites one which he considers "the most fortunate treatise of natural education." It will be the first book read by Émile and for a long time it alone will constitute his library. "This marvelous book," which is to be the text for all conversations on natural science, is not Aristotle, Pliny, or

Buffon, but *Robinson Crusoe* (O.C., 3:326–327). Goethe's admiration for that work is manifest, both from *Dichtung und Wahrheit* (W.A. I, 26:50) and from a letter to Karl Ernst Schubarth (April 2, 1818). Like Rousseau, Goethe avidly read accounts of voyages and travels. "Textbooks," it is stated in *Wilhelm Meisters Lehrjahre*, "should be attractive; they become so only if they present the most cheerful and accessible side of knowledge and science" (W.A. I, 23:256).

"How many things we must know before arriving at a knowledge of Man!" exclaims Rousseau. "Man is the last study of the sage, and you pretend to make it the first one for a child! Before instructing him regarding our sentiments, begin by teaching him to appreciate them" (O.C., 3:331–332). Society, Jean-Jacques continues, must be studied through the medium of mankind, and men through society. "Those who try to treat politics and morality separately will never have any understanding of either" (O.C., 3:433–434). Human nature, Goethe asserts (in the *Lehrjahre*), first becomes intelligible through observation of the child (W.A. I, 23:139). In *Die Wahlverwandtschaften* he also quotes Pope's dictum: "The proper study of mankind is Man" (W.A. I, 20:293). Thus Goethe agrees with Rousseau concerning what both consider a basic principle of education.

Rousseau laments the "dangers" and disadvantages of the study of history. Not only is it difficult to assume a point of view from which one can judge one's fellow man equitably, he says, but one of its chief vices is that it depicts men more often from the bad side than from the good. Interest is centered on revolutions rather than on the quiet development of peoples and governments. Moreover, the facts described in history inevitably fail to give the reader an exact picture of what happened, for they change their aspect in the head of the historian; they are subject to misrepresentation through ignorance or partiality. A general defect of history is its stress on tangible facts which can be fixed in the mind by names, places, and dates, and not on the slow, progressive causes of those facts. Therefore Rousseau prefers the reading of biography for beginning the study of the human heart, above all the lives of great men as depicted by Plutarch with "an inimitable grace" and a happy faculty for making "a single word, a smile or a gesture characterize his hero" (O.C., 4:439–445).

In one of her diary entries Ottilie expresses the belief that a teacher who awakens a feeling for a single good action or a single good poem accomplishes more than one who transmits quantities of factual knowledge

(W.A. I, 20:293). A maxim of Goethe reads: "The best thing we get from history is the enthusiasm that it arouses."[23] Elsewhere he remarks that upon closer inspection one finds that "for the historian himself, history does not readily become historical," since each one merely writes as if he himself had been there, but not about the state of things beforehand and what was in motion at the time (W.A. I, 42¹:188). Hence Rousseau and Goethe voice largely identical objections to history as generally written. Furthermore, Rousseau's comment on the personal bias in historical accounts foreshadows the words of Faust to Wagner about the "Spirit of the Ages:"

> Mein Freund, die Zeiten der Vergangenheit
> Sind uns ein Buch mit sieben Siegeln.
> Was ihr den Geist der Zeiten heisst,
> Das ist im Grund der Herren eigner Geist,
> In dem die Zeiten sich bespiegeln.
>
> (ll. 575–579)

Finally, as previously mentioned, Rousseau and Goethe early delighted in Plutarch. A letter of December 1, 1831, to Wilhelm von Humboldt, tells of Goethe's having his daughter-in-law read to him from the *Lives* in the evenings. Again like Jean-Jacques, he never lost interest in those biographies, which appealed to them both more than history *per se*.

Rousseau and Goethe urge caution in proclaiming religious doctrine to children, since they cannot understand it. Rousseau maintains that to have no idea of the Divinity is preferable to holding base, wrong, fantastic, or other unworthy conceptions (O.C., 3:484). Rather than this potentially misplaced veneration, the Vicar's "respectful doubt" (O.C., 4:107–108) resembles Goethe's elevation of self-reverence in the *Wanderjahre* as the highest degree of all three types (W.A. I, 24:240–241). This supreme veneration of self is like that which caused Jean-Jacques, despite his misanthropic tendencies, to proclaim his worth in the *Confessions*, in the belief that posterity would judge him accordingly. Likewise, the *Rêveries du promeneur solitaire* reveal that same confidence in human dignity and the essentially good and beautiful character of life—at least, in an ultimately better future, when men would appreciate his true worth. And that same lofty reverence sustained Goethe when, against the hard blows of fate and amid the increasing frailties of old age, he strove to complete *Faust*, his testament to mankind, foretelling in the words of the hero his own undying fame:

> *Es kann die Spur von meinen Erdetagen*
> *Nicht in Äonen untergehn.*
>
> (ll. 11,583–11,584)

Both Goethe and Rousseau maintain that woman gains her moral ascendancy through subordination to man and abnegation of self-will. Rousseau states concerning Sophie in *Émile* that "all education of women ought to relate to men. To please them, to be useful to them, to make themselves loved and honored by them, to raise them in youth, to care for them grown up, to counsel them, to console them, to render life agreeable and sweet to them; these are the duties of women in all times, and which should be taught them from childhood on" (O.C., 4:225).

Rousseau insists that women should be taught that in their very duties lie the sources of their pleasures and the foundations of their rights. Woman's dominion "begins with her virtues; hardly do her attractions develop, when she reigns already by the sweetness of her character and makes her modesty commanding." All peoples of moral principles have respected women: Sparta, the ancient Germans, and Rome (O.C., 4:282).

In *Hermann und Dorothea* the heroine similarly declines the help of her supposed future master in carrying water, telling him that woman should early learn to serve, according to her destiny. For only by serving does she finally arrive at the moral ascendancy which is rightfully hers in the household (W.A. I, 50:248).[24] Here she echoes the view of woman's place which Princess Leonore expresses in *Torquato Tasso* (of earlier date):

> *Willst du genau erfahren, was sich ziemt,*
> *So frage nur bei edlen Frauen an.*
>
> (ll. 1013–1014)

Where morality rules, the Princess tells Tasso, women rule, and where insolence prevails, they have no influence. Her characterization of the difference in attitude between the two sexes sums up what both Rousseau and Goethe forcefully depicted (especially as novelists):

> *Nach Freiheit strebt der Mann, das Weib nach Sitte.*
>
> (l. 1022)

Rousseau especially cautions against haste in the educational process. The teacher, he says, should exercise the pupil's body, his senses, and his energies, but keep his mind unoccupied as long as is feasible (O.C., 3:

127–129). Goethe's thoughts on taking one's time in teaching are expressed in *Die Wahlverwandtschaften*, where the assistant at the boarding-school writes to Charlotte concerning Ottilie, whom he greatly admires, as follows:

As long as I instruct her, I see her moving at an even pace slowly, slowly forward, never backward. . . . What does not follow from that which has preceded, she does not comprehend. She is incompetent, even obstinate, in the face of an easily intelligible matter which is out of context for her. Yet if one can find the connecting links and make them clear for her, the most difficult thing is comprehensible to her.

In this slow progress she remains behind her classmates, who, with quite different capacities, always hasten forward, easily grasping everything, even the incoherent, easily retain it, and readily apply it again. . . .

If I am to close with a general observation, I might say: she does not learn as one who is to be educated, but as one who is going to educate; not as a pupil, but as a future teacher.

(W.A. I, 20:38–39)

Many additional examples could be given to illustrate the frequent correspondence of Rousseau's and Goethe's thoughts concerning the training and educating of the young. They would be mainly further details of the general principles already indicated. Neither Rousseau nor Goethe created an instructional system as an end in itself. Plans for education were for them only the means of an endeavor common to both: namely, to mold the human being in accordance with their respective ideas. Not the letter, but the spirit is the concern of each in his precepts for mankind. One's conduct of life in all its stages is the chief pedagogical interest of Rousseau as well as of Goethe; applicable to both is the admonition in the *Lehrjahre*: "Gedenke zu leben!" (W.A. I, 23:198). Both are protagonists of a theory of life in harmony with nature. Émile thanks his teacher for having taught him how to be free, that is, "to yield to necessity."[25] Compare with this Goethe's famous line in the sonnet "Natur und Kunst":

Und das Gesetz nur kann uns Freiheit geben.
(W.A. I, 4:129)

Thus Rousseau and Goethe are revealed as evangelists of timeless cultural ideals, at which they arrived on similar paths in their unceasing quest for higher levels of human existence.

VII

Utopian Visions

This chapter will deal with parallels in the utopias envisioned by Goethe and Rousseau. Special attention will be given to Goethe's mature works, with emphasis on *Wilhelm Meisters Wanderjahre* and *Faust*, and to Rousseau's *Contrat social*.

The impression has stubbornly persisted that Rousseau was from the people and of the people, while Goethe became the creature of aristocrats. Jean-Jacques is often pictured as the fond parent of revolution to come, the implacable hater of the rich and powerful, and the staunch friend of the poor. A distorted view of Goethe, on the other hand, sees him as the defender and flatterer of princes and thus as the enemy of all that is even remotely connected with the French Revolution and with the notion of democracy. Such critics tended to contrast this Goethe, the aloof dispenser of maxims on life to the lowly around him, with Rousseau, the friend to all mankind. Fortunately, a few scholars early saw beyond these limited stereotypes and found a definite connection between their concepts of politics and society; modern studies have vindicated and amplified their conclusions.

Assessment of Goethe's kinship with Rousseau's socio-political ideas has been especially difficult because of the debate surrounding the attitude of both toward revolution. Much has been written concerning Rousseau's role, or lack of it, in the French Revolution. Albert Meynier and many others attribute numerous features of the revolutionary trend to Rousseau's influence.[1] Edme Champion, on the other hand, protests vigorously against the condemning of Rousseau as "a precursor of the terrorists," citing particularly the frequent claim that Jean-Jacques was the "evil genius" of the Revolution and that his preaching of equality engendered the excesses and violence of 1793. Rousseau, Champion maintains, was the victim of a judgment inspired by prejudice and a partisan spirit, as well as of mistaken interpretation; an influence has been attributed to him which he never had.[2] At first, Champion says, the attacks on Rousseau were almost exclusively religious, although the Archbishop of Paris did charge that *Émile* tended to disturb the peace of sovereign states and to incite revolt (p. 1). Champion concludes that little would remain of the accusation if his rhetorical sallies and figures were reduced to their true value and if he were read as he should be read (p. 39). There have been scarcely less frequent arguments about Goethe's reaction to the Revolution. Frank H. Reinsch finally disproved the long-standing misconception that in Weimar Goethe gave up his hitherto-cherished ideals of individualism and equality and accepted the tenets of absolutism.[3] As Eberhard Sauer points out, Goethe's political acumen surpassed that often ascribed to his pro-revolutionary contemporaries, because he was free from prejudice regarding the innovations introduced under the slogans of liberty and equality. His open-mindedness enabled him to foresee, much earlier than his associates, the sudden change from rule by the people to mob rule. Actually, Goethe sided neither with the uprising nor with the countermovement; his primary concern was for humanity—not abstract theory.[4] For, as Edward Dowden emphasizes, Goethe was willing to aid in appropriating and assimilating from foreign nations what would be of real advantage to his fellow countrymen. Efforts to Gallicize the German people, however, were intolerable to him; he had no patience with efforts to transplant the ideas of the French Revolution "into a soil to which they were not native."[5] One is here reminded of Rousseau's criticism of Peter the Great, who "first tried to make Germans and Englishmen" out of his countrymen, instead of beginning by making Russians out of them (O.C., 5:116).

In a statement quoted in our second chapter, Goethe credits Rousseau as well as Diderot with a preparatory function in the revolt, which in Germany mainly assumed a literary form as the "Sturm und Drang" movement. There is no indication, though, that Goethe ever assumed that Rousseau, had he lived until the revolutionary era, would have been in sympathy with the sanguinary violence which repelled many an erstwhile lively supporter of the French upheaval. As we have seen, Goethe's obsession with the Revolution is reflected in numerous works, epic and dramatic, but not even in his initial attempt at literary treatment of it, Der Grosskophta, does he appear as an apologist of the ancien régime.[6] In none of them is his attitude as unequivocal as in Hermann und Dorothea, which, in the words of Adolphus William Ward, offers "the most signal attestation of . . . sympathy" for the noble and elevating aspects of the French reform movement.[7] Melitta Gerhard has shown conclusively that the Revolution is far more than a background for the poem; that in this, Goethe's highest tribute to German middle-class life, the forces of chaos and cosmos are mightily at work.[8] Finally, it contains his strongest, most unmistakable expression of German patriotism (W.A. I, 50:26).

Rousseau and Goethe possessed similar cultural backgrounds in a number of respects. For example, Goethe is known to have read most of the works on politics and economics usually regarded as important for Rousseau. Therefore the two may be said to have had in common an extensive theoretical basis in those areas. Furthermore, although belonging to different generations, both Rousseau and Goethe had opportunity to observe and experience many conditions generally characteristic of eighteenth-century Europe.

Goethe scholarship since World War II has brought about for the first time a broad and comprehensive understanding of Wilhelm Meisters Wanderjahre, according to Hans Joachim Schrimpf.[9] Through this new research the novel has emerged from the relative obscurity to which it had been consigned by nineteenth-century criticism to become the "Kristallisationspunkt" in a widespread reawakening of interest in and appreciation of the works of Goethe's mature years.

The Wanderjahre can be designated the most clearly defined late attempt by Goethe to deal with the problems treated by Rousseau. As one of the two utopias conceived in Goethe's old age (the other is that visualized by Faust in his grandiose philanthropic plan), the novel offers a pattern of communal life which, on a relatively simple basis, is designed to regulate governmental and civic affairs while maintaining a largely self-sufficient economy.

Well over a century ago Karl Rosenkranz designated both parts of Wilhelm Meister together with Die Wahlverwandtschaften as "social novels," inasmuch as they, by their tendency, "force the reader to press toward a grasp of the content and to try to comprehend the idea which governs from within the characters and destinies" in all three works. Rosenkranz states that despite the didactic purpose and prosaic features of the Wanderjahre, Goethe was able to "animate his subject poetically" to an extent not attained by Rousseau in Émile.[10] Thus Rosenkranz finds that Goethe's narrative surpasses its predecessor esthetically; he also sees in it a unity more recently claimed for it by Deli Fischer-Hartmann.[11]

A contemporary of Rosenkranz, Ferdinand Gregorovius, cites a number of ideas in Wilhelm Meister, especially those concerning popular representation, which resemble some very clearly expressed by Rousseau in the Contrat social.[12] His attitude toward Jean-Jacques is not generally sympathetic, yet it seems to rest on a difference of opinion rather than on the prejudice which marked nineteenth-century criticism.[13]

In 1949 Arnold Bergstraesser returned to a more balanced and objective approach to the social views of Goethe and their relationship to Rousseau.[14] Bergstraesser emphasizes Goethe's realism in depicting man and society and his constant study of the ways in which human nature attempts to cope with the world. Bergstraesser finds no irreconcilable difference between the young Goethe's longing for a Rousseau-like "return to nature" and the quieter wisdom of the octogenarian Goethe, who sought a balance between the needs of the individual and the importance of a social order (pp. 9–10). Thus he sees as possible the influence of the Contrat social even upon the mature author of the Wanderjahre. Also, while Rousseau treats theories of education in Émile and the utopian vision of a free society in the Contrat social, Goethe takes up both topics in the Wanderjahre. Bergstraesser sees as an essential difference between Rousseau's image of the ideal state and that of Goethe the fact that Rousseau's ideas remain theoretical while Goethe depicts the actual society he desires (p. 237).

Wilhelm Mommsen, also writing during the immediate postwar years, grants that Goethe in his youth came under influences generally attributed to Rousseau. Yet he is less inclined than Bergstraesser to assign any considerable influence to the Contrat social during any period of Goethe's life, despite the essential agreement of Goethe's Strassburg thesis with Rousseau concerning a ruler's determining the religion of his realm.[15] Perhaps one reason for Mommsen's reluctance lies in the prevalent notion that the Contrat social advocates extreme individualism. This interpretation causes one to overlook the two lines of political thought which intersect in that work, for as Charles Edwyn Vaughan had pointed out decades before, Rousseau champions not merely individual liberty, but state sovereignty as well.[16]

Both Rousseau and Goethe were born as citizens of a free city, hence of a city-state. Whether the former was commiserating with the poor or enjoying the patronage of the great, his proudest title was the self-bestowed designation, "Citizen of Geneva." Rousseau was initially a product of that municipality, and its influence and attraction for him remained indelible. He could see, furthermore, how much better conditions were in the federated cantons of his Swiss homeland than in pre-revolutionary France. Clearly, Rousseau's ideal was a small state, irrespective of the controversy as to how far he had Geneva directly in mind when he wrote the *Contrat social*.[17]

Quite similar is the case of Goethe, who inevitably retained the stamp of his native environment, the Free Imperial City of Frankfurt, which, in its municipal order, differed from that of Geneva more in degree than in kind. His enduring love for the scene of his early years is abundantly evident from his autobiography. Nonetheless, destiny, albeit in a kindlier manner, took Goethe away from Frankfurt just as surely as it removed Rousseau from Geneva.[18] The place of Goethe's administrative activity was the little duchy of Saxe-Weimar, one of the many small states of a preposterously disunited Germany. If its government was a benevolent despotism, that fact alone was enough to single it out in an age when most European despotisms were anything but benevolent. Karl August, whose mentor Goethe became, has repeatedly been called a pupil of Rousseau. The young Duke's innate ability, his solicitude for the welfare of his people, and his readiness to heed Goethe's advice brought about many improvements which would have met with Rousseau's approval. First through his personal influence upon Karl August, then in his ministerial capacities (of immense proportions, as shown by the documentary record of his official acts),[19] Goethe was able to do what Jean-Jacques was not in a position to accomplish directly, in spite of all his brilliantly-conceived plans for Poland, Corsica, and mankind in general.

"If I were a prince or a legislator," Rousseau writes, "I would not waste my time in telling what ought to be done; I would do it, or keep silent" (O.C., 5:6). Goethe followed that precept. Whether he strove to ameliorate the harsh laws concerning unwed mothers, or appealed to the

Duke, in a letter reminiscent of *Émile*, in behalf of the peasants whose crops were being destroyed by hunting parties from court circles (December 26, 1784), or improved the system of fire-fighting, or encouraged measures beneficial to agriculture, everywhere he was engaged in practical activity similar to that advocated by Rousseau. Like the latter, Goethe was a friend to the peasant class and to the poor in general; like him, he gladly helped persons in need. If Rousseau was appalled by the misery of French tillers of the soil, Goethe felt constrained to interrupt the writing of his drama *Iphigenie*, telling Charlotte von Stein (March 6, 1779) that King Thoas must be able to speak as if no stocking-knitter of Apolda were suffering hunger. Rousseau's desire that Frederick the Great might devote his genius to the arts of peace[20] (as indeed he did after the Seven Years' War ended) was a wish for reforms and innovations such as Goethe effected on a smaller scale at Weimar.

Just as Rousseau held steadfastly to his belief in a small, well-governed state, so Goethe returned, long years after his active ministry had ceased, to a similar ideal when he completed *Wilhelm Meisters Wanderjahre*. Half a century earlier he had written the bantering lines for the scene "Auerbachs Keller" in *Faust*:

> *Das liebe heil'ge Röm'sche Reich,*
> *Wie hält's nur noch zusammen?*
> (ll. 2090–2091)

Since that time he had witnessed the final evanescence of a once-proud medieval German empire upon the rise of Napoleon. He had seen the latter's fall and the failure of the Wars of Liberation to bring about a reunited, more democratic Germany. Thus we find Goethe in old age again occupied with the concept of the diminutive state (although that should not lead us to infer that he had despaired of the eventual reunification of his country).[21]

Whether the covenant formed by the prospective citizens of the tiny utopian commonwealth envisioned in the *Wanderjahre* coincides in detail with Rousseau's model or not, in the broader sense it represents a "social contract." Assuredly, its members constitute in some degree a "general will," even though the express designation is lacking. Likewise in keeping with the tenets of Rousseau is the conception of an economy predominantly of artisans, either as outlined for the new settlement across the sea or in the description of the life of the mountain folk. In fact, the rural existence of the latter group is strongly reminiscent of living conditions on Wolmar's estate.[22] Émile's teacher, foreseeing an age of revolutions, prepares the boy to live in future days of uncertainty and shattering of the traditional order. In like manner, Goethe's colonists, having lived through the political upheavals, now face the revolutionizing force of the machine, with its challenge to the whole existing social and economic order.

As previously stated, Rousseau and Goethe shared an intense interest in travel narratives. When the latter, especially in his last decade, was much occupied with America, he was again dealing with a subject which had earlier fascinated Jean-Jacques (one of whose first literary works is the brief dramatic piece entitled *La Découverte du Nouveau Monde*, composed in 1740).[23] So when Moultou wishes he had a bit of Pennsylvania to give to Rousseau,[24] that seems almost a foreshadowing of the plan in the *Wanderjahre* for a new settlement beyond the Atlantic.

In the *Discours sur l'Économie politique* Rousseau says:

From the first moment of life on, one must learn to earn so that one may live; and since one participates in the rights of citizens from the moment of birth on, with this instant the exercise of our duties must begin. . . . Wherever the people love their land, obey the laws, and lead simple lives, there remains little else to do in order to make them happy; and in public administration, where fortune does not play such a role as in the destiny of private persons, wisdom is so near to fortune that both are mingled.

(O.C., 5:3-4)

Similar thoughts are expressed in the *Wanderjahre*, not only in general in the plan for settling in America, as indicated in Odoardo's speech about united effort by the colonists (W.A. I, 25:20), but earlier and more specifically in the account of the "Oheim's" solicitude for just such a simple, industrious, happy existence for his mountain people as Rousseau envisions (W.A. I, 24:96-99).

Rousseau says that, in its absolute sense, a democracy never has existed and never will exist. He continues: "It is against the natural order that the great multitude should rule and the minority be ruled. One cannot imagine that the people would remain in constant assembly to attend to public affairs, and one can easily perceive that they could not install any commissions for this purpose, unless the administration changed" (O.C., 5:143). Goethe maintains that public affairs should be administered with detachment, rather than humanly with likes and dislikes, passion and partiality. The majority, he states, becomes odious through its few energetic pacemakers, scoundrels who accommodate themselves, weaklings who follow suit, and the "crowd that trots along behind without knowing in the least what it wants" (G.A., 9:578). Thus Rousseau and Goethe agree regarding a collective freedom of right-thinking, industrious people, whose fatherland is the scene of their usefulness, but who also receive expert direction from capable leaders. Another instance of such leadership occurs in Goethe's other utopia—that envisioned by the centenarian Faust.

To his famous dictum that man is born free, and everywhere he is in chains, Rousseau adds: "Such a one believes himself to be master of others who does not cease to be more of a slave than they" (O.C., 5:64). Compare Goethe's comment in *Die Wahlverwandtschaften*: "No one is more of a slave than he who thinks he is free without being so" (W.A. I, 20:261).

Rousseau explains that the original meaning of the word "economy" is simply the wise and legitimate government of the household for the good of the whole family. "The sense of this term has subsequently been extended to the government of the great family which is the state" (O.C., 5:1). A companion-piece to this utterance from the *Discours sur l'Économie politique* is the beginning of the second chapter of the *Contrat social*, concerning the first forms of society:

The oldest of all societies, and the only natural one, is that of the family; again, do not the children remain linked to the father only as long as they have need of him for preserving themselves . . . ?
The family is then, if you wish, the first model of political societies: the head is the image of the father; the people, the image of the children; and all, being born equal and free, dispense with their freedom only for their utility. . . .

(O.C., 5:64–65)

In a similar vein, Goethe stresses the concept of the "Volk" as an extension of the "family" in the *Campagne in Frankreich*, long before the inception of the *Wanderjahre*.[25] In the latter work, however, the two concepts find their fullest treatment. The family per se is emphasized throughout the book, not only in the narrative proper, but also in most of the "Novellen" incorporated therein, from *Sankt Joseph der Zweite* on. The utopian project itself rests on the theory of a communal family, as Gregorovius early perceived.[26] Rousseau maintains that:

the right of the first occupant, although more real than that of the strongest, does not become a true right until after the establishment of that of ownership. Every man naturally has a right to all that is necessary for him; but the positive act which renders him the owner of certain property excludes him from all the rest. His part being set off, he must confine himself to it and has no longer any right to the communal holdings. That is why the right of first occupant, so weak in the state of nature, is respectable to every civil man. One respects in this right less what belongs to another than what does not belong to oneself.

(O.C., 5:85–86)

This declaration resembles Odoardo's explanation in the *Wanderjahre* of the New World's advantages concerning possession. There it is easy for the resolute man to win uninhabited areas gradually from nature and to assure himself of partial possession. In the Old World the opposite situation prevails, for everywhere partial possession has already been taken and, more or less, through time immemorial the right to it has been hallowed:

> If there boundlessness appears as an insurmountable obstacle, here simply bounded space opposes hindrances almost harder yet to overcome. . . . If individual ownership is regarded as sacred by society as a whole, then it is still more so for the owner . . . and there are things of a hundred kinds that make the possessor stubborn and opposed to any change. The older, the more intricate, and the more divided such conditions are, the more difficult it becomes to put through a general measure that, while it would take something from the individual, would be beneficial for all and, through retroactive and reciprocal effect, unexpectedly for him also.

(W.A. I, 25:216–217)

Renunciation, says Alexander Jung concerning the book's subtitle, *Die Entsagenden,* "is the discipline of possession. It frees man from the most fearful, dangerous servitude . . . , from servitude through oneself."[27]

It is evident, then, that for Rousseau and Goethe political liberty implies a discipline of conduct which is self-imposed and submissive to the demands of society. Although the sphere of the individual is restricted, since as a citizen he becomes a unit in the collective endeavor of his fellow social beings, his participation is a voluntary one—worlds removed from the heartless compulsion of present-day totalitarianism.[28]

The inviolability of the sovereign power, according to Rousseau, depends upon its not overstepping the proper limits (O.C., 5:96–99). For the avoidance of that very difficulty, we learn, the "higher authority" of the body politic of the emigrants in the *Wanderjahre* will not confine

145

itself to any one place, but will move around constantly, "in order to preserve equality in the principal matters and to grant everyone his will in things of less import." So it was once before in the course of history, the speaker continues: "The German emperors moved about, and this arrangement is most appropriate of all to the concept of free states" (W.A. I, 25:213). (This, of course, refers to the early centuries of the Empire, long before the period of decline portrayed in *Götz* and *Faust*.)

In his sixth chapter, "Concerning the Social Pact," Rousseau states that since men are not able to engender new forces, but only to unite and direct those which exist, their only means of self-preservation lies in the combining of those same forces, putting them into play by a single impulse, and making them act concertedly. Then, remarking that each man's strength and freedom are the first instruments of his preservation, he asks how the individual is to engage them without detriment to the concerns which he owes himself. Rousseau now defines "the fundamental problem," of which the "social contract" offers the solution, as follows: "To find a form of association which will defend and protect, with all the common might, the person and belongings of each associate, and whereby each one, while uniting with all, nevertheless may obey only himself and remain as free as beforehand" (O.C., 5:77).

At the close of his long speech concerning the covenant into which he and his confrères are entering, Lenardo says that whatever the human being may attempt, "the individual is not sufficient to himself; society remains the highest need of a valiant man; . . . we see no one among us who could not at all times perform his activity in a purposeful manner; who would not be assured that everywhere whither chance, inclination, even passion, might lead him, he would find himself well recommended, received, furthered and, indeed, as far as possible, restored from misfortunes" (W.A. I, 25:189). To this the following declaration is later added: "In consideration of the fact that we are just beginning, we lay great stress upon the family circles. We intend to assign great obligations to the housefathers and housemothers; education will be all the easier in our case since everyone must be responsible for himself, farmhand and maid, man-servant and woman-servant" (W.A. I, 25:211). Here, too, Goethe is in agreement with the ideas of Rousseau concerning the foundations of a commonwealth that gives due consideration both to the group and to the individual.

Rousseau places great reliance on the "law of tomorrow," which is to be the work of a state in conformity with the general will and established by the "social contract." A similar train of thought seems to be expressed by Odoardo, who, after having noted people's frequent disagreement about the means of accomplishing generally desired ends, declares: "The century must come to our aid; time must take the place of reason; and, in a broadened heart, the loftier advantage must displace the baser one" (W.A. I, 25:219). Rousseau writes concerning the law (in the *Contrat social*) : "That which is good and in conformance with order is such by the nature of things and independently of human conventions. All justice comes from God; He alone is the source of it; but if we knew how to receive it from so high a plane, we would have no need of government or laws. Without doubt, it is a universal justice, having emanated from reason alone; but this justice, in order to be admitted among us, must be reciprocal" (O.C., 5:104).

The statutes laid down by and for the members of the "Bund" are described: "One notices that stern laws are very soon blunted and gradually become more lax, because nature always asserts its rights. We have lenient laws, in order to be able to become more severe little by little; our punishments consist for the time being in isolation from the citizenry, in a milder or more decisive degree, and for a shorter or longer period, according to the evidence found . . ." (W.A. I, 25:214).

"In order that society might be peaceable and that harmony might be maintained," says Rousseau, "it would be necessary that all citizens should be, without exception, equally good Christians" (O.C., 5:233–234). Likewise, only Christians are acceptable to the company of future American colonists, and the reasons given for that stipulation are similar to those expressed in the *Contrat social* (W.A. I, 25:210).

In his chapter on the "Lawgiver," Rousseau lays down the principle that in order to discover the best rules of society suitable to the nations, there is needed "a superior intelligence who would see all the passions of men and who would not feel any one of them; who would have no relationship with our nature, and who would know it thoroughly; whose happiness would be independent of us, and who nevertheless would wish to be concerned with ours" (O.C., 5:108). Finally, it would have to be someone who, while preparing for himself "a distant glory," might labor in one age and enjoy it in another. Gods would be needed to give laws to men. Then, taking a more realistic tone, Rousseau says that in all respects the legislator is an extraordinary man within the state. If he should be extraordinary because of his genius, he is no less so by reason of his office. The latter is neither that of the government nor that of the sovereign. This office which gives the republic its constitution does not enter into that constitution, being a special and superior function which has nothing in common with authority over men (O.C., 25:109–110).

Faust offers at least a partial resemblance to the lawgiver who establishes the republic. True, he is no god, although he sought to be godlike, only to learn that man achieves his highest level through standing on his human dignity "alone before nature"—a thought certainly acceptable to Rousseau. But at the time of his great philanthropic endeavor Faust is "an extraordinary man" who, despite all the errors of his striving, has gained wisdom during a hundred years of life. He is detached from the ambitions and passions of the people who are to inhabit the land that he is reclaiming from the sea, yet he can realize those feelings and aspirations—he whose experience has embraced, in the greatest measure possible for an individual,

> Was der ganzen Menschheit zugeteilt ist.
> (l. 1770)

Again, like Rousseau's "social contract" and the "Bund" of the prospective New World colonists in Wilhelm Meisters Wanderjahre, it is an ideal enterprise of tomorrow. Faust is occupied with the future well-being of a people for whom, at least in his belief, he is creating the possibility of a commonwealth. For the accomplishment of this undertaking, his supreme ambition, he orders the utmost speed and diligence, to be implemented by stern discipline and promise of reward, all under his direction:

> Dass sich das grösste Werk vollende,
> Genügt ein Geist für tausend Hände.
> (ll. 11,509–11,510)

The many millions who will inhabit the land yet to be wrested from the water are not to be thought of as dwelling in easy security from the elements; rather, their existence will be free through their activity ("tätig-frei"). Whenever the sea threatens their safety, a common urge ("Gemeindrang") will ensure quick repairing of the break in the dike. Thus Faust is content to let the object of his last striving be a "distant glory," which will not perish in aeons. Even though as a mortal he cannot live throughout the course of those generations whose active freedom he foresees, nevertheless, through anticipation he can encompass the spectacle of ages to come:

> Und so verbringt, umrungen von Gefahr,
> Hier Kindheit, Mann und Greis sein tüchtig Jahr:
> Solch ein Gewimmel möcht' ich sehn,
> Auf freiem Grund mit freiem Volke stehn.
> . . . .
> Im Vorgefühl von solchem hohen Glück
> Geniess' ich jetzt den höchsten Augenblick!
> (ll. 11,577–11,580; 11,585–11,586)

Faust's anticipation symbolizes Goethe's own vision of a better future for his still disunited country. He who as a young man in *Götz von Berlichingen*, and more than half a century later, in the first and fourth acts of *Faust II*, so forcefully depicted the unhappy disintegration of the First German Empire (the final gasps of which he himself witnessed), could near the close of his greatest poetic work most appropriately give expression to his hope of a renewed national existence for his German "Volk" on a basis essentially in agreement with Rousseau's theories of government. Earlier, as previously mentioned, in the *Campagne in Frankreich*, Goethe had commended French family life as he observed it, even in wartime (W.A. I, 33:108–110, *passim*). According to Alfred G. Steer, Goethe's praise concerned not individuals but the common people generally whom he encountered while in France during the Revolution (1792). There he admired a "Volkheit" such as could not then exist under the unfavorable conditions of a divided Germany.[29]

We may close on what Faust styles "the last result of wisdom." The men of his utopia, who are to remain free through continued struggle, will be acting in accord with a well-known admonition of Jean-Jacques. "Free peoples," he wrote, "remember this maxim: One can acquire liberty, but one never recovers it" (O.C., 5:115). And after Émile has traveled for two years with his teacher, observing life in sundry lands and noting the duties and rights of citizenship and the workings of the "social contract," he remarks to his mentor: "It seems to me that in order to be free, we must never cease to wish for freedom" (O.C., 4:477–478). Compare Faust's conclusion:

> Ja, diesem Sinne bin ich ganz ergeben.
> Das ist der Weisheit letzter Schluss:

Nur der verdient sich Freiheit wie das Leben,
Der täglich sie erobern muss.

(ll. 11,573–11,576)

Clearly, this is an ideal in the spirit of Rousseau as well as of Goethe. The kinship of their respective aspirations for mankind thus appears especially manifest in the socio-political aims which they direct toward an enlightened era yet to come.

VIII

God, Man, and Cosmos

Rousseau and Goethe both early departed from the conventionality of orthodox Christian belief in which they were brought up. Yet, despite their rejection of dogma, they were both profoundly religious and remained so until the end of their lives, as will be demonstrated in the course of this chapter.

For Rousseau as for Goethe mankind finds in itself the preferred object of study and contemplation. Both cherish the ideal of elevating Man to a higher plane. As previously noted, neither Rousseau nor Goethe would have the human being subordinated to mechanical aids for the sake of expediency. Theirs is an anthropocentric Weltanschauung which inevitably embraces Man's relation to the surrounding universe and its Creator. God and nature are inseparable concepts denoting the background and setting of human existence.[1] Religion is not to be thought of as divorced from the physical world about us—a tenet stressed alike in the profession of faith of Rousseau's Savoyard Vicar and in the cosmic poems of Goethe's later years.

A recent commentator on the religious thought of Rousseau makes the observation that everything pertaining to Jean-Jacques "seems to be charged with electrical force and to arouse passion."[2] The polarity of viewpoints is strikingly evinced, for example, by the exhaustively doc-

umented, three-volume treatise of Pierre-Maurice Masson,[3] who emphasizes the supposed Catholic elements in Rousseau's writings, and Albert
Schinz' survey of early twentieth-century Protestant interpretations of his
works. Whereas Masson asserts that Rousseau, despite his return to the
Calvinist fold, aided the Catholic revival in post-Revolutionary France,
Schinz sees a concerted effort by a number of critics, including Masson,
to monopolize "the impious Rousseau, the heretic of yesterday" for the
profit of Catholicism.[4] The succeeding decades have added innumerable
titles to the vast array of studies dealing with Rousseau and religion.

Though less heated, the discussions of Goethe's religious ideas are
almost as numerous. In 1932, the centenary of the poet's death, two noteworthy books on that theme appeared, one by Erich Franz on Goethe as
a religious thinker,[5] the other by Franz Koch concerning his conceptions
of death and immortality.[6] A still greater number of contributions to the
subject signalized the Goethe Bicentennial of 1949, among them Wilhelm Flitner's exposition of the elderly Goethe's religious and ethical
thought,[7] and Robert Hering's interpretation of the idea of God as developed in *Wilhelm Meister* and *Faust*.[8]

Just as the religious views of both Rousseau and Goethe are difficult
to define precisely, so the position of each in the realm of philosophy remains a widely debated issue. Neither of the two can be fitted into the
Procrustean bed of any restricted philosophical system. Many erudite
volumes have set forth the philosophical aspects of their respective works,
without being able to establish a sharply delineated scheme of philosophy
for either. Among those who discover a unity of thought in Rousseau's
work is the famous literary historian Gustave Lanson.[9] Ernst Cassirer also
finds such a unity, but he admits that Jean-Jacques' personality and world
of ideas still defy easy classification for histories of philosophy.[10] After
endless portrayals as the exponent of irrationalism, Robert Dérathé sees
Rousseau as a rationalist, within limits.[11]

Goethe has proved equally embarrassing company for those who
would systematize his all-embracing thought. Large numbers of interpretations attest the intense preoccupation of scholars in many lands with
the philosophical content of his works. A recent notable instance is
Ferdinand Weinhandl's treatment of Goethe's metaphysics.[12] Yet, as
Bruno Bauch remarks in his excellent general lecture on Goethe and
philosophy, it is an inexhaustible subject which can never be brought to
a definitive close.[13]

The enormous scope of controversial discussions of both the religious and the philosophical concepts of Rousseau and Goethe concern us here only insofar as such analyses shed light upon correspondences between the respective positions taken by the two toward religion, especially the "Gottesidee" and "Gott-Natur." As in the preceding chapters dealing with educational and socio-political ideas, the comparison of basic concepts in the religious passages of Rousseau and Goethe must be confined to certain representative examples. Furthermore, in this brief survey only slight attention can be given to the numberless theories—some debatable —regarding the indebtedness of Rousseau and Goethe to predecessors and contemporaries. Nevertheless, it should be borne in mind that both possessed the same heritage of eighteenth-century European culture, as well as a similar background in religious, ethical, and philosophical thought from Plato down to their own respective eras.

As succinctly outlined by Kurt Rossmann, the young Goethe's own philosophical way of thinking proceeded from and was nourished by the totality of the French philosophical spirit of the Enlightenment, i.e., the spirit of Voltaire, Rousseau, Diderot and the Encyclopedists. Goethe, who comprehended life, his own as well as nature in general, through the simile of the diastole and systole, found himself likewise alternately attracted and repelled by that French spirit. One must not forget, says Rossmann, that the way to what Goethe himself called his true relationship to the "Gott-Natur" was prepared for him by Rousseau. The latter brought Goethe "back to himself" (as Kant declared concerning his own case), and the turning toward nature which Rousseau effected in his case made him receptive to the pantheistic metaphysics of belief of Giordano Bruno and Spinoza.[14] If Rossmann's thesis is true, we may expect to find a kinship of ideas on the part of Rousseau and Goethe with respect to religious matters, especially "natural religion."

Let us gain a perspective on the comparison of the religious ideas of Goethe and Rousseau by first glancing at certain similarities in the religious background and early experience of each. Calvinism in the Geneva of Rousseau's boyhood, if somewhat less austere than formerly, was still rigorous enough. The elders maintained close moral surveillance over the citizens, persistently exhorting them to live righteously and in strict observance of religious demands. Although Rousseau later imagined the family into which he was born as more remarkable for its "piety and morals" than was probably the case, it seems safe to characterize the surroundings of his earliest years as devout. Indeed, he could scarcely have escaped the ethical sternness of Genevan life.[15] When he wandered forth into the world, his formal Protestantism came to an abrupt end, a break which lasted for many years. His eventual reinstatement in the faith of his fathers ultimately caused him much trouble and also inspired many a subsequent dispute about the true character of his religion.

Goethe's Frankfurt was almost as inexorably Lutheran as Geneva was Calvinistic; in fact, it had been so ever since the Reformation, ecclesiastically as well as politically. The Reformed families—some of them, like that of Lili Schönemann, quite wealthy—could be seen driving out to Bockenheim to attend the Sunday service, for they had no churches within the city wall. They were not allowed to hold office, nor were the Catholics, who at least possessed churches and monasteries in Frankfurt, while the Jews had their synagogues in their quarter. Thus the customs and patterns of life in the old Imperial city were determined by Lutherans. In the home of Goethe's parents the prescribed order of Sunday worship and church festivals was conscientiously observed.

There was one more religious body that had unostentatiously but steadily gained in numbers (largely at the expense of Lutheranism): the Pietists. Frankfurt, the city of Spener, had long been an international center of that movement.[16] The Quaker leader William Penn had solicited colonists there for Pennsylvania, with the result that in 1683 a group of Pietists led by Franz Daniel Pastorius founded the first German settlement in the New World, namely, Germantown. When Zinzendorf, the last great representative of Pietism, was forced to leave Herrnhut, he had taken refuge in Frankfurt and lived there for a considerable length of time. Goethe therefore experienced in childhood and youth an atmosphere of conflicting religious trends, and he was to share with Rousseau the influence of one of these sects.

Jean-Jacques' rather fortuitous entrance into the circles in which Mme de Warens moved brought him directly into the Mother Church, to which she was a convert, and also, through "Maman" herself, to some acquaintance with Pietism. In the sixth book of the *Confessions* Rousseau gives the reader an exposé of her religious beliefs. As mentioned above (chapter four), François Magny, prominent in the Pietist movement in the Pays de Vaud, had been her tutor, and even after her conversion to Catholicism she was still imbued with certain of his theological principles. Hence, as Eugène Ritter and Philippe Godet point out, an echo of Spe-

ner's ideas reached the future author of *Émile* through these two inter-
mediaries.[17] Masson, while acknowledging the correctness of Ritter's
statement concerning the action of Spener upon the Protestant commu-
nities of Zurich and Bern, thinks it probable that Mme de Warens came
into contact with other Pietists in her youth beside Magny, since at the
beginning of the eighteenth century all Switzerland was obsessed with
Pietistic influences, from both French and German quarters (1:69–70).[18]
She had therefore acquired a strange medley of religious persuasions,
which she gradually communicated to Rousseau.

When the sixteen-year-old Goethe left home to study at Leipzig, he
also bade farewell to formal Protestant worship. The short verses on the
Communion, addressed to his mother, seem to symbolize that break. Like
Faust, he is not known to have felt any longing for the sacrament during
his Leipzig sojourn. Despite Goethe's tribute to the proselyting efforts of
his friend Langer, the latter did not quite succeed in leading him back to
the paths of orthodox Christianity. Upon his return to Frankfurt, phys-
ically ill and spiritually adrift, it was not in the church of his upbringing,
but with the Pietists that Goethe found comfort and inspiration, chiefly
under the tutelage of Susanna von Klettenberg. As Hans von Schubert
asserts, Pietism was for the young Goethe and for many people of all
classes in part an actual rediscovery of religion (p. 20). He shortly passed
beyond the bounds of Pietistic credence, even as he had earlier departed
from the ritualism of the Lutheran Church.

Singular circumstances, therefore, removed both Rousseau and
Goethe in their early years from the practice of denominational worship
and subsequently took them into situations where the precepts of Pietism
significantly affected their respective outlooks upon religious questions.
Through partly similar experiences, both arrived at an unconventionality
of belief which made them uncomfortable associates for their orthodox
contemporaries. The discord which arose between Jean-Jacques and
the pastors of Geneva, even between him and his friend Jacob Vernes,
foreshadowed the shocked attitude of Lavater and Jacobi at Goethe's
pantheistic concepts. Just as Rousseau found himself under attack by
Catholics and Protestants, so Goethe lived to see himself (and Schiller)
bitterly assailed by his former companion during his first journey to Switzerland, the poet Friedrich Leopold zu Stolberg, whose ardent Catholicism caused him to view with horror the classical ideals of art and life
championed by the "Dioscuri" of Weimar. The credo espoused succes-

sively by Rousseau and Goethe often seemed more dangerous to the proponents of orthodoxy than atheism, against which one could take a forthright stand, whereas a profession of Christianity rising above denomination and prescribed dogma offered a problem too complex for a ready solution. Nonetheless, Rousseau has been credited with important influence as a religious teacher and reformer,[19] and he was not unaware of that position. Goethe, who in old age cited his "Christianity" as the reason for not belonging to any sect, was likewise conscious of having left indelible traces in the sphere of religion.

The lack of even the slightest dogmatic precision in Rousseau's faith was often noted. One might think, says D. Parodi, that Jean-Jacques' concept of a common religion, detached from all particular creeds, was simply expressive of his own religious experience and the ease with which he seems to have passed, without inward crises, from the Protestantism of his early childhood to the exterior Catholicism of the seminary at Turin, to the liberalism of the Abbé Gaime (in part the prototype of his Savoyard Vicar), and to the "indulgent and accommodating" religion of Mme de Warens.[20] Notably absent from Rousseau's religious views, as Peyre reminds us, are strictness of doctrine, repentance, redemption, and even revelation, and his admission of the divinity of Christ, if it occurs at all, seems poetic or figurative rather than literal. Finally, in his ethics Rousseau may be considered more stoic than Christian; he detaches morality from religion when he maintains that one should practice the good instinctively from the heart, rather than from an intellectual understanding of it (pp. 355–356).

Like Rousseau, Goethe decidedly rejects the dualism and transcendence of Christian dogmatism and ethics. Robert d'Harcourt aptly refers to the "extreme mobility" of Goethe's religious thought, its incessant evolution, and the difficulty of confining it within formulas.[21] Franz maintains that Goethe's frequent designation of himself as a "pagan" is more than a jocular brusqueness toward pious friends. Rather, he feels related to the conception of life held by classical antiquity, with its orientation toward this world. He emphatically declines to accept the dualistic metaphysics of Christianity. It is not ultimately a question of his opposing the Christian religion, but of his opposition to any religious or philosophical Weltanschauung which would seek its values outside of reality. The emphasis is not on negation or polemics, but on positive affirmation of a deep feeling of "Weltfrömmigkeit," an all-embracing love for human beings (pp. 254–255). Franz avers that from the period of his Pietistic experience to the end of his life Goethe retained a personally warm relationship to Christianity in its purity, that is, to the Scriptures and to the person of Christ, in an entirely undogmatic, nonecclesiastical, purely human way (p. 255). We can see the striking similarity of attitude which this comparison reveals.

The apparent connection of Goethe's Strassburg thesis for the licentiate and the *Contrat social* has already been mentioned briefly (in the second chapter). Few passages in Rousseau's writings have occasioned as much controversy as his chapter advocating a "civil religion." Otto Vossler, for instance, says it is no wonder that the severest reproaches were leveled at the proponent of such "bloody theories," which, in a time of triumphantly progressing enlightenment and tolerance, seemed an "unheard-of relapse" into the periods of cruelest religious persecution.[22] One marveled that this proposal to punish nonconformity with banishment should come from a writer who had previously expressed his conviction that men's spiritual needs could be fully met through "natural religion." The latter, Charles W. Hendel maintains, was easier to find for Man in general than the civil religion for the citizen of the state. Even so, Hendel adds later, it was the practical intention of that chapter in the *Contrat social* to prevent intolerance and to establish religious freedom.[23] Thus there arose a dilemma in Rousseau's reasoning which, as Pierre Burgelin notes, he never really solved.[24]

Interestingly enough, Goethe's no longer extant thesis, of which he gives an account in *Dichtung und Wahrheit* (W.A. I, 28:40–45), dealt with the idea "that the state, the lawgiver, had the right to determine a form of worship according to which the clergy should teach and conduct themselves, and to which on the other hand the laymen would outwardly have to conform exactly; however, there was to be no question of what each one thought, felt or meditated within himself." For the disputation Goethe chose the first half of this theme, namely, "that the legislator was not only authorized but obligated to establish a certain form of worship from which neither the clergy nor the laity would be allowed to deviate." Robert Hering believes that Goethe must have cited Rousseau in the historical part of the treatise.[25] In any event, their agreement is even more striking than that obtaining between Rousseau's Vicar and the *Brief des Pastors* . . . , which drew Lavater's attention to Goethe.[26]

Rousseau's love for the Bible is well-known. It was his nightly reading before he retired, and he drew inspiration from it for his *Lévite d'Éphraïm*. Inevitably, reflections of the Scriptural narrative and phraseology in his writings are many. Goethe's reverence for the Bible, especially for the story of Man as related in Genesis, could not even be shaken by his first rationalistic doubts; that and the memory of his mother's spiritual attitude, says Schubert, were the two solid religious values which the youth of sixteen took with him to Leipzig (p. 27). In his boyhood he had already treated several biblical subjects, one of which, *Höllenfahrt Christi*, has been preserved. Much of Book Four of *Dichtung und Wahrheit* is given up to his commentary on the Children of Israel in their pastoral stage. Elsewhere in that work Goethe expresses his great fondness for the Scriptures, to which, he states, he owed his moral education almost entirely, while the stories, doctrines, symbols, and parables all deeply impressed and affected him (W.A. I, 27:96–97).

Rousseau and Goethe also agree about a limited acceptance of the Gospels. Notwithstanding his veneration for the Evangel, the Vicar of Savoy declares: "With all that, this same Gospel is full of incredible things, of things that are repugnant to reason, and which it is impossible for any sensible man to conceive of or admit" (O.C., 4:107). "One might as well drink of the ocean," Goethe told Eckermann (February 13, 1831), "as become involved in a historical and critical investigation of the Gospels. It is far better to adhere, with no further ado, to what is given and to appropriate what one can use for one's own ethical culture and support."

Neither Rousseau nor Goethe can approve of barren speculation. The Vicar of Savoy shows little inclination toward "abstract notions of philosophy and purely intellectual ideas" (O.C., 4:31). Mephistopheles voices much the same attitude when he admonishes Faust (hitherto engrossed in "gray theory") as follows:

> *Ich sag' es dir: ein Kerl, der spekuliert,*
> *Ist wie ein Tier, auf dürrer Heide*
> *Von einem bösen Geist im Kreis herumgeführt,*
> *Und rings umher liegt schöne grüne Weide.*
> (ll. 1830–1833)

For both Goethe and Rousseau reverence begins with the contemplation of nature. Since they believe that God is the Creator and animating Spirit of nature, they seek and find Him there, much to the disquiet of orthodox souls who would close every nondogmatic approach to the Deity. God and nature are therefore indissoluble components of the Weltanschauung of both Rousseau and Goethe. Inasmuch as they discover the Divine in nature generally, they necessarily find it in Man, as nature's highest achievement. This standpoint also dismays the adherents of dogma, for it constitutes a rejection of the doctrine of original sin.

"I believe . . ." says the Vicar, "that the world is governed by a powerful and wise will; I see it, or rather I feel it, and that is important for me to know" (O.C., 4:37). "I do not inquire whether this highest being has understanding," Goethe told Eckermann (February 23, 1831). "I feel that it *is* understanding, it *is* reason."

"One must believe in God in order to be saved," Rousseau quotes, adding that "this badly misunderstood dogma is the principle of bloodthirsty intolerance and the cause of all those vain instructions which deal a death-blow to human reason by accustoming it to be satisfied with words" (O.C., 3:481–482). In one of the Maximen und Reflexionen Goethe remarks: " 'I believe in a God'—this is a fine, laudable thing to say. Yet to acknowledge God wherever and however He is manifested, that indeed is the bliss of heaven on earth." [27] Moreover, Goethe observed to Eckermann (December 31, 1823): " 'God, the dear God, the good God'— to those who use the expression daily, especially the clergy, it becomes but a phrase, a mere name thoughtlessly used. Were they imbued with a sense of His greatness, they would grow mute and be unable to utter the name for sheer reverence."

Thus it becomes evident that neither Rousseau nor Goethe can approve of a purely verbal confession of faith. When Saint-Preux expresses astonishment that the children of such a pious mother as Julie are not learning their catechism and asks her why, she replies, "In order that they may one day believe it; I wish to make Christians of them some day" (O.C., 9:285). Also in *Émile* we read:

The obligation to believe implies the possibility of it. The philosopher who does not believe is wrong, because he makes poor use of the reason he has cultivated, and because he is in a position to understand the truths which he rejects. But what does the child who professes the Christian religion believe? That which he understands; and he has so slight an understanding of what he is made to say, that if you tell him the opposite thing, he will adopt it quite as willingly. The faith of children and of many men is a matter of geography. Shall they be rewarded for having been born at Rome rather than at Mecca?

(O.C., 3:482)

Reverence, the elders of the Pedagogical Province declare to Wilhelm Meister, is something all-important for the complete man, but it is not among the attributes which one brings with him into the world; it must be acquired. In words suggestive of agreement with Rousseau's advice about not exceeding the child's capacity for belief, they explain to Wilhelm that the first of the gestures he has noticed is exacted of the very young children, who in this way give testimony to the primary form of reverence, namely, that there is a God above, reflected and revealed in parents, teachers, and superiors (W.A. I, 24:240).

"Let us avoid proclaiming the truth to those who are not capable of understanding it," Rousseau admonishes, "for that is to attempt to substitute error." He then states that it would be better to have no idea of the Divinity than to have "low, fantastic, harmful, and unworthy ideas" of that Being (O.C., 3:484). "If our horizon is wide," says Goethe, "God is all; if our horizon is narrow, then God is a supplement to our wretchedness" (W.A. I, 42^2:212).

The Vicar recounts the following about his consulting the philosophers: "I leafed through their books; I examined their diverse opinions; I found them all proud, self-assertive, and dogmatic, even in their pretended skepticism, unwilling to admit not knowing anything, proving nothing, making fun of one another; and this common point seemed to me the only one about which they all are right" (O.C., 4:17–18). "Since poetry," Goethe writes in his autobiography, "presupposes a certain belief in the impossible, and since religion is based on a like belief in what passes the understanding, the philosophers seemed to me to be in an awkward position in their attempts at proving and explaining them both within their sphere. A glance at the history of philosophy was enough to demonstrate that each philosopher sought a different basis, and that the skeptic knocked the bottom out of all efforts to explain" (W.A. I, 27:11).

What redoubled the Vicar's embarrassment, he relates, was being born into a Church which decided everything, which permitted no doubt whatever; one point rejected made him reject all the rest; and the impossibility of admitting so many absurd decisions cut him off also from those which were not. "In telling me: 'Believe all,' they prevented me from believing anything, and I did not know where to stop" (O.C., 4:17). In *Dichtung und Wahrheit* Goethe contrasts "general, natural religion," which needs no specific belief, since it holds that "a great creating, ordering, and guiding Being" is concealed behind nature, with particular religion, which is founded upon a faith that must be unshakable, if it is not to be destroyed at once in its essentials. "Every doubt regarding such a religion is deadly" (W.A. I, 26:218–219).

The first benefit which the Vicar derived from his reflections was learning to limit his inquiries to what was of immediate interest and importance to him, and to remain in profound ignorance regarding all the rest, without worrying himself to the point of doubt (O.C., 4:19). Goethe expressed a similar thought to Eckermann (October 15,1825): "Man was not born to solve the problems of the universe, but rather to try to lay bare the heart of the problem and then to keep within the limits of what is amenable to the understanding." Another one of Goethe's maxims reads: "The highest happiness of Man as a thinking being is to have fathomed what is knowable and to revere quietly the unknowable" (G.A., 17:695).

Rousseau's Vicar tells us that he has remained in a "voluntary skepticism." Defining his position, he comments further: "I serve God in the simplicity of my heart. I do not seek to know anything except what concerns my conduct. As for the dogmas which influence neither actions nor morality, and with which so many people torment themselves, I do not trouble myself about them at all" (O.C., 4:108). In a conversation with Johann Daniel Falk (January 25, 1813) Goethe declared: "As soon as we proceed from the principle that knowledge and faith are not designed to cancel each other out, but rather to supplement each other, then that which is right will be ascertained throughout."

Piety is a fundamental trait of these two deeply religious men. Goethe often encountered just as little understanding of his "Naturfrömmigkeit" as the Genevan had experienced from those who insisted on keeping nature and religion apart. The objections to *Émile* raised by the Archbishop of Paris are similar to the retort of the Archbishop-Chancellor in *Faust II*, when Mephistopheles refers to the power of nature and mind of a talented man (namely, Faust):

> *Natur und Geist—so spricht man nicht zu Christen.*
> *Deshalb verbrennt man Atheisten,*
> *Weil solche Reden höchst gefährlich sind.*
> *Natur ist Sünde, Geist ist Teufel,*
> *Sie hegen zwischen sich den Zweifel,*
> *Ihr missgestaltet Zwitterkind.*
>
> (ll. 4897–4902)

In the *Marienbader Elegie* Goethe delineates human striving to yield itself voluntarily, out of gratitude, to a higher, purer, unknown Being, thus unriddling for itself the Ever Nameless One; thereupon he adds: "Wir heissen's: fromm sein!" (W.A. I, 3:24). That was not the sort of piety that Fritz Jacobi, for example, expected of him. Goethe had replied nearly four decades earlier (June 9, 1785) to his friend's chiding of his Spinozistic (ergo, pantheistic) leanings as follows: "Forgive me for preferring to keep silent when you talk of a divine being. Such a one I discern only in and from individual things, and no one can encourage the closer and deeper contemplation of these than Spinoza himself. . . . Here am I, on and under mountains, seeking the divine *in herbis et lapidibus*." "In plants and stones"—even as Jean-Jacques himself had done, not very many years before. Although Rousseau is not named at this point, Goethe's utterance suggests a kindred spirit. In his letter of January 31, 1812 to Adolf von Schlichtegroll, Goethe draws the following contrast between their respective views: "Jacobi . . . handles my beloved nature rather too unceremoniously to suit me, but I do not bear him any grudge on that account. In keeping with the trend of his development, his God must detach himself more and more from the world, whereas mine is becoming more and more intertwined with it. . . ." Here, at the very time of writing *Dichtung und Wahrheit*, Goethe reaffirms his pristine enthusiasm for nature in its outward manifestations. Throughout his latter decades, then, he retains and intensifies this concept of the interrelation of God and nature—a concept shared with Rousseau.

The Vicar's apprehension of the Divinity is defined thus:

This Being who will and can; this Being, active through himself; this Being, finally, whoever he may be, who moves the universe and orders all things, him I call God. To this name I join the ideas of intelligence, power, and will which I have gathered, and that of goodness, which is a necessary consequence of them; but I do not know the Being to whom I have given it any better. . . . I perceive God everywhere in His works; I feel Him in me; I see Him all around me; but as soon as I try to contemplate Him within Himself, as soon as I wish to seek where He is, what He is, and what His substance is, He escapes me, and I see nothing more.

(O.C., 4:37–38)

Compare Goethe's "Proœmion," in the cycle *Gott und Welt*:

> *Im Namen dessen, der sich selbst erschuf,*
> *Von Ewigkeit in schaffendem Beruf;*

In seinem Namen, der den Glauben schafft,
Vertrauen, Liebe, Tätigkeit und Kraft;
In jenes Namen, der, so oft genannt.
Dem Wesen nach blieb immer unbekannt:

Soweit das Ohr, soweit das Auge reicht,
Du findest nur Bekanntes, das ihm gleicht,
Und deines Geistes höchster Feuerflug
Hat schon am Gleichnis, hat am Bild genug;
Es zieht dich an, es reisst dich heiter fort,
Und wo du wandelst, schmückt sich Weg und Ort;
Du zählst nicht mehr, berechnest keine Zeit,
Und jeder Schritt ist Unermesslichkeit.

(W.A. I, 3:73)

This again, essentially, is "der Allumfasser, der Allerhalter" of the first version of *Faust*, written in the "Sturm und Drang" era. This does not sound as if Goethe had "renounced" Rousseau.

The Vicar expresses horror at the spectacle of the crucifixion of Christ. By contrast, the death of Socrates, "philosophizing tranquilly with his friends," is the gentlest that one could desire. The death of Jesus, "expiring in torments, injured, mocked, cursed by a whole people," is the most horrible that could be feared. "Socrates, taking the poisoned cup, blesses him who presents it to him, and who is weeping; Jesus, in the midst of frightful suffering, prays for his implacable executioners. Yes, if the life and death of Socrates are those of a wise man, the life and death of Jesus are those of a God" (O.C., 4:107).

A passage in *Wilhelm Meisters Wanderjahre* is reminiscent of the Vicar's view of Christ's death. After learning that the preceptors of the Pedagogical Province have set the life of Jesus before their pupils as a guiding precept and model, Wilhelm asks whether they have likewise held up His suffering and death as an example of sublime endurance. The eldest one answers: "Certainly. We make no mystery out of this, but we draw a veil over these sufferings, just because we revere them so highly. We consider it a damnable insolence to expose that framework of torture and the Hallowed One enduring agony thereon to the sight of the sun that hid its countenance when a ruthless world forced this spectacle upon it" (W.A. I, 24:255).

The idea of hell plays little part in the religious thinking of Rousseau and Goethe. Neither of them can reconcile the concept of eternal punishment with the infinite goodness attributed to God. The Vicar professes

163

not to know whether the souls of the wicked are annihilated when they die, or whether their ultimate salvation is made possible through Divine clemency (O.C., 4:50). Goethe's final belief in immortality postulates a positive, affirmative personality—a concept which would seem to exclude *ipso facto* the negativism of evil. Both vigorously deny the damnation of untold millions of non-Christians. For Rousseau as well as for Goethe evil finds its punishment in this life. Thus the Vicar asks what need there is to seek hell in the life to come, since it already exists on earth in the hearts of the wicked (O.C., 4:51). He states a few pages earlier that while God does not will the evil committed by Man in the abuse of his freedom, He does not prevent Man's committing it. Similar thoughts are expressed in the Harper's song (in *Wilhelm Meisters Lehrjahre*) addressed to the "Heavenly Powers":

> Ihr führt ins Leben uns hinein,
> Ihr lasst den Armen schuldig werden,
> Dann überlasst ihr ihn der Pein;
> Denn alle Schuld rächt sich auf Erden.[28]
>   (W.A. I, 21:218)

Just as Rousseau took pride in having written a novel without a villain or any wickedness in the usual sense, so Goethe likewise created hardly any villainous characters. At most, they are weak, like Weislingen or Clavigo in the early dramatic works, and in the novels from *Werther* to the *Wanderjahre* they are virtually as nonexistent as in *La Nouvelle Héloïse*. Even Mephistopheles is the spirit of negation, rather than the medieval Devil of the Faust tradition before Goethe. It is significant of the small role which hell itself plays in *Faust* that we see only the "Höllen-rachen" that the devils bring with them (ll. 11,639–11,653). As described by Mephisto, it is a Dantesque vision, reminiscent also of the "fireworks" emphasized in extant notices of the lost German Faust play.

Rousseau, says Grimsley, was constantly preoccupied in his later years with the hope and ever deepening conviction of immortality, believing that only in the afterlife could a man of his nature become free of earthly insufficiencies and attain to completeness of self (p. 33). His Vicar had indeed long since declared: "I aspire to the moment when, delivered from the trammels of the body, I shall be *I* without contradiction, without division, and I shall have need only of myself in order to be happy" (O.C., 4:72).

In a conversation with Falk (January 25, 1813) Goethe commented on the continuance of personal existence after death: "It is in no way contradictory to the observations of many years' standing that I have made concerning the character of us and of all creatures in nature; on the contrary, it even proceeds from them with new power of demonstration." Furthermore, "it is always only the same metamorphosis and capacity for transformation on the part of nature which produces a flower, a rose, from the leaf, a caterpillar from the egg, and a butterfly from the caterpillar."

This last thought brings to mind Goethe's *West-östlicher Divan*, which he was soon to create. Flitner views the poet's later writings in their totality as vehicles for expressing his religious and ethical ideals, beginning with *Dichtung und Wahrheit*. Goethe felt, says Flitner, an ever stronger urge to complete his literary endeavors. This "Drang zum Gesamtwerk" lent a cyclic character to Goethe's style in old age. Consequently, the poems of the *Divan* form a cycle, as do also the verses of cosmic import collected under the title *Gott und Welt*, and to some extent the *Sprüche* and the *Maximen und Reflexionen*. Although conceived originally as "highly independent plants," the major works were now destined to be related to one another, Flitner asserts, as the author proceeded toward their completion. Therefore they became vessels for his most important utterances concerning the mysteries of life and for revelations of his Weltanschauung, as well as of his interpretation of existence. Yet there is never an entire unveiling through any single one of these works; rather, they refer to one another, and they must be considered together if their author's intention is to be grasped (pp. 10–11). This is true especially of the "Gottesidee," which must likewise be sought in Rousseau's "Gesamtwerk," but particularly in his chief literary works.

Konrad Burdach, one of the first Goethe scholars to appreciate the greatness of the *Divan*, calls Rousseau's concept of nature one of the basic elements from which this lyric cycle was derived.[29] Indeed, it is replete with thoughts and concepts suggestive of Rousseau. The religious-mystical pantheism, which Burdach finds almost equally represented in all twelve books (p. xli), is similar to Rousseau's idea of a divinely-permeated nature, as expressed by the Vicar. Love, which, as Albert Fuchs has ably shown, informs the entire work,[30] is represented in every gradation, from the sensual to the spiritualized and transcendent form. This is the same wide range of degrees of love that we find in Rousseau's novel and in his autobiographical works. Personality, which is characterized (in the words of Suleika) as "höchstes Glück der Erdenkinder" (W.A. I, 6:162), is a favorite and ever-recurring theme for depiction by Rousseau as well as by Goethe, both in their creative writings and in their memoirs. The idea of metamorphosis, which alike informs Goethe's poetry and his treatises on natural science, is expressed in endless variations. We see how thoroughly akin to Rousseau's world of concepts that element is from Romain Rolland's assertion (cited above) that the idealism of Rousseau leads to Goethe's "Stirb und werde!" But the oft-quoted poem "Selige Sehnsucht" is not alone in its kind. Among other examples, one thinks of the previously mentioned figure of the diastole and systole:

> Im Atemholen sind zweierlei Gnaden:
> Die Luft einziehen, sich ihrer entladen;
> Jenes bedrängt, dieses erfrischt;
> So wunderbar ist das Leben gemischt.
> Du danke Gott, wenn er dich presst,
> Und dank' ihm; wenn er dich wieder entlässt.
>
> (W.A. I, 6:11)

Above all, let us note the search for God and immortality and consequently for the "supreme happiness" that Rousseau actively sought. If, as Grimsley suggests (p. 87), Rousseau's portrayal of the idealistic possibilities of humankind was in part inspired by a personal need, and if the ideal of perfection was for him both a universal one and a result of personal experience, then a parallel condition is abundantly evident in Goethe's later works, and particularly in the *Divan*. Where, except in *Faust* itself, can we find more evidences of a quest for that "highest bliss" than in this, Goethe's greatest sustained lyric achievement? Here, too, as in Rousseau's idealizations, is a search for Paradise—both earthly and celestial.

Several aspects of *Faust II* correspond to certain ideas of Rousseau. First, Rousseau's dictum in *Émile* about the incomprehensibility of the Creator, whose works are in evidence around us (O.C., 3:476), expresses the basic concept of Faust's famous line about the sunlight, unbearable in its direct brightness but manifested by refraction in the rainbow colors of the waterfall:

> Am farbigen Abglanz haben wir das Leben.
>
> (l. 4727)

For Faust the sun is the symbol of the infinite. Just as the eye cannot bear the direct light of the sun, so the human mind is not capable of perceiving the Divine directly, but rather through its "Abglanz," the manifestations of nature. This is a fundamental idea in Goethe's Weltanschauung.[31]

The symbolic figures, the "Mothers," reflect the maternal influences in Goethe's own life, according to Harold Jantz' analysis.[32] The similarity in Rousseau's life tempts one to draw a parallel. Maurice Bémol has gone even further, suggesting the direct influence of Rousseau in *Faust II*.

Bémol conjectures that Goethe may have taken from Rousseau his rather strange idea of facilitating Faust's entrance into heaven by the intervention of a woman who has sinned but received forgiveness.[33] He connects Rousseau's poignant tribute to the memory of Mme de Warens in the *Confessions* to the conclusion of *Faust II*. Although he readily admits that there are no external proofs or evidences of a direct connection here, he nevertheless asserts that internal resemblances invite critical reflections conducive to such a hypothesis. Rousseau, after expressing his profound sense of loss at the departure of "the best of women and mothers" from this "vale of tears," continues: "Allez, âme douce et bienfaisante . . . , allez goûter le fruit de la vôtre, et préparer à votre élève la place qu'il espère avoir un jour près de vous." And if he did not believe that he would see her again in heaven, his feeble imagination would deny itself the perfect happiness which he promises himself there (O.C., 16:98).

Goethe, Bémol says, makes it clear that Faust's ascension to heaven has long since been prepared by the intervention of Gretchen, who considers him her pupil and who represents the Eternal Feminine, and by that of the Mater Gloriosa (p. 16). Gretchen is thus the intermediary of the Divine Love of which Faust's angel escorts sing:

> Gerettet ist das edle Glied
> Der Geisterwelt vom Bösen,
> Wer immer strebend sich bemüht,
> Den können wir erlösen.
> Und hat an ihm die Liebe gar
> Von oben teilgenommen,
> Begegnet ihm die selige Schar
> Mit herzlichem Willkommen.
> (ll. 11,934–11,941)

Gretchen pleads:

> Vergönne mir, ihn zu belehren,
> Noch blendet ihn der neue Tag
> (ll. 12,092–12,093)

167

The Virgin replies:

> *Komm! hebe dich zu höhern Sphären!*
> *Wenn er dich ahnet, folgt er nach.*
>
> (ll. 12,094–12,095)

The resemblance is strengthened, according to Bémol, by Rousseau's description in Book Six of the *Confessions* of the essential role played by Mme de Warens in the formulation of his beliefs concerning salvation and heaven. The feelings of assurance and security which "Maman" inspired in him are such as Faust experiences, even in the presence of Mephistopheles; "this climate of merciful indulgence," Bémol concludes, is indeed the one which reigns in Paradise, where Faust is to encounter the achievement of his destiny (p. 17).

A further parallel between Rousseau's religious views and those of Goethe as expressed in *Faust II* may be seen in the figures of Julie and Gretchen, although we would not go as far as Bémol to suggest any direct influence. Julie's role may be taken as analogous to Gretchen's. Saint-Preux writes to Bomston about Julie's sorrow that Wolmar is an unbeliever: "What horror for a tender spouse to imagine the Supreme Being as the avenger of His unrecognized divinity, to think that the happiness of him who constitutes her own must end with his life!" (O.C., 9:298–299). In similar words Faust defends Gretchen against Mephistopheles:

> *Du Ungeheuer siehst nicht ein,*
> *Wie diese treue liebe Seele*
> *Von ihrem Glauben voll,*
> *Der ganz allein*
> *Ihr selig machend ist, sich heilig quäle,*
> *Dass sie den liebsten Mann verloren halten soll.*
>
> (ll. 3528–3533)

Although Julie promises to await Saint-Preux' arrival in heaven, as mentioned above in connection with Goethe's concluding remark on the coming glad awakening of Eduard and Ottilie, she continues to feel concern for her husband. "If heaven," she says, "refuses me the conversion of this honest man, I have only one more favor to ask of it: that is, to die first" (O.C., 9:299). On her deathbed she makes her profession of faith (which antedates that of the Vicar of Savoy), and it is Wolmar who reports her discourse and conversation with the minister to Saint-Preux. Although the reader can have no certainty of what will follow in this regard, one gains the impression that Wolmar feels so deeply moved by his dying wife's expression of her beliefs, that with the help of those who remain he may yet succeed in accepting Christianity. Julie's intercession for him after reaching heaven could well be assumed, if only in the light of Rousseau's own convictions. Thus Julie, herself a fallen woman who has repented, also exemplifies "das Ewig-Weibliche" in a redemptive role.

The transcendence which Rousseau accords to Julie in his novel and, later, by intimation, to "Maman" in the *Confessions* and the *Rêveries*, partially paralleled by Goethe's Ottilie, finds fulfillment in the apotheosis of Gretchen, who represents "das Ewig-Weibliche" and under whose guidance Faust is destined to continue growing spiritually and striving in "the highest existence." Makarie in the *Wanderjahre*, that mystic elder sister, so to speak, of Mignon and Ottilie,[34] reaches a different, albeit complementary, plane of the transcendental. In the interpretation of Hering, the poet once again faces the cosmos, but in a situation other than that of Faust, beholding the Macrocosm. Whereas here it was the "Sturm und Drang" figure, whose urge for deeds could not be satisfied by contemplation of the beautiful harmony of the All, and who was searching for ethical values, in Makarie the human being appears incorporated in the cosmos itself. She bears within herself a mirror of the universe and its cosmic harmony, which is transformed into an ethical one—just as ethical reflections impose themselves upon Wilhelm Meister when he views the planets through a telescope at the observatory.[35] In the course of his conversation with the astronomer concerning the splendor of Venus, he tells of a remarkable dream, the imparting of which causes those near Makarie to reveal to him (Wilhelm) her mysterious relationship to the cosmos. This had first become evident through her intuitive perception of planetary bodies then not yet discovered. Later, by means of the "Universum im Innern," she had, as it were, passed beyond the orbit of Mars and approached that of Jupiter, observing with wonder the giant planet and its satellites (W.A. I, 24:185–187).

Here, then, is a transcendence even before death. In this instance, too, the one who accomplishes it represents the principle of the "Eternal Womanly" that draws mankind upward. Again, whether or not Goethe was conscious by "reminiscence" of dreams and longings expressed by Rousseau cannot be definitely ascertained. But when one recalls the Solitary Walker's intention to recapture happiness through his "reveries" (O.C., 16:281), the above-quoted yearning for reunion with "Maman" in

Paradise, and the Vicar's discourse on the Divine harmony of the universe (C.G., pp. 331–336), it seems reasonable to suggest that with Gretchen and Makarie Goethe attained the ultimate projection of beatific visions which might have been congenial to Jean-Jacques.

From the foregoing it should be evident that Goethe's religious beliefs and experiences show remarkable parallels to those of Rousseau. Both proceeded from an orthodox training in early youth to unconventional views of God, Man, and the universe. Both perceived God in the manifestations of Nature, and both believed implicitly in His benevolence toward mankind. Although both were firmly convinced of a future life, they rejected the idea of eternal punishment. Lastly, both gave expression to their views on religion principally in two of their chief works: Rousseau in *La Nouvelle Héloïse* and *Émile*, Goethe in *Wilhelm Meisters Wanderjahre* and *Faust*. One cannot determine with certainty how far Goethe, who knew Rousseau's ideas, may have been inspired by them, but a general affinity of their religious concepts is indisputable.

Goethe, who grew to manhood in a Germany permeated by Rousseau's ideas, could not have escaped contact with them in some form. We have seen that Goethe's own statements demonstrate a lifelong veneration for Rousseau, despite a still persistent scholarly tradition to the contrary. The extent to which Rousseau inspired Goethe cannot be measured in quantitative terms. But the multiplicity of likenesses and analogies in their works proves that Goethe possessed a profound affinity with Rousseau— too profound to be gauged adequately in terms of external influence in the usual sense. The Philosopher of Geneva and the Sage of Weimar shared a wealth of ideas and a fundamental concern with the ethical and cultural advancement of mankind.

Abbreviations of Titles
Used in Notes and Bibliography

AJJR	Annales de la Société Jean-Jacques Rousseau
Archiv	Archiv für das Studium der Neueren Sprachen und Literaturen
CL	Comparative Literature
DVLG	Deutsche Vierteljahrsschrift für Literaturwissenschaft und Geistesgeschichte
EG	Études Germaniques
FR	French Review
GJb	Goethe-Jahrbuch
Goethe	Goethe: Neue Folge des Jahrbuchs der Goethe-Gesellschaft
GQ	German Quarterly
GR	Germanic Review
GRM	Germanisch-romanische Monatsschrift
ISLL	Illinois Studies in Language and Literature
IUHS	Indiana University Humanities Series
JbGG	Jahrbuch der Goethe-Gesellschaft
JEGP	Journal of English and Germanic Philology
LSUSHS	Louisiana State University Studies, Humanities Series
MLN	Modern Language Notes
MLQ	Modern Language Quarterly
MLR	Modern Language Review
MP	Modern Philology
NS	Die Neueren Sprachen
PEGS	Publications of the English Goethe Society
PMLA	Publications of the Modern Language Association of America

RDM	Revue des Deux Mondes
RMM	Revue de Métaphysique et de Morale
RomN	Romance Notes
SCB	South Central Bulletin
SR	Sewanee Review
TSLL	Texas Studies in Literature and Language
UCPMP	University of California Publications in Modern Philology
UNCSCL	University of North Carolina Studies in Comparative Literature
UNCSGLL	University of North Carolina Studies in Germanic Languages and Literatures
YFS	Yale French Studies
ZDP	Zeitschrift für Deutsche Philologie
ZFSL	Zeitschrift für Französische Sprache und Literatur

Notes

INTRODUCTION

1. Bernard Groethuysen, *Jean-Jacques Rousseau*, 4th ed. (Paris, 1949).

2. Jean Guéhenno, *Jean-Jacques Rousseau: Histoire d'une conscience* (Paris, 1962).

3. Léon Émery, *Rousseau: L'Annonciateur* (Lyon, n.d.). For a well-written "popular" appreciation of Jean-Jacques, see Ernst Glaeser, "Rousseau—fast ein Heiliger," *Merian*, 16, No. 1 (1963):65–69.

4. Saint-Marc Girardin, *J.-J. Rousseau: Sa vie et ses œuvres* (Paris, 1875).

5. Jules Lemaître, *J.-J. Rousseau* (Paris, n.d.).

6. Georg Brandes, *Main Currents in Nineteenth-Century Literature* (New York, 1906), pp. 15–26, *passim*. Compare Oskar Seidlin, "Georg Brandes," *Essays on German and Comparative Literature*, UNCSCL, No. 30 (Chapel Hill, 1961), pp. 1–29.

7. Bernard Bouvier, "Rapport de la commission initiative," *AJJR*, 1 (1905):14. Bouvier cites the "Goethe-Schiller-Archiv" at Weimar as the model for the "Société."

8. Surprisingly enough, a recent, widely circulated Goethe book by Richard Friedenthal, *Goethe: Sein Leben und seine Zeit* (Munich, 1963), is expressly devoted to destroying the so-called "Goethelegende," namely, the uncritical admiration of an idolized "Olympier" (see the "Nachwort," pp. 735–738). While claiming to dethrone an image already long since nonexistent for Goethe scholarship, he attempts to introduce a negative counter-legend of eroticism and selfishness. Compare Erich Franz, "Entweder—Oder? Bemerkungen zu dem Goethebuch von Richard Friedenthal," *Goethe*, 26 (1964):136–143, and Andreas B. Wachsmuth, "Ein neues Goethebild? Zu dem Buch von R. Friedenthal," *Goethe*, 27 (1965):279–308. See also Hippolyte Loiseau, "La légende de l'olympisme de Goethe," *Mélanges Henri Lichtenberger* (Paris, 1934), pp. 49–69. Equally surprising is the fact that the two-volume work of K. R. Eissler, *Goethe: A Psycho-Analytic Study, 1776–1786* (Detroit, 1963), almost completely forgoes the pathological comparisons of Goethe with Rousseau which the reader might have expected.

9. Emil Staiger, *Goethe* (Zurich, 1952–1956).

10. Heinrich Meyer, *Goethe: Das Leben im Werk* (Hamburg-Bergedorf, 1949). Compare Meyer's collective review article, "Der alte und der neue Goethe," *Merkur: Zeitschrift für europäisches Denken*, 3 (1949):3–11; also, Heinz Kindermann, *Das Goethebild des zwanzigsten Jahrhunderts* (Vienna, 1952).

11. Barker Fairley, *A Study of Goethe* (London, 1947).

12. Albert Fuchs, *Goethe: Un homme face à la vie* (Paris, 1946); cited below as Fuchs.

13. Ulrich Weisstein, *Einführung in die Vergleichende Literaturwissenschaft* (Stuttgart, 1968), p. 88.

14. Erich Schmidt, *Richardson, Rousseau und Goethe* (Jena, 1875).

15. "Obraldruck" of the original edition of 1875 (Jena, 1924). See review by Walter Müller, *AJJR*, 16 (1925):267–268.

16. Compare Albert W. Aron, "The Mature Goethe and Rousseau," *JEGP*, 35 (1936):180; cited below as Aron.

17. Lucien Lévy-Bruhl, "L'Influence de J.-J. Rousseau en Allemagne," *Annales de l'École Libre des Sciences Politiques*, 2 (1875):342–343.

18. Wilhelm Scherer, *Geschichte der deutschen Literatur* (Berlin, n.d.), p. 549. (The first edition appeared in 1883.)

19. Jules Barbey d'Aurevilly, *Goethe et Diderot* (Paris, 1880), pp. 36–37.

20. John Grand-Carteret, *La France jugée par l'Allemagne* (Paris, 1896), pp. 129–130, 266–272.

21. Joseph Texte, *Jean-Jacques Rousseau et les origines du cosmopolitisme littéraire* (Paris, 1895), pp. 109–110, *passim*.

22. Virgile Rossel, *Histoire des relations littéraires entre la France et l'Allemagne* (Paris, 1897), p. 435.

23. Armand Caumont, "Goethe et la littérature française," *Programm des städtischen Gymnasiums zu Frankfurt am Main* (Frankfurt, 1885), pp. 1–37.

24. C. Sachs, "Goethes Beschäftigung mit französischer Sprache und Literatur," *ZFSL*, 23 (1901):34–68.

25. Isaac Benrubi, "Goethe et Schiller continuateurs de Rousseau," *RMM*, 20 (1912):442.

26. Louis Reynaud, *Histoire générale de l'influence française en Allemagne*, 2nd ed. (Paris, 1915), p. 431. In his later work, *L'Influence allemande en France au XVIIIe et au XIXe siècle* (Paris, 1922), Reynaud emphasizes the purely German characteristics of *Werther*, which, he says, at first hindered its ready acceptance in France (pp. 67–69).

27. Max Kommerell, *Jean Pauls Verhältnis zu Rousseau*, Beiträge zur deutschen Literaturwissenschaft, ed. Ernst Elster, No. 23 (Marburg, 1925), p. 47.

28. Herbert Smith, "Goethe and Rousseau," *PEGS*, n.s., 3 (1926):31, 44–47, *passim*. Smith attaches excessive importance to Johann Christian Kestner's remark (in a letter to August von Hennings, November 18, 1772): "He is not yet fixed in his principles and is still striving for a sure system. To say something about that, he thinks very highly of Rousseau, but is no blind worshiper of him" (p. 55). For the original of this statement, see Wilhelm Bode, *Goethe in vertraulichen Briefen seiner Zeitgenossen* (Berlin, 1921), 1:36.

29. Eduard Spranger, "Einführung" to Rousseau, *Kulturideale: Eine Zusammenstellung aus seinen Werken . . .* , trans. Hedwig Jahn (Jena, 1922), pp. 1–25.

30. Hippolyte Loiseau, *Goethe et la France: ce qu'il en a connu, pensé et dit* (Paris, 1930), pp. 139–141.

31. E. Preston Dargan, "Goethe and France," *Goethe Centenary Papers*, ed. Martin Schütze (Chicago, 1932), pp. 45–64. Konrad Gaiser's essay, "Goethes Auseinandersetzung mit der französischen Kultur," *Neue Jahrbücher für Wissenschaft und Jugendbildung*, 8 (1932):113–127, likewise strongly reflects Loiseau with reference to Jean-Jacques.

32. Valentin Brunet, *L'Influence de Rousseau sur les idées politiques et sociales et sur la sentimentalité de Goethe* (Toulouse, 1932).

33. Aron, p. 170 (see note 16 above); page references hereafter in text.

34. Bertram Barnes, *Goethe's Knowledge of French Literature* (Oxford, 1937), pp. 56–62. Barnes also quotes Kestner's comment on Goethe's attitude toward Rousseau (p. 60). See note 28 above.

35. Rudolf Buck, *Rousseau und die deutsche Romantik* (Berlin, 1939), pp. 5–6. At this point Buck quotes Oskar Walzel concerning Rousseau's importance for Goethe's *Werther*. Compare Walzel, "Einleitung" to *Die Leiden des jungen Werther*, *Goethes Werke*, Festausgabe (Leipzig, 1926–1927), 9:31.

36. René Michéa, *Le "Voyage en Italie" de Goethe* (Paris, 1945).

37. In *Les Travaux scientifiques de Goethe* (Lille, 1946), pp. 69–79.

38. Fuchs, pp. 243–257, 446–447, *passim*.

39. Fritz Strich, *Goethe und die Weltliteratur* (Bern, 1946), pp. 11–13, 56.

40. Roy Pascal, "Goethe's Autobiography and Rousseau's *Confessions*," *Studies in French Language and Literature Presented to R. L. Graeme Ritchie* (Cambridge,

Eng., 1949), pp. 147–162. Compare Ernst Cassirer, *Goethe und die geschichtliche Welt* (Berlin, 1932), pp. 15–16.

41. Edmond Vermeil, "Goethe et Rousseau," *AJJR*, 31 (1946–1949): 57–77. Compare the following essays of related content by Vermeil: "Goethe: homme du milieu," *Comparative Literature*, 1 (1949): 324–336; "Goethe and the West," trans. W. E. Delp, *MLR*, 44 (1949): 504–513.

42. "*La Nouvelle Héloïse* et son influence sur l'œuvre de Goethe," *Goethe et l'esprit français: Actes du Colloque International de Strasbourg, 23–27 Avril 1957* (Paris, 1958), pp. 57–68.

43. Maurice Bémol, "Goethe, Rousseau et Faust," *EG*, 13 (1958): 1–17. See also Bémol's article, "Goethe et Rousseau, ou la double influence," *EG*, 9 (1954): 257–277.

I The Cultural Background

1. Ernst Cassirer, "Kant and Rousseau," *Rousseau, Kant, Goethe*, trans. James Gutmann et al. (Princeton, 1947), p. 1. The second of the two essays in this book is entitled "Kant and Goethe"; little attention is given to Rousseau and Goethe, but see Cassirer's monograph *Goethe und die geschichtliche Welt* (Berlin, 1932), pp. 15–16.

2. *Correspondance générale*, ed. Théophile Dufour and Paul-Pierre Plan (Paris, 1924–1934), 6:81. Compare S. Moreau-Rendu, *L'Idée de bonté naturelle chez J.-J. Rousseau* (Paris, 1929), p. 316.

3. Roland Mortier, *Diderot en Allemagne, 1750–1850* (Paris, 1954).

4. Jacques Voisine, *J.-J. Rousseau en Angleterre à l'époque romantique* (Paris, 1956).

5. Herbert Dieckmann, "Goethe und Diderot," *DVLG*, 10 (1932): 478–503.

6. Karl S. Guthke, "Zur Frühgeschichte des Rousseauismus in Deutschland," *ZDP*, 77 (1958): 384; cited below as Guthke.

7. At the conclusion of his article (pp. 395–396) Guthke emphasizes the significance of Johann Heinrich Füssli's appraisal of Rousseau—probably the fairest contemporaneous estimate of Jean-Jacques. Compare Henri Fuseli, *Remarks on the Writings and Conduct of J.-J. Rousseau* (London, 1767), ed. Karl S. Guthke, Augustan Reprint Society Publications, No. 82 (Los Angeles, 1960), pp. i–vi and 1–30.

8. For this review, see Gotthold Ephraim Lessing, *Sämtliche Schriften*, ed. Karl Lachmann and Franz Muncker, 3rd ed. (Stuttgart, Berlin, Leipzig, 1886–1915), 4:394–395; cited below as *Sämtliche Schriften*.

9. Fredcric C. Tubach, "Perfectibilité: der zweite Diskurs Rousseaus und die deutsche Aufklärung," *EG*, 12 (1960): 144; cited in text as Tubach.

10. Compare Friedrich Sengle, *Christoph Martin Wieland* (Stuttgart, 1949) p. 230; cited below as Sengle.

11. Lessing, *Sämtliche Schriften*, 7:37–38.

12. The letter is found in Moses Mendelssohn, *Gesammelte Schriften*, ed. G. E. Mendelssohn (Leipzig, 1843), 5:22; the comment from the *Sendschreiben* occurs in the same edition, 1:313 (both quoted by Tubach, p. 146).

13. In his monograph *Rousseau und die deutsche Geschichtsphilosophie* (Leipzig, 1890), Richard Fester asserts that Lessing derived "positive inspiration" from *La Nouvelle Héloïse* and *Émile* for his religious thinking, as evidenced by his *Nathan der Weise* (p. 34).

14. Hans M. Wolff, "Der junge Herder und die Entwicklungsidee Rousseaus," *PMLA*, 57 (1942): 756. For the poem, see Herder's *Sämtliche Werke*, ed. Bernhard Suphan (Berlin, 1877–1913), 29:254–258; cited below as *Sämtliche Werke*.

15. Herder, *Sämtliche Werke*, 29:264–265.

16. In a letter to Scheffner, Oct. 31, 1767.

17. Robert T. Clark, Jr., *Herder: His Life and Thought* (Berkeley and Los Angeles, 1955), p. 46; page references hereafter in text.

18. Sengle, pp. 220–230.

19. Victor Michel, *C.-M. Wieland: La forme et l'évolution de son esprit jusqu'en 1772* (Paris, n.d.), p. 161; cited below as Michel.

20. Sengle, pp. 202, 263–264.

21. To cite several instances, by L. John Parker, *Christoph Martin Wielands dramatische Tätigkeit* (Bern, 1961), pp. 45–46; Sengle, pp. 284–285; Michel, p. 390; and Alfred R. Neumann, "The Changing Concept of the *Singspiel* in the Eighteenth Century," *Studies in German Literature*, ed. Carl Hammer, Jr., LSUSHS, No. 13 (Baton Rouge, 1963), p. 67.

22. *Der Teutsche Merkur*, 30 (April, 1780):90; 31 (August, 1780):146.

23. Quoted by Michel, p. 316.

24. Compare Erich Schmidt, *Richardson, Rousseau und Goethe* (Jena, 1875), p. 57.

25. Kuno Ridderhoff, *Sophie von LaRoche, die Schülerin Richardsons und Rousseaus* (Einbeck, 1895), pp. 58–59.

26. Max Kommerell, *Jean Pauls Verhältnis zu Rousseau*, Beiträge zur deutschen Literaturwissenschaft, ed. Ernst Elster, No. 23 (Marburg, 1925), p. 47.

27. Heinz Kindermann, ed., *Kampf um das soziale Ordnungsgefüge*, Deutsche Literatur in Entwicklungsreihen, Reihe Irrationalismus, vol. 8 (Leipzig, 1939):16.

28. See Karl Weinhold, "Anfang eines fantastischen Romans, von Lenz, von dessen eigener Hand," *GJb*, 10 (1889):65.

29. Erich Schmidt, *Lenz und Klinger* (Minden, 1904), pp. 55–56 (quoted by Wyneken; see note 30).

30. F. A. Wyneken, *Rousseaus Einfluss auf Klinger*, UCPMP, No. 3 (Berkeley, 1912), pp. 1–85.

31. Henry Wood, "Die Faustromane F. M. Klingers und Goethes *Faust*," *Fauststudien* (Berlin, 1912), pp. 264–265.

32. H. M. Waidson, "Goethe and Klinger: Some Aspects of a Personal and Literary Relationship," *PEGS*, n.s., 23 (1954):110.

33. Hans M. Wolff, "Der Rousseaugehalt in Klingers Drama *Das leidende Weib*," *JEGP*, 39 (1940):365–366.

34. Rudolf Unger, *Hamann und die Aufklärung* (Halle, 1925), 1:396; page references hereafter in text.

35. Hans M. Wolff, "Rousseau, Möser und der Kampf gegen das Rokoko," *Monatshefte*, 34 (1942):115–125; page references hereafter in text.

36. Ludwig Bäte, *Justus Möser: Advocatus patriae* (Frankfurt, 1961), pp. 91–97.

37. Hermann Hettner, *Geschichte der deutschen Literatur im achtzehnten Jahrhundert*, rev. Gotthard Erler (Berlin, 1961), 2:245–249.

38. Isaac Benrubi, "Goethe et Schiller continuateurs de Rousseau," *RMM*, 20 (1912):450; page references hereafter in text.

39. Wolfgang Liepe, "Der junge Schiller und Rousseau: Eine Nachprüfung der Rousseaulegende um den *Räuber*-Dichter," *ZDP*, 51 (1926):308–309. For the eulogy (contained in an essay) to which Liepe refers, see Johann Georg Jacobi, "Ueber J.J. Rousseau," *Der Teutsche Merkur*, 23 (1778):201–218. Compare Carl Hammer, Jr., "Jacobi's Memorial to Rousseau," *Die Neueren Sprachen*, No. 6 (Jahrgang 1965):280–283.

40. Roger Ayrault, "Schiller et Rousseau: Sur la genèse des *Brigands*," *EG*, 10 (1955):97–104.

41. E. L. Stahl, *Schiller's Dramas* (Oxford, 1954), p. 9.

42. Joachim Ulrich, "Goethes Einfluss auf Schillers Schönheitsbegriff," *JbGG*, 20 (1934):175.

43. William F. Mainland, *Schiller and the Changing Past* (London, 1953), p. 115.

44. Kommerell devotes his second chapter (pp. 35–60) to Rousseau's importance for German writers other than Jean Paul.

45. Oskar Ritter von Xylander, *Heinrich von Kleist und J.-J. Rousseau*, Germanische Studien, No. 193 (Berlin, 1937). Xylander offers a preliminary discussion of Rousseau's significance for the literary generation in Germany to which Kleist belonged (see especially pp. 10–29).

46. Lately, for instance, by Walter Silz, *Hölderlin's Hyperion: A Critical Reading* (Philadelphia, 1969), pp. 3 and 11.

47. Bernard Böschenstein, "La Transfiguration de Rousseau dans la poésie allemande à l'orée du XIXᵉ siècle: Hölderlin—Jean Paul—Kleist," *AJJR*, 36 (1963–1965):153–171.

48. Jacques Voisine, "L'Influence de la *Nouvelle Héloïse* sur la génération de *Werther*," *EG*, 5 (1950):120–133.

49. Anne-Louise Germaine de Staël-Holstein, *Dix années d'exil* (Paris, n.d.), p. 26.

50. See my article, "Goethe's Silence Concerning Ronsard," *MLN*, 75 (1960): 697–698.

51. Compare Carl Hammer, Jr., "Re-examining Goethe's Views of Corneille," *GR*, 29 (1954):260–268.

52. See Louis Morel, "Influence de la littérature française chez Goethe," III, *GJb*, 32 (1911):91.

53. Geneviève Bianquis, "Goethe et Voltaire," *Études sur Goethe* (Paris, 1951), p. 97.

54. Johann Peter Eckermann, *Gespräche mit Goethe in den letzten Jahren seines Lebens*, Goethes Werke, Gedenkausgabe (Zurich, 1949–1960), 24:383.

55. See *Diderot Studies*, ed. Otis Fellows and Norman L. Torrey, vol. 1 (Syracuse, 1949), p. IX.

56. *Diderot Studies*, vol. 2 (Syracuse, 1952), p. 20.

57. Herbert Dieckmann, "Goethe und Diderot," *DVLG*, 10 (1932):480; cited below as Dieckmann. Conversely, Arthur M. Wilson says that Diderot's later writings indicate that he penetrated farther and more deeply into the mysteries of life than any other man of his century except Goethe (*Diderot: The Testing Years, 1713–1759* [New York, 1957], p. 346).

58. Compare my article, "The 'Philosophers' Quarrel' as Seen by Goethe," *RomN*, 9, No. 2 (Spring, 1968):232–234.

59. Norman L. Torrey, "Rousseau's Quarrel with Grimm and Diderot," *Essays in Honor of Albert Feuillerat*, ed. Henri Peyre, Yale Romanic Studies, No. 22 (New Haven, 1943), p. 164; cited below as Torrey.

60. George Brereton, ed., *French Thought in the Eighteenth Century: Rousseau–Voltaire–Diderot* (New York, 1953), p. v.

61. Hippolyte Loiseau, *Goethe et la France: ce qu'il en a connu, pensé et dit* (Paris, 1930), pp. 125–126.

62. Torrey, p. 163.

63. Compare Dieckmann, pp. 478–479. See also Roland Mortier, *Diderot en Allemagne, 1750–1850* (Paris, 1954), pp. 183–184.

64. "Holbach According to Goethe," *RomN*, 1, No. 1 (November, 1959):18–21.

65. See Charles-Augustin Sainte-Beuve, *Causeries du lundi*, 7 (Paris, 1853), p. 288, and Edmond Scherer, *Melchior Grimm: L'homme de lettres—le factotum—le diplomate* (Paris, 1887), pp. 97, 143–146, passim.

66. René Wellek, *A History of Modern Criticism* (New Haven, 1955–1967), vol. 1: *The Later Eighteenth Century*, p. 71.

67. See Jeanne R. Monty, "The Criticism of Rousseau in the *Correspondance littéraire*," *MLQ*, 24 (1963):99–103.

68. Compare Heinrich Bauer, *Jean-François Marmontel als Literarkritiker* (Leipzig, 1937), p. 149.

69. *Goethes Gespräche*, ed. Flodoard von Biedermann (Leipzig, 1909–1911), 2:101.

70. In his essay, "The Theme of Genius in Diderot's *Neveu de Rameau*," *Diderot Studies*, vol. 2 (Syracuse, 1952), Otis Fellows describes Diderot's reply to Palissot in *Le Neveu de Rameau* as "some of the most violent invective of the age" (p. 176).

71. Goethe remarks that the première (in 1760) of such a public, personal satire as *Les Philosophes* must have caused a great sensation in an animated city like Paris. Whereas, Goethe continues, a German of real merit could keep on living and working undisturbed while awaiting eventual understanding by his compatriots, the Frenchman is a man of social instincts who lives, acts, stands, or falls in society (W.A. I, 41^2:77–78).

72. Théophile Gautier, *Histoire de l'art dramatique en France depuis 25 ans*, No. 3 (Paris, 1859), p. 315; quoted by Hermann Sauter, *Goethe in Lob und Tadel seiner französischen Zeitgenossen* (Speyer, n.d.), p. 130.

II JEAN-JACQUES ACCORDING TO GOETHE

1. *Correspondance générale*, ed. Théophile Dufour and Paul-Pierre Plan (Paris, 1924–1934), 2:303–324; cited below as *Correspondance générale*.

2. Voltaire, *Œuvres complètes*, ed. Louis Moland (Paris, 1877–1888), 9:465–480.

3. See George R. Havens, "Voltaire, Rousseau, and the 'Lettre sur la Providence,'" *PMLA*, 59 (1944):109–130.

4. Bettina von Arnim (née Brentano), *Goethes Briefwechsel mit einem Kinde* (Stuttgart, n.d.), 2:132.

5. "The pastor at Berlin": Jean-Louis-Samuel Formey, French Protestant clergyman and "homme de lettres" then living in the Prussian capital. Compare note 3, above.

6. See Bertram Barnes, *Goethe's Knowledge of French Literature* (Oxford, 1937), p. 58, where the passages, quoted in the original, are placed side by side.

7. Hippolyte Loiseau, *Goethe et la France: ce qu'il en a connu, pensé et dit* (Paris, 1930), p. 139; cited below as Loiseau.

8. Albert W. Aron, "The Mature Goethe and Rousseau," *JEGP*, 35 (1936): 170; cited below as Aron.

9. Edmond Jaloux, *Goethe*, rev. ed. (Paris, 1949), p. 140. Compare Wilhelm Bode, *Goethes Schweizer Reisen* (Leipzig, 1922), p. 80.

10. Wilhelm Bode, *Die Tonkunst in Goethes Leben* (Berlin, 1912), 1:89–90.

11. Flodoard von Biedermann, ed., *Goethes Gespräche* (Leipzig, 1909–1911), 5:187.

12. For the original, see Anne-Louise Germaine de Staël-Holstein, *Œuvres* (Paris, 1858), 1:127–147.

13. Compare Aron, p. 178.

14. "Why," Goethe asked Eckermann (January 18, 1825), "should I take the trouble to invent one (i.e., a song) of my own, when that of Shakespeare was the very thing and said just what it should?"

15. See Henry H. H. Remak, "Goethe on Stendhal: Development and Significance of his Attitude," *Goethe Bicentennial Studies by Members of the Faculty of Indiana University*, ed. Hubert J. Meessen, IUPHS, No. 22 (Bloomington, 1950), p. 207.

16. Michel Bréal, *Deux Études sur Goethe: . . . 2. Les Personnages originaux de la "Fille naturelle"* (Paris, 1898), p. 135.

17. Charles-Augustin Sainte-Beuve, *Les grands écrivains français: Études des lundis* (Paris, n.d.), 2:1–20.

18. Goethe's translation of this passage from Rousseau reads as follows:

"Man muss in Herrn Rameau ein sehr grosses Talent anerkennen, viel Feuer, einen wohlklingenden Kopf, eine grosse Kenntnis harmonischer Umkehrungen und aller Mittel, die Wirkung hervorbringen; man muss ihm die Kunst zugestehen, sich fremde Ideen zuzueignen, ihre Natur zu verändern, sie zu verzieren, zu verschönern und seine eigenen auf vielseitige Weise umzudrehen. Dagegen hatte er weniger Leichtigkeit, neue zu erfinden, mehr Geschicklichkeit als Fruchtbarkeit, mehr Wissen als Genie, oder wenigstens ein Genie, erstickt durch zu vieles Wissen; aber immer Stärke, Zierlichkeit und sehr oft einen schönen Gesang."

Compare the original French, as given in *Œuvres complètes de J.-J. Rousseau*, ed. P. R. Auguis (Paris, 1825), 15:357:

"Il faut reconnoître dans M. Rameau un très grand talent, beaucoup de feu, une tête bien sonnante, une grande connoissance des renversements harmoniques et de toutes les choses d'effet; beaucoup d'art pour s'approprier, dénaturer, orner, embellir les idées d'autrui, et retourner les siennes; assez peu de facilité pour en inventer de nouvelles; plus d'habilité que de fécondité, plus de savoir que de génie, ou du moins un génie étouffé par trop de savoir; mais toujours de la force et de l'élégance, et très souvent du beau chant."

19. Rousseau's letter is dated Nov. 10, 1763 (*Correspondance générale*, 10:205–216).

20. Loiseau, p. 137.

21. Compare note 15 above.

22. Goethe's supposed quotation from Rousseau reads: "Und zu den Füssen seiner Geliebten sitzend, wird er Hanf brechen, und er wird wünschen Hanf zu brechen, heute, morgen und übermorgen, ja sein ganzes Leben."

I have not found an identical passage in *La Nouvelle Héloïse*. Apparently, Goethe, who was so fond of the words, "today, tomorrow, the day after tomorrow, and all his life," that he repeated them on several occasions at long intervals, failed to recall the exact situation. But Saint-Preux ends his account of the vintage festival at Clarens (Part Five, Letter Seven) with the following sentence: "Ensuite on offre à boire à toute l'assemblée: chacun boit à la santé du vainqueur [in a work contest conducted by Julie], et va se coucher content d'une journée passée dans le travail, la gaieté, l'innocence, et qu'on ne serait fâché de recommencer le lendemain, le surlendemain, et toute sa vie" (C.G., p. 564).

23. See Elise von Keudell, *Goethe als Benutzer der Weimarer Bibliothek* (Weimar, 1931), p. 334.

24. Aron, pp. 178–179. Compare Adolph Hansen, *Goethes Metamorphose der Pflanzen: Geschichte einer botanischen Hypothese* (Giessen, 1907), pp. 267–268.

25. From the second of the "Lettres adressées à M. de la Tourette" on botany, 1770 (O.C., 7:129–130).

26. The following treatises discuss, with varying emphasis, Rousseau's importance for Goethe's botanical studies: René Berthelot, *Science et philosophie chez Goethe* (Paris, 1932); Valentin Haecker, *Goethes morphologische Arbeiten und die neuere Forschung* (Jena, 1927); Maurice Hocquette, *Les Fantaisies botaniques de Goethe* (Lille, 1946); Rudolf Magnus, *Goethe als Naturforscher* (Leipzig, 1906); René Michéa, *Les Travaux scientifiques de Goethe* (Paris, 1943); and Günther Schmid, "Goethes Metamorphose der Pflanzen," *Goethe als Seher und Forscher der Natur*, ed. Johannes Walter (Halle, 1930).

III Literary Echoes from Four Decades

1. Isaac Benrubi, "Goethe et Schiller continuateurs de Rousseau," *RMM*, 20 (1912):442; cited below as Benrubi.

2. Hippolyte Loiseau, *Goethe et la France: ce qu'il en a connu, pensé et dit* (Paris, 1930), p. 16; cited below as Loiseau. According to Heinz Kindermann ("Einleitung" to *Der Rokoko-Goethe*, Deutsche Literatur in Entwicklungsreihen, Reihe Irrationalismus, 2 [Leipzig, 1932]:42), the opening lines of Goethe's third Ode addressed to Behrisch:

> *Sei gefühllos!*
> *Ein leichtbewegtes Herz*
> *Ist ein elend Gut*
> *Auf der wankenden Erde*
> (W.A. I, 4:185)

echo the following passage in *La Nouvelle Héloïse* (Part One, Letter Twenty-Six): "O Julie! que c'est un fatal présent du ciel qu'une âme sensible! Celui qui l'a reçue doit s'attendre à n'avoir que peine et douleur sur terre" (C.G., p. 74).

3. Richard M. Meyer, "Einleitung" to *Dichtung und Wahrheit*, *Goethes Werke*, Jubiläums-Ausgabe (Stuttgart, 1902–1912), 21:xvii.

4. Édouard Rod, *Essai sur Goethe* (Paris, 1898), p. 80.

5. Loiseau, p. 326. Eduard von der Hellen, on the contrary, regards these features as positively Rousseauesque ("Anmerkungen" to *Götz von Berlichingen*, *Goethes Werke*, Jubiläums-Ausgabe [Stuttgart, 1902–1912], 10:263).

6. Christian Gauss, ed., *Selections from the Works of Jean-Jacques Rousseau*, 2nd ed. (Princeton, 1920), p. 93.

7. William Witte, "Goethe and the 'Ius Naturale,'" *Schiller and Burns and Other Essays* (Oxford, 1959), pp. 81–94.

8. According to Wolfgang Martini, the appearance and loving depiction of so many persons from among the common folk in Goethe's youthful dramas was inspired by Rousseau (*Die Technik der Jugenddramen Goethes* [Weimar, 1932], p. 164).

9. Compare W. H. Bruford, *Theatre, Drama, and Audience in Goethe's Germany* (London, 1950), p. 206, where it is stated that for the contemporaneous audience *Götz von Berlichingen* was a picture of the Empire in their time, still weak, disunited, and torn by class struggles. For them, Frenchified manners and "personal intrigues" were reflected in the court of the Bishop of Bamberg, in contrast to plain, straightforward German country ways. Bruford further mentions Bruder Martin's frustration, and Karl's having been taught words—not things, as called for by the pedagogy of Basedow, who had learned it from Rousseau (p. 207).

10. Albert Fuchs, *Goethe: Un homme face à la vie*, 1 (Paris, 1946):257. That line extends, says Fuchs, to the cry of the hero of *Des Epimenides Erwachen* (1814):

> *Nun sind wir Deutsche widerum,*
> *Nun sind wir wieder gross!*
> (W.A. I, 16:380)

11. Edith Braemer, *Goethes Prometheus und die Grundpositionen des Sturm und Drang*, 3rd rev. ed. (Berlin and Weimar, 1968), p. 170.

12. Richard M. Meyer, "Literarhistorische Bemerkungen, I: Zu Goethe," *Euphorion*, 3 (1896):106.

13. Loiseau, p. 329.

14. Bertram Barnes, *Goethe's Knowledge of French Literature* (Oxford, 1937), p. 60.

15. Hans M. Wolff, "Satyros," *GR*, 24 (1949):170; page references hereafter in text.

16. Imitation of *La Nouvelle Héloïse* is claimed by Louis Reynaud, *Histoire générale de l'influence française en Allemagne*, 2nd ed. (Paris, 1915), p. 431, and lack of significant relationship by Herbert Smith, "Goethe and Rousseau," *PEGS*, n.s., 3 (1926): 52; cited below as Herbert Smith.

17. See Stuart P. Atkins, "J. C. Lavater and Goethe: Problems of Psychology and Theology in *Die Leiden des jungen Werthers*," *PMLA*, 63 (1948): 545.

18. Quoted from Wilhelm Bode, *Goethe in vertraulichen Briefen seiner Zeitgenossen* (Berlin, 1921), 1:123–124.

19. Fernand Baldensperger, *Goethe en France: Étude de littérature comparée*, 2nd rev. ed. (Paris, 1920), especially pp. 13–39; compare Ferdinand Gross, *Goethes "Werther" in Frankreich* (Leipzig, n.d.).

20. Émile Montégut, "Types modernes en littérature: Werther," *RDM*, 11 (1855): 333–344 (a very appreciative estimate).

21. Joachim Merlant, *Le Roman personnel de Rousseau à Fromentin* (Paris, 1905), p. 32.

22. Erich Schmidt, *Richardson, Rousseau und Goethe* (Jena, 1875), p. 159.

23. Hans Heinrich Borcherdt, *Der Roman der Goethezeit* (Urach and Stuttgart, 1949), p. 7.

24. Compare Daniel Mornet, *Le Romantisme en France au XVIIIᵉ siècle* (Paris, 1912), p. 52; Herbert Smith, pp. 35–36; and Wolfgang Leppmann, *The German Image of Goethe* (Oxford, 1961), p. 16. Concerning the vast array of adaptations (other than novels) of the Werther theme, see Stuart P. Atkins, *The Testament of Werther in Poetry and Drama* (Cambridge, Mass., 1949).

25. Friedrich Gundolf, *Goethe*, 7th ed. (Berlin, 1920), pp. 179–180.

26. Hans Gose, *Goethes "Werther"* (Halle, 1921), p. 100.

27. In Russia, too, *Werther* encountered readers who, thoroughly conditioned by Richardson and Rousseau, received Goethe's novel as just another work in the familiar sentimental vein. See André von Gronicka, *The Russian Image of Goethe* (Philadelphia, 1968), p. 11.

28. Helene Herrmann, *Die psychologischen Anschauungen des jungen Goethe* (Berlin, 1904); Max Herrmann, "Einleitung" to *Werther*, Goethes Werke, Jubiläums-Ausgabe (Stuttgart, 1902–1912), 17:v–lix.

29. Ernst Feise, "Goethes Werther als nervöser Charakter," *GR*, 1 (1926): 185–253.

30. Robert T. Clark, Jr., "The Psychological Framework of Goethe's *Werther*," *JEGP*, 46 (1947): 273–278.

31. Marc Eigeldinger, *Jean-Jacques Rousseau et la réalité de l'imaginaire* (Neuchâtel, 1962); cited below as Eigeldinger.

32. Loiseau, p. 327.

33. Eduard Bodemann, *Julie von Bondeli und ihr Freundeskreis* (Hanover, 1874), p. 25.

34. Wilhelm Nowack, *Liebe und Ehe im deutschen Roman zu Rousseaus Zeiten, 1747 bis 1774* (Bern, 1906), p. 39.

35. Martin Lauterbach, *Das Verhältnis der zweiten zur ersten Ausgabe von "Werthers Leiden*," Quellen und Forschungen, No. 110 (Strassburg, 1910). Lauterbach regards the two versions as monuments of different epochs of Goethe's poetic art (p. 128). Gerhard Storz designates *Werther* as a "diary novel" (*Goethe-Vigilien* [Stuttgart, 1953], p. 23).

36. Hans Reiss, "*Die Leiden des jungen Werthers*: A Reconsideration," *MLQ*, 20 (1959): 92.

37. J. Firmery, *Goethe* (Paris, 1894), p. 84.

38. Arthur Kutscher, *Das Naturgefühl in Goethes Lyrik bis zur Ausgabe der Schriften 1789*, Breslauer Beiträge zur Literaturgeschichte, No. 8 (Leipzig, 1906), p. 58.

39. Maurice Bémol, "Goethe et Rousseau, ou la double influence," *EG*, 9 (1954):262–266. Compare L. A. Willoughby, "The Image of the 'Wanderer' and the 'Hut' in Goethe's Poetry," *EG*, 6 (1951):212–214.

40. H. J. Meessen, "*Clavigo* and *Stella* in Goethe's Personal and Dramatic Development," *Goethe Bicentennial Studies by Members of the Faculty of Indiana University*, ed. H. J. Meessen, IUHS, No. 22 (Bloomington, 1950), pp. 153, 179; cited below as Meessen.

41. Georg Grempler, *Beiträge zu Goethes "Clavigo"* (Halle, 1911), pp. 59–60.

42. Meessen, p. 153.

43. Compare Elmar Bötcher, *Goethes Singspiele "Erwin und Elmire" und "Claudine von Villa Bella" und die "opera buffa"* (Marburg, 1912), p. 63.

44. See Albert Jansen, *Jean-Jacques Rousseau als Musiker* (Berlin, 1884), pp. 158–187; Max Friedländer, "Goethe und die Musik," *JbGG*, 3 (1916):280–281; Robert Petsch, "Einleitung" to *Proserpina, Goethes Werke*, Festausgabe (Leipzig, 1926–1927), 8:192; Hans Joachim Moser, *Goethe und die Musik* (Leipzig, 1949), p. 20; Ernst Beutler, "Corona Schröter," *Essays um Goethe*, 6th ed. (Bremen, 1957), p. 477; and Wolfgang Kayser, "Anmerkungen" to *Proserpina, Goethes Werke* (Hamburg, 1948–1960), 4:596.

45. Albert W. Aron, "The Mature Goethe and Rousseau," *JEGP*, 35 (1936): 180; cited below as Aron.

46. R. M. Browning, "The Humanity of Goethe's *Iphigenie*," *GQ*, 30 (1957): 98, 110–112.

47. Lester G. Crocker, "*Julie* ou la nouvelle duplicité," *AJJR*, 26 (1963–1965):152.

48. Edmond Vermeil, "*La Nouvelle Héloïse* et son influence sur l'œuvre de Goethe," *Goethe et l'esprit français: Actes du Colloque International de Strasbourg, 23–27 Avril 1957* (Paris, 1958), p. 63.

49. Recorded by Eckermann, May 6, 1827 (G.A., 24 [*Gespräche mit Goethe*]: 635).

50. Paola Ambri Berselli, "Influences italiennes sur *La Nouvelle Héloïse*," *AJJR*, 32 (1950–1952):156–162.

51. James Sime, *The Life of Johann Wolfgang Goethe* (London, n.d.), p. 124.

52. Valentin Brunet, *L'Influence de Rousseau sur les idées politiques et sur la sentimentalité de Goethe* (Toulouse, 1932), p. 43; page references hereafter in text.

53. Ernst Jockers, "Soziale Polarität in Goethes Klassik," *Mit Goethe: Gesammelte Aufsätze* (Heidelberg, 1957), p. 71.

54. Certain aspects of Goethe's greatest "Revolutionsdichtung," the idyllic epic *Hermann und Dorothea*, are discussed in the last two chapters.

55. Hugo von Hofmannsthal, "Wilhelm Meister in der Urform," *Corona*, 1 (1930):633–641.

56. Madeleine B. Ellis, *Julie ou La Nouvelle Héloïse: A Synthesis of Rousseau's Thought (1749–1759)* (Toronto, 1949).

57. Melitta Gerhard, *Der deutsche Entwicklungsroman bis zu Goethes "Wilhelm Meister"* (Halle, 1926), p. 125.

58. Benrubi, p. 447.

59. Henri Lichtenberger, *Goethe* (Paris, 1937), 2:152.

60. Ronald Gray, *Goethe: A Critical Introduction* (Cambridge, Eng., 1967), p. 186.

61. Benrubi, p. 447.

62. Vermeil, "Goethe et Rousseau," *AJJR*, 21 (1946–1949):65.

63. Rodolfo Mondolfo, *Rousseau e la coscienza moderna* (Florence, 1954), p. 13.

64. W. H. Bruford, "Goethe's *Wilhelm Meister* as a Picture and as a Criticism of Society," *PEGS*, n.s., 9 (1933):28.

65. Benrubi, pp. 447–448.
66. George Santayana, *Three Philosophical Poets: Lucretius, Dante and Goethe* (Cambridge, Mass., 1910), p. 154.
67. Benrubi, pp. 448–449.
68. See Werner Kohlschmidt, "Rousseau und Goethe," *Zeitschrift für den deutschen Unterricht*, 18 (1904):139–140.
69. Original of *Faust* quotation:

> Werd' ich zum Augenblicke sagen:
> Verweile doch! du bist so schön!
> (ll. 1699–1700);

source of passage from *Rêveries du promeneur solitaire*, O.C., 16:348. Compare Martha Langkavel, "Eine Parallelstelle zu den Worten der Wette des Goetheschen Faust mit Mephisto," *Archiv*, 3 (1904):156; Aron, p. 182; Benjamin Woodbridge, "Rousseau and Faust," *MLN*, 55 (1940):582–583; and Maurice Bémol, "Goethe, Rousseau et Faust," *EG*, 13 (1958):4–9.

IV MEMORIES AND MEMOIRS

1. Rudolf Lehmann, "*Anton Reiser* und die Entstehung des *Wilhelm Meister*," *JbGG*, 3 (1916):123.
2. Marcel Raymond, "J.-J. Rousseau: Deux aspects de sa vie intérieure (intermittence et permanence du 'moi')," *AJJR*, 29 (1941–1942):50–51. Compare Raymond's book, *Jean-Jacques Rousseau: La quête de soi et la rêverie* (Paris, 1962), esp. pp. 13–75.
3. Gustav von Loeper, "Einleitung" to *Dichtung und Wahrheit, Goethes Werke*, Hempel-Ausgabe (Berlin, n.d., 23:xxxv–xxxvi.
4. Richard M. Meyer, "Einleitung" to *Dichtung und Wahrheit, Goethes Werke*, Jubiläums-Ausgabe (Stuttgart, 1902–1912) 21:xvii; cited below as Richard M. Meyer.
5. Karl Alt, *Studien zur Entstehungsgeschichte von Goethes "Dichtung und Wahrheit"* (Munich, 1898), p. 41.
6. Kurt Jahn, *Goethes "Dichtung und Wahrheit"* (Halle, 1908), pp. 119–120.
7. "Famous Autobiographies," *Edinburgh Review*, 214 (1911):331–356.
8. Martin Sommerfeld, "Jean-Jacques Rousseaus Bekenntnisse und Goethes Dichtung und Wahrheit," *Goethe in Umwelt und Folgezeit* (Leiden, 1935), pp. 10–12.
9. Arthur Franz, "Die literarische Porträtzeichnung in Goethes *Dichtung und Wahrheit* und in Rousseaus *Confessions*," *DVLG*, 6 (1928):507–509.
10. Ewald A. Boucke, "Einleitung" to *Dichtung und Wahrheit, Goethes Werke*, Festausgabe (Leipzig, 1926–1927), 15:53.
11. Hippolyte Loiseau, *Goethe et la France: ce qu'il en a connu, pensé et dit* (Paris, 1930), pp. 345–346.
12. Ernst Beutler, "Einleitung" to *Dichtung und Wahrheit, Goethes Werke*, Gedenkausgabe (Zurich, 1948–1954), 10:891–892.
13. Roy Pascal, "Goethe's Autobiography and Rousseau's *Confessions*," *Studies in French Language and Literature, Presented to R. L. Graeme Ritchie* (Cambridge, Eng., 1949), pp. 147–162; page references hereafter in text.
14. Gustav Roethe, "Dichtung und Wahrheit," *Goethe: Gesammelte Vorträge und Aufsätze* (Berlin, 1932), p. 5.
15. Friedrich Hiebel, *Goethe: Die Erhöhung des Menschen* (Bern, 1961), pp. 12–13.
16. Édouard Rod, *Essai sur Goethe* (Paris, 1898), pp. 22, 40.
17. Albert Cahen, "La vie," *Jean-Jacques Rousseau: Leçons faites à l'École des*

Hautes Études (Paris, 1912), p. 12. In contrast to all predecessors among autobiographers (including Rousseau), Goethe, in the opinion of Emil Staiger, makes the hero of *Dichtung und Wahrheit*—not the book itself—appear as an organic and consistently developed work of art (*Goethe* [Zurich, 1952–1956], 3:254).

18. Compare Ernst Beutler, "Einleitung" to *Annalen, Goethes Werke*, Gedenkausgabe (Zurich, 1948–1954), 15:1027–1028.

19. François Jost, *Jean-Jacques Rousseau Suisse* (Fribourg, 1961), 1:5; page references hereafter in text.

20. Friedrich Maschek, "Goethes Reisen," Part 2, *Fünfzehnter Jahres-Bericht der k.k. Staatsmusikhochschule in Reichenberg* (Reichenberg, 1887), p. 3.

21. René Michéa, *Le "Voyage en Italie" de Goethe* (Paris, 1945), p. 19; page references hereafter in text.

22. Eugène Ritter, "Les douze métiers de Jean-Jacques," *AJJR*, 11 (1916–1917):17–24. Rousseau's intensive study of chemistry is emphasized by Maurice Gautier, editor of "Les *Institutions chymiques* de Jean-Jacques Rousseau," *AJJR*, 12 (1918–1919):iii–xxiii, 1–164; and 13 (1920–1921): 1–118.

23. Léon Herrmann, "Jean-Jacques Rousseau Traducteur de Sénèque," *AJJR*, 13 (1920–1921):215–224.

24. I. Grünberg, "Rousseau joueur d'échecs," *AJJR*, 3 (1907):157–174.

25. To cite a minor example of related experiences, Rousseau's account of hearing a retired "chevalier de Saint-Louis" pretend acquaintance with the *Devin du village* and its author (O.C., 15:164) finds a parallel in Goethe's description of a retired "Ludwigsritter" at Strassburg, "one of the many to whom life yields no results" (W.A. I, 27:263). Furthermore, by an interesting coincidence the "Wirtshaus zum Geist," where Goethe put up on arriving in Strassburg, was the very inn at which Rousseau had stopped some five years earlier.

26. Alexis François, "Les provincialismes suisses-romands et savoyards de Jean-Jacques Rousseau," *AJJR*, 3 (1907):1–67.

27. Eugène Ritter, *La Famille et la jeunesse de Rousseau* (Paris, 1896), pp. 293–296.

28. See my article, "Goethe, Prévost, and Louisiana," *MLQ*, 16 (1955):232–238.

29. Henry H. H. Remak, "Goethes Gretchenabenteuer und Manon Lescaut: Dichtung oder Wahrheit?" *Formen der Darstellung: Festgabe für Fritz Neubert* (Berlin, 1956), pp. 394–395.

30. Compare William H. Blanchard, *Rousseau and the Spirit of Revolt* (Ann Arbor, 1967).

31. See Richard M. Meyer, p. xiii.

32. E.g., Eduard von der Hellen, "Stackelberg bei Goethe, 1829," *GJb*, 13 (1892):91.

33. Günter Schulz, "Der ländliche Wesenszug des jungen Goethe," *Goethe*, 5 (1940):115–117.

34. Lawrence M. Price, "Goldsmith, Sesenheim, and Goethe," *GR*, 4 (1929):238.

35. See my article, "Goethe's Estimate of Oliver Goldsmith," *JEGP*, 44 (1945):131–138.

36. Compare my monograph *Goethes "Dichtung und Wahrheit,"* 7. Buch—Literaturgeschichte oder Bildungserlebnis? ISLL, 30, No. 1 (Urbana, 1945), especially pp. 9, 39–41, 64–66.

37. See Jean de Pange, "Les voyages de Herder en France," *EG*, 2 (1947):51.

38. Henri Peyre, *Literature and Sincerity* (New Haven, 1963), p. 80; page references hereafter in text.

39. Madeleine B. Ellis, *Rousseau's Venetian Story: An Essay upon Art and Truth in "Les Confessions"* (Baltimore, 1966), pp. viii, 32; cited hereafter as Ellis.

40. Compare Mark J. Temmer, "Art and Love in the Confessions of Jean-Jacques Rousseau," *PMLA*, 73 (1958):215–220.
41. Georg Witkowski, *Goethe*, 2nd ed. (Leipzig, 1912), pp. 140–141.
42. Ellis, p. viii.
43. Jürg Fierz, *Goethes Porträtierungskunst in "Dichtung und Wahrheit"* (Frauenfeld, 1945), p. 11.
44. Sir John Morley, *Rousseau* (London, 1886), 1:63. (The first edition appeared in 1873.)
45. Compare, for instance, Adriana Petronella Roose, *Het karakter van Jean-Jacques Rousseau* (Groningen, 1919), pp. 50–51.
46. The passage quoted is from *Egmont*, Act II (W.A. I, 8:220).

V OF LOVE AND MARRIAGE

1. Martin Sommerfeld, "Goethes Wahlverwandtschaften im neunzehnten Jahrhundert," in *Goethe in Umwelt und Folgezeit* (Leiden, 1935), p. 209.
2. Compare Heinrich Meyer, *Goethe: Das Leben im Werk* (Hamburg-Bergedorf, 1949), p. 533; cited below as Heinrich Meyer.
3. E.g., Peter Ammann, *Schicksal und Liebe in Goethes "Wahlverwandtschaften"* (Bern, 1962); H. G. Barnes, *Goethe's "Die Wahlverwandtschaften"* (Oxford, 1967); Humphrey Trevelyan, "Goethe's Wahlverwandtschaften," *The Gate*, 1 (1949):13–22. By contrast, Thomas Mann relates one of Ottilie's educational ideas to Rousseau. See "Goethes Laufbahn als Schriftsteller," *Leiden und Grösse der Meister* (Berlin, 1935), p. 62.
4. Compare Edith Aulhorn, "Der Aufbau von Goethes Wahlverwandtschaften," *Zeitschrift für den deutschen Unterricht*, 33 (1918):337–355. Benedetto Croce calls *Die Wahlverwandtschaften* a drama (*Goethe*, Bari, 1939, p. 113). The "modernity" of this novel is stressed by Ernst Barthel (*Goethes Wissenschaftslehre in ihrer modernen Tragweite*, Bonn, 1922, p. 252).
5. Otto Harnack, "Briefe von und an Wilhelm von Humboldt," *Biographische Blätter*, 2 (1896):52–71.
6. See Heinrich Meyer, pp. 534–568, where the poet's infatuation with Silvie von Ziegesar is set forth with convincing detail.
7. Max Morris, "Über die Quelle der Wahlverwandtschaften," in *Goethe-Studien* (Berlin, 1897), pp. 129–130.
8. Erich Schmidt, *Richardson, Rousseau und Goethe* (Jena, 1875), pp. 167–168.
9. Friedrich Lienhard, "Goethes Elsass," *JbGG*, 7 (1920):291.
10. August Vetter, "Wahlverwandtschaft," *JbGG*, 17 (1931):98–113.
11. Paul Stöcklein suggests that Goethe objectifies certain phases of his own character in Eduard. The tendency to yield to all one's impulses as utterances of nature is seen as Rousseauesque ("Einleitung" to *Die Wahlverwandtschaften*, Goethes Werke, Gedenkausgabe, Zurich, 1949, 9:696).
12. Albert W. Aron, "The Mature Goethe and Rousseau," *JEGP*, 35 (1936):170–182.
13. Hanna Fischer-Lamberg, "Frau von Stein—ein 'Bildungserlebnis' Goethes," *DVLG*, 15 (1937):385–402.
14. In his article, "Goethes Polaritätsidee und die Wahlverwandtschaften," *PMLA*, 58 (1939):1105–1123, Hubert J. Meessen stresses the author's fondness for juxtaposing "Gefühls- und Verstandesmenschen" in his works (p. 1108). Rousseau did likewise in his novel; e.g., Saint-Preux and Wolmar (also Bomston), Julie and Claire.
15. André François-Poncet, *Les "Affinités électives" de Goethe* (Paris, 1910), p. 73.

16. E.g., Albert Bielschowsky, *Goethe: Sein Leben und seine Werke* (Munich, 1928), 2:275, 290; Christian Semler, *Goethes "Wahlverwandtschaften" und die sittliche Weltanschauung des Dichters* (Hamburg, 1887), pp. 32–33; and Oskar Walzel's article, "Goethes Wahlverwandtschaften im Rahmen ihrer Zeit," *GJb*, 27 (1906):166–205. See, however, Walzel's commentary in his "Einleitung to *Die Wahlverwandtschaften*," *Goethes Werke*, Festausgabe (Leipzig, 1926–1927), 13: 7–10, where he emphasizes Goethe's own great love for Ottilie, his fondest creation. Julie was, of course, Rousseau's favorite character.

17. Hans Reiss, *Goethes Romane* (Bern, 1963), p. 169.

18. John Morley, *Rousseau* (London, 1873), 2:29–30.

19. Paul Hankamer, *Spiel der Mächte: Ein Kapitel aus Goethes Leben und Goethes Welt* (Tübingen, 1947), pp. 1–3. What Goethe called "das Dämonische" figures prominently in Hankamer's book. See also Humphrey Trevelyan, "Goethe's Awareness of the Unconscious and the Elemental," *The Gate*, 1 (1947):28–36.

20. Hans M. Wolff, *Goethe in der Periode der "Wahlverwandtschaften,"* 1802–1809 (Bern, 1952), pp. 211–212.

21. Compare E. L. Stahl, *"Die Wahlverwandtschaften,"* PEGS, n.s., 15 (1946): 85.

22. Romain Rolland, ed., *Living Thoughts of Rousseau*. Trans. Julie Kernan (Philadelphia, 1939), p. 28.

23. Compare Heinrich Meyer, p. 567.

24. See my article, "Goethe and Marianne—After the *Divan*," *SCB*, 28 (1968): 134–138; also, the concluding paragraphs of Albert Fuchs' essay, "Le *West-östliche Divan*: Livre de l'amour," *PEGS*, n.s., 22 (1952–1953):1–30.

25. Hans-J. Weitz, ed., *Briefwechsel Goethe-Willemer* (Frankfurt/Main, 1965), p. 871.

VI IDEALS OF CULTURE

1. Josef Rattner, *Grosse Pädagogen* (Munich, 1956), p. 69.

2. E.g., Kurt Jahn, *Goethes "Dichtung und Wahrheit"* (Halle, 1908), p. 118; Felix Steinmetz, *Die pädagogischen Grundgedanken in Goethes Werken* (Greifswald, 1910), p. 4; Ludwig Kiehn, *Goethes Begriff der Bildung* (Hamburg, 1932), p. 194.

3. Rudolf Lehmann, "Goethe und das Problem der Erziehung," *JbGG*, 4 (1917):42–58.

4. Elisabeth Caspers, *Goethes pädagogische Grundanschauungen im Verhältnis zu Rousseau* (Langensalza, 1922).

5. For Müller's review, see *AJJR*, 16 (1924–1925):251–252.

6. Oskar Walzel, "Einleitung" to *Wilhelm Meisters Wanderjahre*, *Goethes Werke*, Festausgabe (Leipzig, 1926–1927), 12:21.

7. E.g., by Fester, *Rousseau und die deutsche Geschichtsphilosophie* (Leipzig, 1890), pp. 151–152, and Eduard Spranger, *Pestalozzis Denkformen* (Stuttgart, 1947), p. 3, passim.

8. "Zu den Wanderjahren," *GJb*, 26 (1905):275–276.

9. E. L. Stahl, "Goethe as Novelist," *Essays on Goethe*, ed. William Rose (London, 1949), p. 62.

10. August Raabe, "Das Dämonische in den Wanderjahren," *Goethe*, 1 (1936): 119–127.

11. Wilhelm Flitner, *Goethes pädagogische Ideen* (Godesberg, 1948), p. 7.

12. Compare Friedrich August Hüller, *Natur- und Gesellschaftsprinzip in Rousseaus Pädagogik* (Leipzig, 1898), pp. 1–3.

13. Émile Durkheim, "La 'Pédagogie' de Rousseau," *RMM*, 26 (1919):157.

14. Compare Paul Sakmann, *Jean-Jacques Rousseau* (Berlin, 1913), p. 46: ". . . Wolmar und Julie sind auch Mustererzieher." Sakmann then suggests that the discussion of educational principles in *La Nouvelle Héloïse*—a "Vorstudie" of *Émile*—was originally intended as the introduction to a special part of the novel which would have corresponded to the Pedagogical Province in *Wilhelm Meisters Wanderjahre* (p. 46).

15. Karl Muthesius, *Goethe ein Kinderfreund*, 2nd ed. (Berlin, 1910), pp. 23–24. Compare Adolf Langguth, *Goethe als Pädagog* (Halle, 1887), p. 5.

16. Arnold Bork, *Goethe der Jugendbildner* (Berlin, 1947), p. 133. How closely Charlotte associated Goethe with Rousseau seems apparent from the fact that on a trip to visit Fritz in Breslau she read *Faust* and the *Confessions*. See Wilhelm Bode, *Charlotte von Stein* (Berlin, 1910), p. 471.

17. Barker Fairley, *A Study of Goethe* (Oxford, 1947), pp. 49–50.

18. Compare Joseph Fabre, *Les Pères de la Révolution* (Paris, 1910), pp. 320–322.

19. *Maximen und Reflexionen*, ed. Max Hecker, Schriften der Goethe-Gesellschaft, No. 21 (Weimar, 1907), p. 126; cited below as *Maximen und Reflexionen*.

20. See Carl Diem, *Körpererziehung bei Goethe* (Frankfurt, 1948), p. 105, passim.

21. Compare Arthur Hoffmann, *Werktätiges Leben im Geiste Goethes* (Weimar, 1950), especially pp. 126–128.

22. See Albert W. Aron, "The Mature Goethe and Rousseau," *JEGP*, 35 (1936):181.

23. *Maximen und Reflexionen*, p. 107.

24. In *Die Wahlverwandtschaften* we read that the girls who are destined later to assume a guiding position in the household and to be mainly dependent on themselves must be trained for their truest, most natural calling: to bring up children and to be housewives (W.A. I, 20:283–284). "Is there a sight in the world," Rousseau asks in his *Lettre à M. d'Alembert*, "as touching, as worthy of respect, as that of a mother of a family, surrounded by her children, directing the work of her servants, making a happy life for her husband, and wisely ruling the household? It is there that she appears in all the dignity of an upright woman; it is there that she truly inspires respect and beauty shares with honor the homage rendered to virtue" (O.C., 2:122). How thoroughly Goethe is in accord with these sentiments is manifest from his descriptions of his mother; from his characters modeled after her, e.g., Frau Elisabeth in *Götz von Berlichingen* and the mother in *Hermann und Dorothea*; and from some of his letters to his wife, Christiane.

25. *Émile*, V, Garnier edition (Paris, n.d.), p. 605. Cf. Léon Émery, "Rousseau and the Foundations of Human Regeneration," *YFS*, 28 (1962):6–7.

VII UTOPIAN VISIONS

1. Albert Meynier, *Jean-Jacques Rousseau révolutionnaire* (Paris, 1910), p. 77, passim.

2. Edme Champion, *J.-J. Rousseau et la Révolution Française* (Paris, 1909), pp. vii–viii; page references hereafter in text. For a recent, balanced account of the entire controversy, see Joan McDonald, *Rousseau and the French Revolution, 1762–1791* (London, 1965).

3. Frank H. Reinsch, *Goethe's Political Interests prior to 1787*, UCPMP, Vol. 10, No. 3 (Berkeley and Los Angeles, 1923), pp. 273–276, passim. Compare Rudolf Alexander Schröder, "Das politische Weltbild im Werk und Leben Goethes," *Goethe-Kalender auf das Jahr 1934*, ed. Ernst Beutler (Leipzig, 1933), pp. 121–131; cited below as Schröder.

4. Eberhard Sauer, "Goethe und die französische Revolution," *Jahrbuch des Freien Deutschen Hochstifts* (Frankfurt, 1913), p. 173.

5. Edward Dowden, "Goethe and the French Revolution," *PEGS*, 5 (1889): 10.

6. Compare G. P. Gooch, "The Political Background of Goethe's Life," *PEGS*, n.s., 3 (1924):7.

7. Adolphus William Ward, "Goethe and the French Revolution," *PEGS*, 14 (1912):5–7.

8. Melitta Gerhard, "Chaos und Kosmos in Goethes *Hermann und Dorothea*," *Monatshefte*, 34 (1942):415–424. Compare Pierre-Paul Sagave, "Französische Politik in deutscher Dichtung," *Jahresring 64/65* (Stuttgart, 1964), pp. 269–280.

9. Hans Joachim Schrimpf, *Das Weltbild des späten Goethe* (Stuttgart, 1956), p. 7.

10. Karl Rosenkranz, *Goethe und seine Werke*, 2nd ed. (Königsberg, 1856), p. 404.

11. Deli Fischer-Hartmann, *Goethes Altersroman: Studien über die innere Einheit von "Wilhelm Meisters Wanderjahren"* (Halle, 1941), pp. 7–14.

12. Ferdinand Gregorovius, *Goethes "Wilhelm Meister" in seinen sozialistischen Elementen*, 2nd ed. (Schwäbisch Hall, 1855), pp. 96–97, *passim*; cited below as Gregorovius.

13. For a typical example of such views, see Otto Harnack, *Goethe in der Epoche seiner Vollendung, 1805–1832*, 3rd ed. (Leipzig, 1905), pp. 274–275.

14. Arnold Bergstraesser, *Goethe's Image of Man and Society* (Chicago, 1949); page references hereafter in text.

15. Wilhelm Mommsen, *Die politischen Anschauungen Goethes* (Stuttgart, 1948), p. 24; cited below as Mommsen. Compare Gertrud Schubart-Fikentscher, *Goethes sechsundfünfzig Strassburger Thesen vom 6. August 1771* (Weimar, 1949), pp. 39–40.

16. Charles Edwyn Vaughan, *The Political Writings of Jean-Jacques Rousseau* (Cambridge, Eng., 1915), 2:4.

17. For conflicting views in this regard, see John S. Spink, *J.-J. Rousseau et Genève* (Paris, 1934), pp. 89–90; Gaspard Vallette, *J.-J. Rousseau, Génevois* (Paris, 1911), pp. 176 and 434–450; and Guglielmo Ferrero, "Genève et le *Contrat social*," *AJJR*, 14 (1934):137–152. Whereas Spink tends to minimize the Genevan influence, Vallette and Ferrero strongly emphasize it. Moreover, Ferrero calls Geneva "an aristocratic republic." Rousseau is characterized as a Genevan rather than a Swiss by Georges-Paul Collet in his article, "Jean-Jacques Rousseau et Genève," *Symposium*, 18 (1964):79–89. The opposite standpoint is convincingly and exhaustively presented by François Jost in his two-volume work, *Jean-Jacques Rousseau Suisse* (Fribourg, 1961), previously cited with reference to Goethe and his interest in Rousseau.

18. Compare Friedrich Bothe, *Goethe und seine Vaterstadt Frankfurt* (Frankfurt, 1948), p. 9, *passim*; Mommsen, pp. 21–23.

19. *Amtliche Schriften: Goethes Tätigkeit im Geheimen Consilium, I* (1776–1786), ed. Willi Flach (Weimar, 1950). See also Joseph A. von Bradish, *Goethes Beamtenlaufbahn* (New York, 1937). Those who wonder how Goethe's devotion to Karl August can be reconciled with the ideas of Rousseau, should read the latter's funeral oration for the Duke of Orléans, eloquent in its praise of that prince (*O.C.*, 1:393–414).

20. *Correspondance générale*, ed. Théophile Dufour and Paul-Pierre Plan (Paris, 1924–1934), 8:224; cited below as *Correspondance générale*.

21. See Alfred G. Steer, *Goethe's Social Philosophy as Revealed in "Campagne in Frankreich" and "Belagerung von Mainz,"* UNCSGLL, No. 15 (Chapel Hill, 1955), p. 148; cited below as Steer.

22. Compare Henri Sée, *Economic and Social Conditions in France during the*

Eighteenth Century, trans. Edwin H. Zeydel (New York, 1927), p. 54; also, C. A. Fusil, *L'Anti-Rousseau ou les Égarements du coeur et de l'esprit* (Paris, 1929). Fusil considers Rousseau's economics better than his pedagogy (p. 87).

23. See Gilbert Chinard, *L'Amérique et le rêve exotique dans la littérature française au XVIIᵉ et au XVIIIᵉ siècle* (Paris, 1934), pp. 341–358.

24. *Correspondance générale*, 13:115–116.

25. Compare Steer, esp. pp. 9–20, 69–71, 165–168.

26. Gregorovius, p. 104.

27. Alexander Jung, *Goethes "Wanderjahre" und die wichtigsten Fragen des 19. Jahrhunderts* (Mainz, 1854), p. 54.

28. See Lester G. Crocker, *An Age of Crisis: Man and World in Eighteenth-Century French Thought* (Baltimore, 1959), p. 251.

29. Steer, pp. 69–70. Compare Schröder, pp. 129–130. See also Johann Georg Sprengel, *Der Staatsgedanke in der deutschen Dichtung vom Mittelalter bis zur Gegenwart* (Berlin, 1953), pp. 225–226.

VIII GOD, MAN, AND COSMOS

1. Compare Gaston Graul, "Über Goethe, den kosmischen Menschen," *JbGG*, 8 (1921):23.

2. Henri Peyre, "Religion and Literary Scholarship in France," *PMLA*, 77 (1962):355; page references hereafter in text.

3. Pierre-Maurice Masson, *La Religion de J.-J. Rousseau* (Paris, 1916); page references hereafter in text.

4. Albert Schinz, *La Pensée religieuse de Rousseau et ses récents interprètes* (Paris, 1927).

5. Erich Franz, *Goethe als religiöser Denker* (Tübingen, 1932); page references hereafter in text.

6. Franz Koch, *Goethes Stellung zu Tod und Unsterblichkeit* (Weimar, 1932); cited below as Koch.

7. Wilhelm Flitner, *Goethe im Spätwerk: Glaube, Weltsicht, Ethos* (Hamburg, 1947); page references hereafter in text.

8. Robert Hering, *Wilhelm Meister und Faust und ihre Gestaltung im Zeichen der Gottesidee* (Frankfurt, 1952).

9. Gustave Lanson, "L'Unité de la pensée de J.-J. Rousseau," *AJJR*, 8 (1912): 1–32.

10. Ernst Cassirer, *The Question of Jean-Jacques Rousseau*, trans. Peter Gay (Bloomington, Ind., 1963), p. 35.

11. Robert Dérathé, *Le Rationalisme de J.-J. Rousseau* (Paris, 1948). Dérathé concludes that Rousseau's rationalism is a matter of relativism (p. 176).

12. Ferdinand Weinhandl, *Die Metaphysik Goethes* (Darmstadt, 1965).

13. Bruno Bauch, *Goethe und die Philosophie*, Philosophie und Geschichte, No. 20 (Tübingen, 1928), p. 3.

14. Kurt Rossmann, "Goethe und der Geist der französischen Philosophie," *Goethe et l'esprit français*, ed. Albert Fuchs (Paris, 1958), pp. 207–208.

15. Compare Ronald Grimsley, *Rousseau and the Religious Quest* (Oxford, 1968), pp. 1–2; page references hereafter in text.

16. See Hans von Schubert, *Goethes religiöse Jugendentwicklung* (Leipzig, 1925), pp. 20–25; page references hereafter in text.

17. Eugène Ritter, *La Famille et la jeunesse de Rousseau* (Paris, 1896), pp. 243–244; also Philippe Godet, *Histoire littéraire de la Suisse Française* (Paris, 1890), p. 201.

18. Compare François Mugnier, *Madame de Warens et J.-J. Rousseau* (Paris,

n.d.), pp. 22–23. Mugnier tends to minimize the importance of Magny's influence.

19. For a discussion of varying opinions, see Roger D. Masters, *The Political Philosophy of Rousseau* (Princeton, 1968), pp. 54–73.

20. D. Parodi, "Des idées religieuses de Rousseau," *RMM*, 9 (1912):124.

21. Robert d'Harcourt, *La Religion de Goethe* (Paris, 1949), p. 73.

22. Otto Vossler, *Rousseaus Freiheitslehre* (Göttingen, 1963), p. 352.

23. Charles W. Hendel, *Jean-Jacques Rousseau, Moralist* (London, 1934), 1:231 and 243.

24. Pierre Burgelin, *La Philosophie de l'existence de J.-J. Rousseau* (Paris, 1952), pp. 444–445.

25. Robert Hering, *Spinoza im jungen Goethe* (Leipzig, 1897), pp. 11–12.

26. See O. Guinadeau, "Les Rapports de Goethe et de Lavater," *EG*, 4 (1949):214.

27. *Maximen und Reflexionen*, ed. Max Hecker, Schriften der Goethe-Gesellschaft, No. 21 (Weimar, 1907), p. 179.

28. Compare Koch, pp. 280–282.

29. Konrad Burdach, "Einleitung" to *West-östlicher Divan*, Goethes sämtliche Werke, Jubiläums-Ausgabe (Stuttgart, 1902–1912), 5:xxxiii.

30. Albert Fuchs, "Der West-östliche Divan als Buch der Liebe," *Goethe-Studien* (Berlin, 1968), pp. 82–96.

31. See Goethes Werke, Hamburger Ausgabe, ed. Erich Trunz et al. (Hamburg, 1948–1960), 3:534, for note (by Trunz) on this passage from *Faust*.

32. Harold Jantz, *The Mothers in "Faust": The Myth of Time and Creativity* (Baltimore, 1969), pp. 31–46.

33. Maurice Bémol, "Goethe, Rousseau et Faust," *EG*, 13 (1958):14–15; page references hereafter in text.

34. See Julius Schiff, "Mignon, Ottilie, Makarie im Lichte der Goetheschen Naturphilosophie," *JbGG*, 9 (1922):133–147.

35. Compare Hering, *Faust und Meister*, p. 443.

Selected Bibliography

I. WORKS, CORRESPONDENCE, CONVERSATIONS

A. Goethe.

Goethe, Johann Wolfgang von. *Amtliche Schriften: Goethes Tätigkeit im Geheimen Consilium, I* (1776–1786). Ed. Willy Flach. Weimar: H. Böhlaus Nachfolger, 1950.

———. *Botanical Writings*. Trans. Bertha Mueller. Honolulu: University of Hawaii Press, 1952.

———. *Der junge Goethe*. Ed. Max Morris. 6 vols. Leipzig: Inselverlag, 1909–1912; new rev. ed., ed. Hanna Fischer-Lamberg. 5 vols. Berlin: de Gruyter, 1963–1969.

———. *Der Rokoko-Goethe*. Ed. Heinz Kindermann. Deutsche Literatur in Entwicklungsreihen, Reihe Irrationalismus. Vol. 2. Leipzig: Reclam, 1932.

———. *Maximen und Reflexionen*. Ed Max Hecker. Schriften der Goethe-Gesellschaft, No. 21. Weimar: Verlag der Goethe-Gesellschaft, 1907.

———. *Romans*. Bibliothèque de la Pléiade, No. 103. Trans. Bernard Groethuysen. Paris: Colombier & Brod, 1954.

———. *Werke*. Festausgabe. Ed. Robert Petsch et al. 13 vols. Leipzig: Bibliographisches Institut, 1926–1927.

———. *Werke*. Gedenkausgabe. Ed. Ernst Beutler et al. 24 vols. Zurich: Artemis-Verlag, 1949–1960.

———. *Werke*. Hamburger Ausgabe. Ed. Erich Trunz et al. 14 vols. Hamburg: Wegener, 1948–1960; *Briefe*. Ed. Karl Robert Mandelkow et al. 4 vols. 1966–1967.

———. *Werke*. Hempel-Ausgabe. Ed. Woldemar von Biedermann et al. 23 vols. Berlin: Hempel, 1868–1879.

———. *Werke*. Jubiläums-Ausgabe. Ed. Eduard von der Hellen et al. 40 vols. Stuttgart: Cotta, 1902–1904.

———. *Werke*. Weimarer Ausgabe. Weimar: Böhlau, 1887–1919. In four sections: I. *Werke*, 55 vols.; II. *Naturwissenschaftliche Schriften*, 13 vols.; III. *Tagebücher*, 15 vols.; IV. *Briefe*, 50 vols.

Biedermann, Flodoard von, ed. *Goethes Gespräche*. 5 vols. Leipzig: Biedermann, 1909–1911; revised as *Goethe: Begegnungen und Gespräche*, ed. Ernst Grumach and Renate Grumach, Vol. 1 (1749–1776). Berlin: de Gruyter, 1956; Vol. 2 (1777–1785), 1966.

Bode, Wilhelm, ed. *Goethe in vertraulichen Briefen seiner Zeitgenossen*. 3 vols. Berlin: Mittler, 1921.

Bradish, Joseph A. von. *Goethes Beamtenlaufbahn*. New York: Westermann, 1937.

Burkhardt, C. A., ed. *Goethes Unterhaltungen mit Kanzler Friedrich von Müller*. 2nd ed. Stuttgart: Cotta, 1898.

Eckermann, Johann Peter. *Gespräche mit Goethe in den letzten Jahren seines Lebens*. Ed. H. H. Houben, 8th original edition. Leipzig: Brockhaus, 1909.

Gräf, Hans Gerhard. *Goethe über seine Dichtungen*. 9 vols. Frankfurt/Main: Rütten & Loening, 1901–1914.

Soret, Frédéric. *Zehn Jahre bei Goethe*. Trans. H. H. Houben. Leipzig: Brockhaus, 1929.

B. Rousseau.

Rousseau, Jean-Jacques. *Œuvres complètes*. Ed. V. D. Musset-Pathay. 25 vols. Paris: Dupont, 1823–1826.

————. *Discours sur les Sciences et les Arts*. Ed. George R. Havens. New MLA Monograph Ser., No. 15, 1946.

————. *Kulturideale: Eine Zusammenstellung aus seinen Werken*. Trans. Hedwig Jahn. Jena: Diederichs, 1922.

————. *La Nouvelle Héloïse*. Nouvelle édition publiée d'après les manuscrits et les éditions originales avec des variantes, une introduction, des notices et des notes, par Daniel Mornet. 4 vols. Paris: Hachette, 1925.

————. *Les Rêveries du Promeneur solitaire*. Édition critique publiée d'après les manuscrits autographes par John S. Spink. Paris: Didier, 1948.

————. *Living Thoughts of Rousseau*, presented by Romain Rolland. Trans. Julie Kernan. Philadelphia: McKay, 1939.

————. *Pages choisies*. Ed. S. Rocheblave. Paris: Colin, 1931.

————. *Selections from the Writings of Rousseau*. Ed. Christian Gauss. 2nd ed. Princeton: Princeton University Press, 1920.

————. *The Political Writings of Rousseau*. Ed. Charles Edwyn Vaughan. 2 vols. Cambridge, Eng.: Cambridge University Press, 1915.

————. *Correspondance générale*. Collationnée sur les manuscrits originaux, annotée et commentée par Théophile Dufour and Paul-Pierre Plan. 20 vols. Paris: Colin, 1924–1934.

Streckeisen-Moultou, G. *J. J. Rousseau. Ses amis et ses ennemis*. 2 vols. Paris: Calmann-Lévy, 1864.

II. Bibliographies

Baldensperger, Fernand. *Bibliographie critique de Goethe en France*. Paris: Hachette, 1907.

Betz, Louis P. *La Littérature comparée: Essai bibliographique*. Strassburg: Trübner, 1904.

Cabeen, David C., General Editor. *A Critical Bibliography of French Literature.* Vol. 4: "The Eighteenth Century," ed. George R. Havens and Donald F. Bond. Syracuse: Syracuse University Press, 1951.

Giraud, Jeanne. *Manuel de bibliographie littéraire pour les XVIe, XVIIe et XVIIIe siècles français* (1921–1935). Paris: Vrin, 1939.

Goedeke, Karl. *Grundriss zur Geschichte der deutschen Dichtung*, Vol. 4, Sects. ii–iv. Dresden: Ehlermann, 1910–1913.

Körner, Josef. *Bibliographisches Handbuch des deutschen Schrifttums.* 3rd ed. Bern: Francke, 1949.

Lanson, Gustave. *Manuel bibliographique de la littérature française moderne.* New, rev. ed. Paris: Hachette, 1931.

Oswald, Eugene. "Goethe in England and America: Bibliography." *PEGS*, Vol. 9 (1909).

Pyritz, Hans, et al., eds. *Goethe-Bibliographie.* 2 vols. Heidelberg: Winter, 1955–1968.

Schinz, Albert. *État présent des travaux sur J.-J. Rousseau.* New York: MLA, 1941.

Sénelier, Jean *Bibliographie générale des œuvres de J.-J. Rousseau.* Paris: Édition "Encyclopédie Française," 1950.

Spurlin, Paul M. "Jean-Jacques Rousseau." *A Critical Bibliography of French Literature.* Vol. 4, pp. 208–251. (See "Cabeen" above.)

III. Books

Alt, Carl. *Goethes "Dichtung und Wahrheit": Studien zur Entstehungsgeschichte.* Munich: Haushalter, 1898.

Altenberg, Paul. *Goethe: Versuch einer morphologischen Darstellung.* Berlin: Colloquium Verlagsgesellschaft, 1949.

Amman, Peter. *Schicksal und Liebe in Goethes "Wahlverwandtschaften,"* Basler Studien zur deutschen Sprache und Literatur, ed. Walter Muschg, No. 25. Bern: Francke, 1962.

Angelloz, Joseph-François. *Goethe.* Trans. R. H. Blackley. New York: Orion Press, 1958.

Arber, Agnes. *Natural History of Plant Form.* London: Cambridge University Press, 1950.

Arnim, Bettina von. *Goethes Briefwechsel mit einem Kinde.* 3 vols. Stuttgart: Spemann, n.d.

Atkins, Stuart P. *The Testament of Werther in Poetry and Drama.* Cambridge, Mass.: Harvard University Press, 1949.

Babbitt, Irving. *Rousseau and Romanticism.* Boston: Houghton Mifflin, 1919.

Badelt, Otto. *Das Rechts- und Staatsdenken Goethes.* Bonn: Bouvier, 1966.

Bäte, Ludwig. *Justus Möser: Advocatus patriae.* Frankfurt/Main: Athenäum Verlag, 1961.

Baldensperger, Fernand. *Goethe en France*. Paris: Hachette, 1904.

Barbey d'Aurevilly, Jules. *Goethe et Diderot*. Paris: Dentu, 1880.

Barnard, F. M. *Herder's Social and Political Thought*. Oxford: Clarendon Press, 1965.

Barnes, Bertram. *Goethe's Knowledge of French Literature*. Oxford: Clarendon Press, 1937.

Barnes, H. G. *Goethe's "Die Wahlverwandtschaften": A Literary Interpretation*. Oxford: Clarendon Press, 1967.

Barthel, Ernst. *Goethes Wissenschaftslehre in ihrer modernen Tragweite*. Bonn: Cohen, 1922.

Bauch, Bruno. *Goethe und die Philosophie*, Philosophie und Geschichte, No. 20. Tübingen: Möhr, 1928.

Bauer, Heinrich. *Jean-François Marmontel als Literarkritiker*. Diss. Leipzig. Dresden: Dittert, 1937.

Béguin, Albert. *L'Âme romantique et le rêve*. New ed. Paris: Corti, 1928.

Benjamin, Walter. *Goethes "Wahlverwandtschaften."* Frankfurt/Main: Insel-Verlag, 1955.

Benrubi, Isaak. *Rousseaus ethisches Ideal*. Langensalza: Beyer, 1905.

Berend, Eduard. *Jean-Paul und die Schweiz*. Frauenfeld: Huber, 1943.

Berendt, Hans. *Untersuchungen zur Entstehungsgeschichte von "Wilhelm Meisters theatralischer Sendung."* Diss. Bonn. Dortmund: Ruhfus, 1910.

Bergstraesser, Arnold. *Goethe's Image of Man and Society*. Chicago: Regnery, 1949.

——, ed. *Goethe and the Modern Age* (International Convocation, Aspen, Colorado, 1949). Chicago: Regnery, 1950.

Berthelot, René. *Science et philosophie chez Goethe*. Paris: Alcan, 1932.

Bertrand, Louis. *La Fin du classicisme et le retour à l'antique dans la seconde moitié du XVIIIe siècle et les premières années du XIXe siècle en France*. Paris: Hachette, 1897.

Beutler, Ernst. *Essays um Goethe*. 6th ed. Bremen: Schünemann, 1957.

Bielschowsky, Albert. *Goethe: Sein Leben und seine Werke*, rev. Walther Linden. 2 vols. Munich: Beck, 1928.

Black, Frank G. *The Epistolary Novel in the Late Eighteenth Century*, University of Oregon Studies in Literature and Philology, No. 2. Eugene, 1940.

Blanchard, William H. *Rousseau and the Spirit of Revolt: A Psychological Study*. Ann Arbor: University of Michigan Press, 1967.

Blaze de Bury, Ange Henri. *Les Maîtresses de Goethe*. Paris: Lévy, 1873.

Bode, Wilhelm. *Charlotte von Stein*. Berlin: Mittler, 1910.

——. *Die Franzosen und Engländer in Goethes Leben und Urteil*. Berlin: Mittler, 1915.

——. *Goethes Sohn*. Berlin: Mittler, 1910.

——. *Die Tonkunst in Goethes Leben*. 2 vols. Berlin: Mittler, 1912.

——. *Goethes Schweizer Reisen*. Leipzig: Haessel-Verlag, 1922.

194

Bodemann, Eduard. *Julie von Bondeli und ihr Freundeskreis.* Hanover: Hahn, 1874.

Bötcher, Elmar. *Goethes Singspiele "Erwin und Elmire" und "Claudine von Villa Bella" und die "opera buffa."* Marburg: Elwert, 1912.

Bollert, Martin. *Beiträge zu einer Lebensgeschichte von Franz Michael Leuchsenring.* Diss. Strassburg. Strassburg: Heitz, 1901.

Borcherdt, Hans Heinrich. *Der Roman der Goethezeit.* Stuttgart: Port-Verlag, 1949.

Bork, Arnold. *Goethe als Jugendbildner.* Berlin: Minerva-Verlag, 1947.

Boschann, Johannes. *Die Spontaneitätsidee bei J.-J. Rousseau.* Diss. Würzburg. Berlin: Ebering, 1928.

Bothe, Friedrich. *Goethe und seine Vaterstadt Frankfurt.* Frankfurt/Main: Kramer, 1948.

Boucher, Maurice. *La Révolution de 1789 vue par les écrivains allemands, ses contemporains.* Paris: Didier, 1954.

Boucke, Ewald A. *Wort und Bedeutung in Goethes Sprache.* Berlin: Felber, 1901.

Boy-Ed, Ida. *Das Martyrium der Charlotte von Stein: Versuch ihrer Rechtfertigung.* Stuttgart: Cotta, 1925.

Braemer, Edith. *Goethes Prometheus und die Grundpositionen des Sturm und Drang.* 3rd rev. ed. Berlin and Weimar: Aufbau-Verlag, 1968.

Brandes, Georg. *Main Currents in Nineteenth Century Literature.* 6 vols. New York: Macmillan, 1906.

Bréal, Michel. *Deux Études sur Goethe: Un Officier de l'ancienne France; Les Personnages originaux de la "Fille naturelle."* Paris: Hachette, 1898.

Brédif, L. *Du Caractère intellectuel et moral de Rousseau, étudié dans sa vie et ses écrits.* Paris: Hachette, 1906.

Brereton, George, ed. *French Thought in the Eighteenth Century: Rousseau—Voltaire—Diderot.* New York: McKay, 1953.

Bretonneau, Gisèle. *Valeurs humaines de J.-J. Rousseau.* Paris: La Colombe, 1961.

Brockerhoff, Ferdinand. *Jean-Jacques Rousseau: Sein Leben und seine Werke.* 3 vols. Leipzig: Wigand, 1863–1874.

Bruford, Walter H. *Theatre, Drama, and Audience in Goethe's Germany.* London: Routledge & Kegan Paul, 1950.

———. *Culture and Society in Classical Weimar (1775–1806).* Cambridge, Eng.: Cambridge University Press, 1962.

Brunet, Valentin. *L'Influence de Rousseau sur les idées politiques et sociales et sur la sentimentalité de Goethe.* Thèse complémentaire Toulouse. Toulouse: Imprimerie Régionale, 1932.

Buck, Rudolf. *Rousseau und die deutsche Romantik.* Berlin: Junker & Dünnhaupt, 1939.

Buffenoir, Hippolyte. *Les Charmettes et J.-J. Rousseau.* Paris: Corman, 1911.

———. *Le Prestige de J.-J. Rousseau.* Paris: Émile-Paul, 1909.

Burgelin, P. *La Philosophie de l'existence de J.-J. Rousseau.* Paris: Presses Universitaires de France, 1952.

Butler, E. M. *The Tyranny of Greece over Germany.* Cambridge, Eng.: Cambridge University Press, 1935.

Caspers, Elisabeth. *Goethes pädagogische Grundanschauungen im Verhältnis zu Rousseau.* Langensalza: Beyer, 1922.

Cassirer, Ernst. *Die Philosophie der Aufklärung.* Tübingen: Mohr, 1932.

———. *Rousseau, Kant, Goethe.* Trans. James Gutmann et al. Princeton Princeton University Press, 1947.

———. *The Question of Jean-Jacques Rousseau.* Trans. Peter Gay. Bloomington: Indiana University Press, 1963.

Champion, Edme. *J.-J. Rousseau et la Révolution française.* Paris: Colin, 1910.

Chinard, Gilbert. *L'Amérique et le rêve exotique dans la littérature française au XVIIᵉ et au XVIIIᵉ siècle.* Paris: Droz, 1934.

Chuquet, Arthur. *J.-J. Rousseau.* 7th rev. ed. Paris: Hachette, n.d.

Claretie, Léo. *J.-J. Rousseau et ses amies.* Paris: Chailly, 1896.

Clark, Robert T., Jr. *Herder: His Life and Thought.* Berkeley: University of California Press, 1955.

Cobban, Alfred. *Rousseau and the Modern State.* London: Allen & Unwin, 1934.

Compayré, Gabriel. *Jean-Jacques Rousseau and Education from Nature.* Trans. R. P. Jago. New York: Crowell, 1907.

Courtois, Louis J. *Chronologie critique de la vie et des œuvres de Jean-Jacques Rousseau, AJJR, Vol. 15.* Geneva, 1923.

Croce, Benedetto. *Goethe.* 3rd ed. Bari: Laterze, 1939.

Crocker, Lester G. *An Age of Crisis: Man and World in Eighteenth-Century French Thought.* Baltimore: The Johns Hopkins Press, 1959.

Cuendet, William. *La Philosophie religieuse de J.-J. Rousseau et ses sources.* Geneva: Jullien, 1913.

Dechent, Hermann. *Goethes "Schöne Seele": Susanna Katharina von Klettenberg.* Gotha: Perthes, 1896.

Dérathé, R. *Le Rationalisme de Jean-Jacques Rousseau.* Paris: Presses Universitaires de France, 1948.

d'Harcourt, Robert. *Éducation sentimentale de Goethe.* Paris: Colin, 1931.

———. *La Religion de Goethe.* Paris: Le Roux, 1949.

Diderot, Denis. *Œuvres complètes.* Ed. Assézat-Tourneux. 20 vols. Paris: Garnier, 1875–1877.

Diem, Carl. *Körpererziehung bei Goethe.* Frankfurt/Main: Kramer, 1948.

Droz, J. *L'Allemagne et la Révolution française.* Paris: Presses Universitaires de France, 1949.

Ducros, Louis. *Jean-Jacques Rousseau.* 3 vols. Paris: Fontemoing, 1908–1917.

Eigeldinger, Marc. *Jean-Jacques Rousseau et la réalité de l'imaginaire.* Neuchâtel: La Baconnière, 1962.

Einaudi, Mario. *The Early Rousseau.* Ithaca: Cornell University Press, 1967.
Eissler, K. R. *Goethe: A Psycho-Analytic Study, 1775–1786.* 2 vols. Detroit: Wayne University Press, 1966.
Ellis, Madeleine B. *Julie or La Nouvelle Héloïse: A Synthesis of Rousseau's Thought (1749–1759).* Toronto: University of Toronto Press, 1949.
————. *Rousseau's Venetian Story: An Essay upon Art and Truth in "Les Confessions."* Baltimore: The Johns Hopkins Press, 1966.
Émery, Léon. *Rousseau: L'Annonciateur.* Lyon: Les Cahiers libres, n.d.
Fabre, Jean, ed. *Jean-Jacques Rousseau et son œuvre: Problèmes et Recherches: Commémoration et Colloque de Paris, 16–20 octobre 1962.* Paris: Klinksieck, 1964.
Fabre, Joseph. *Les Pères de la Révolution.* Paris: Alcan, 1910.
Fairley, Barker. *Goethe as Revealed in His Poetry.* Chicago: University of Chicago Press, 1932.
————. *A Study of Goethe.* London: Oxford University Press, 1947.
Fellows, Otis L. and Torrey, Norman L., ed. *Diderot Studies,* Vol. 1. Syracuse: Syracuse University Press, 1949; Vol. 2, 1952.
Ferval, Claude. *Jean-Jacques Rousseau et les femmes.* Paris: Fayard, 1934.
Fester, Richard. *Rousseau und die deutsche Geschichtsphilosophie.* Leipzig: Meyer, 1890.
Fierz, Jürg. *Goethes Porträtierungskunst in "Dichtung und Wahrheit,"* Wege zur Dichtung, ed. Emil Ermatinger, No. 48. Frauenfeld: Huber, 1945.
Firmery, J. *Gocthe.* Paris: Lecène-Oudin, 1894.
Fischer-Hartmann, Deli. *Goethes Altersroman: Studien uber die innere Einheit von "Wilhelm Meisters Wanderjahren."* Halle: Niemeyer, 1941.
Flitner, Wilhelm. *Goethe im Spätwerk: Glaube, Weltsicht, Ethos.* Hamburg: Claassen & Goverts, 1947.
————. *Goethes pädagogische Ideen.* Godesberg: Kupper, 1948.
Flores d'Arcais, Giuseppe. *Il problema pedagogico nell' Emilio di G. G. Rousseau.* Padua: Editoria Liviana, 1951.
Fränkel, Jonas. *Goethes Erlebnis der Schweiz.* St. Gallen: Tschudy, 1949.
François-Poncet, André. *Les "Affinités électives" de Goethe.* Paris: Alcan, 1910.
Franz, Erich. *Goethe als religiöser Denker.* Tübingen: Mohr, 1932.
Friedenthal, Richard. *Goethe: Sein Leben und seine Zeit.* Munich: Piper, 1963.
Fuchs, Albert. *Goethe: Un homme face à la vie,* 1. Paris: Aubier, 1946.
————, ed. *Goethe et l'esprit français: Actes du Colloque International de Strasbourg, 23–27 Avril 1957.* Paris: Société d'Éditions: Les Belles Lettres, 1958.
————. *Goethe-Studien.* Berlin: de Gruyter, 1968.
Fuseli, Henri. *Remarks on the Writings and Conduct of J.-J. Rousseau (1767),* ed. Karl S. Guthke Augustan Reprint Society Publications, No. 82. Los Angeles: Clark Memorial Library, University of California, 1960.

Fusil, C. A. *L'Anti-Rousseau ou les Égarements du coeur et de l'esprit.* Paris: Plon-Nourrit, 1929.

Gerhard, Melitta. *Der deutsche Entwicklungsroman bis zu Goethes "Wilhelm Meister,"* DVLG, Buchreihe, Vol. 9. Halle: Niemeyer, 1926.

Girardin, Saint-Marc. *J.-J. Rousseau, sa vie et ses œuvres.* Paris: Charpentier, 1875.

Gloël, Heinrich. *Goethe und Lotte.* Berlin: Mittler, 1922.

Glum, Friedrich. *Jean-Jacques Rousseau—Religion und Staat: Grundlegung einer demokratischen Staatslehre.* Stuttgart: Kohlhammer, 1956.

Godet, Philippe. *Histoire littéraire de la Suisse Française.* Paris: Fischbacher, 1890.

Goschen, George Joachim, Viscount. *The Life and Times of Georg Joachim Göschen, Publisher and Printer of Leipzig, 1752–1828.* 2 vols. London: Murray, 1903.

Gose, Hans. *Goethes "Werther,"* Bausteine zur Geschichte der deutschen Literatur, No. 18. Halle: Niemeyer, 1921.

Grand-Carteret, John. *La France jugée par l'Allemagne.* Paris: Perrin, 1896.

Grappin, Pierre. *La Théorie du génie dans le préclassicisme allemand.* Paris: Presses Universitaires de France, 1952.

Gray, Ronald. *Goethe: A Critical Introduction.* Cambridge, Eng.: Cambridge University Press, 1967.

Green, F. C. *Jean-Jacques Rousseau: A Critical Study of His Life and Writings.* Cambridge, Eng.: Cambridge University Press, 1953.

Gregorovius, Ferdinand. *Goethes "Wilhelm Meister" in seinen sozialistischen Elementen.* Schwäbisch-Hall: Fischhaber, 1853.

Grempler, Georg. *Beiträge zu Goethes "Clavigo."* Diss. Halle-Wittenberg. Halle: Karras, 1911.

Grimm, Friedrich Melchior et al. *Correspondance littéraire, philosophique et critique.* 16 vols. Paris: Buisson, 1812–1814.

Grimsley, Ronald. *Rousseau and the Religious Quest.* Oxford: Clarendon Press, 1968.

Groethuysen, Bernard. *Jean-Jacques Rousseau.* 4th ed. Paris: Gallimard, 1949.

Gross, Ferdinand. *Goethes "Werther" in Frankreich: Eine Studie.* Leipzig: Heitz, n.d.

Guéhenno, Jean. *Jean-Jacques Rousseau: Histoire d'une conscience.* Paris: Éditions Gallimard, 1962. Trans. (as *Jean-Jacques Rousseau*) John and Doreen Weightman. 2 vols. London: Routledge & Kegan Paul, 1966.

Guillemin, Henri. *Un homme, deux ombres.* Geneva: Éditions du Milieu du Monde, 1943.

Gundolf, Friedrich. *Goethe,* 3rd ed. Berlin: Bondi, 1930.

Guttmann, Alfred. *Musik in Goethes Wirken und Werken.* Berlin-Halensee: Deutscher Musikliteratur-Verlag, 1949.

Haecker, Valentin, *Goethes morphologische Arbeiten und die neuere Forschung.* Jena: Fischer, 1927.

Hale, William Harlan. *Challenge to Defeat: Modern Man in Goethe's World and Spengler's Century.* New York: Harcourt Brace, 1932.

Hammer, Carl, Jr. *Goethes "Dichtung und Wahrheit," 7. Buch: Literaturgeschichte oder Bildungserlebnis?* Illinois Studies in Language and Literature, Vol. 30, No. 1, Urbana, 1945.

————, ed. *Goethe after Two Centuries,* Louisiana State University Studies, Humanities Series, No. 1, Baton Rouge, 1952.

Hankamer, Paul. *Spiel der Mächte. Ein Kapitel aus Goethes Leben und Goethes Welt.* Tübingen: Wunderlich, 1947.

Hansen, Adolph. *Goethes Metamorphose der Pflanzen: Geschichte einer botanischen Hypothese,* Part I. Giessen: Töpelmann, 1907.

Harnack, Otto. *Goethe in der Epoche seiner Vollendung (1805–1832).* 3rd ed. Leipzig: Hinrichs, 1905.

Havens, George R. *The Age of Ideas: From Reaction to Revolution in Eighteenth-Century France.* New York: Holt, 1955.

Hendel, Charles W. *Jean-Jacques Rousseau, Moralist.* 2 vols. London: Oxford University Press, 1934.

Henkel, Arthur. *Entsagung: Eine Studie zu Goethes Altersroman,* Hermaea, Germanistische Forschungen, n.s., No. 3. Tübingen: Niemeyer, 1954.

Herder, Johann Gottfried. *Sämtliche Werke.* Ed. Bernhard Suphan. 33 vols. Berlin: Weidmann, 1877–1913.

Hering, Robert. *Spinoza im jungen Goethe.* Diss. Leipzig. Leipzig: Schmidt und Baumann, 1897.

————. *Wilhelm Meister und Faust und ihre Gestaltung der Gottesidee.* Frankfurt/Main: Schulte-Buhnke, 1952.

Herrmann, Helene. *Die psychologischen Anschauungen des jungen Goethe und seiner Zeit,* Part I. Diss. Berlin. Berlin: Imberg und Lefson, 1904.

Hertz, G. W. *Natur und Geist in Goethes "Faust,"* Deutsche Forschungen, No. 25. Frankfurt/Main: Diesterweg, 1931.

Herzfelder, J. *Goethe in der Schweiz.* Leipzig: Hirzel, 1891.

Hettner, Hermann. *Geschichte der deutschen Literatur im achtzehnten Jahrhundert.* 2 vols. Berlin: Aufbau-Verlag, 1961.

Hiebel, Friedrich. *Goethe: Die Erhöhung des Menschen.* Bern: Francke, 1961.

Hocquette, Maurice. *Les Fantaisies botaniques de Goethe.* Paris: Aubier, 1943.

Höfer, Klara. *Goethes Ehe.* 6th ed. Stuttgart: Cotta, 1922.

Höffding, Harald. *Rousseau und seine Philosophie.* Stuttgart: Frommann, 1897.

Hoffmann, Arthur. *Werktätiges Leben im Geiste Goethes.* Weimar: H. Böhlaus Nachfolger, 1950.

Holbach, Paul, Baron d'. *Système de la nature.* 2 vols. Paris: Ledou, 1821.

Hüller, Friedrich August. *Natur- und Gesellschaftsprinzip in Rousseaus Pädagogik*. Diss. Leipzig. Leipzig-Plagwitz: Stefan, 1898.

Istel, Edgar. *Jean-Jacques Rousseau als Komponist seiner lyrischen Scene "Pygmalion."* Diss. Leipzig. Leipzig: Breitkopf und Härtel, 1901.

Jahn, Kurt. *Goethes "Dichtung und Wahrheit": Vorgeschichte–Entstehung –Kritik–Analyse*. Halle: Niemeyer, 1908.

Jaloux, Edmond. *Goethe*. New, rev. ed. Paris: Fayard, 1949.

Jansen, Albert. *Jean-Jacques Rousseau als Musiker*. Berlin: Reimer, 1884.

Jantz, Harold. *The Mothers in "Faust": The Myth of Time and Creativity*. Baltimore: The Johns Hopkins Press, 1969.

Jockers, Ernst. *Mit Goethe: Gesammelte Aufsätze*. Heidelberg: Winter, 1957.

Josephson, Matthew. *Jean-Jacques Rousseau*. New York: Harcourt Brace, 1931.

Jost, François. *Jean-Jacques Rousseau Suisse*. 2 vols. Fribourg: Éditions universitaires, 1961.

Jung, Alexander. *Goethes "Wanderjahre" und die wichtigsten Fragen des 19. Jahrhunderts*. Mainz: Kunze, 1854.

Keudell, Elise von. *Goethe als Benutzer der Weimarer Bibliothek*. Weimar: H. Böhlaus Nachfolger, 1931.

Kiehn, Ludwig. *Goethes Begriff der Bildung*. Hamburg: Boysen, 1932.

Kindermann, Heinz. *Goethes Menschengestaltung: Versuch einer literarischen Anthropologie*, 1. Berlin: Junker und Dünnhaupt, 1932.

————, ed. *Kampf um das soziale Ordnungsgefüge*, Deutsche Literatur in Entwicklungsreihen, Reihe Irrationalismus, Vol. 8. Leipzig: Reclam, 1939.

————. *Das Goethebild des zwanzigsten Jahrhunderts*. Vienna: Humboldt-Verlag, 1952.

Klein, Timotheus. *Wieland und Rousseau*. Diss. Berlin. Berlin: Duncker, 1903.

Kluckhohn, Paul. *Die Auffassung der Liebe in der Literatur des 18. Jahrhunderts und der deutschen Romantik*. Halle: Niemeyer, 1922.

Koch, Franz. *Goethes Stellung zu Tod und Unsterblichkeit*, Schriften der Goethe-Gesellschaft, No. 45. Weimar: Verlag der Goethe-Gesellschaft, 1932.

Kommerell, Max. *Jean Pauls Verhältnis zu Rousseau*. Marburg: Elwert, 1925.

Korff, H. A. *Die Dichtung von Sturm und Drang im Zusammenhange der Geistesgeschichte*. Leipzig: Quelle und Meyer, 1928.

————. *Geist der Goethezeit*. 3 vols. Leipzig: Weber, 1930.

Kutscher, Arthur. *Das Naturgefühl in Goethes Lyrik bis zur Ausgabe der Schriften 1789*, Breslauer Beiträge zur Literaturgeschichte, No. 8. Leipzig: Hesse, 1906.

Langguth, Adolf. *Goethe als Pädagog*. Halle: Niemeyer, 1887.

Lanson, Gustave. *Histoire de la littérature française*. 12th rev. ed. Paris: Hachette, 1912.

Lauterbach, Martin. *Das Verhältnis der zweiten zur ersten Ausgabe von "Werthers Leiden,"* Quellen und Forschungen, No. 10. Strassburg: Trübner, 1910.

Lemaître, Jules. *J.-J. Rousseau*. Paris: Calmann-Lévy, n.d.

Leppmann, Wolfgang. *The German Image of Goethe*. Oxford: Oxford University Press, 1961.

Lessing, Gotthold Ephraim. *Sämtliche Schriften*. Ed. Karl Lachmann and Franz Muncker. 3rd ed. 22 vols. Stuttgart, Berlin, Leipzig: Göschen, 1886–1915.

Lichtenberger, Henri. *Goethe*. 2 vols. Paris: Didier, 1937.

Lienhard, Friedrich. *Wege nach Weimar: Gesammelte Monatsblätter*, Vol. 3. Stuttgart: Greiner und Pfeiffer, 1907.

Loiseau, Hippolyte. *L'Évolution morale de Goethe*. Paris: Alcan, 1911.

———. *Goethe et la France: ce qu'il en a connu, pensé et dit*. Paris: Attinger, 1930.

———. *Goethe: L'homme, l'écrivain, le penseur*. Paris: Aubier, 1944.

Magnus, Rudolf. *Goethe als Naturforscher*. Leipzig: Barth, 1906; *Goethe as a Scientist*. Trans. Heinz Norden. New York: Schumann, 1949.

Mainland, William F. *Schiller and the Changing Past*. London: Heinemann, 1953.

Marmontel, Jean-François. *Mémoires*. 4 vols. Paris: Xhrouet, 1804.

Martin, Kingsley. *French Liberal Thought in the Eighteenth Century*. Boston: Little, Brown, 1929.

Martini, Wolfgang. *Die Technik der Jugenddramen Goethes*. Weimar: H. Böhlaus Nachfolger, 1932.

Masson, Pierre-Maurice. *La Religion de J.-J. Rousseau*. 3 vols. Paris: Hachette, 1916.

Masters, Roger D. *The Political Philosophy of Rousseau*. Princeton: Princeton University Press, 1968.

Mauzi, Robert. *L'Idee du bonheur dans la littérature et la pensée françaises au XVIIIe siècle*. Paris: Colin, 1960.

McDonald, Joan. *Rousseau and the French Revolution, 1762–1791*. London: Athlone Press, 1965.

Mentzel, E. *Der Frankfurter Goethe*. Frankfurt/Main: Rütten und Loening, 1900.

Merlant, Joachim. *Le Roman personnel de Rousseau à Fromentin*. Paris: Hachette, 1905.

Meyer, Heinrich. *Goethe: Das Leben im Werk*. Hamburg-Bergedorf: Strom-Verlag, 1949.

Meyer, Richard M. *Goethe*. 3rd ed. Berlin: Hofmann, 1905.

Meynier, Albert. *Jean-Jacques Rousseau révolutionnaire*. Paris: Schleicher, 1910.

Mézières, Alfred. *Wolfgang Goethe: Les œuvres expliquées par la vie*. Paris: Didier, 1872.

Michéa, René. *Le "Voyage en Italie" de Goethe*. Paris: Aubier, 1945.

———. *Les Travaux scientifiques de Goethe*. Lille: Demailly, 1946.

Michel, Victor. *C.-M. Wieland: La forme et l'évolution de son esprit jusqu'en 1772*. Paris: Boivin, n.d.

Mommsen, Wilhelm. *Die politischen Anschauungen Goethes*. Stuttgart: Deutsche Verlags-Anstalt, 1948.

Mondolfo, Rodolfo. *Rousseau e la coscienza moderna*. Florence: La Nuova Italia, 1954.

Moreau-Rendu, S. *L'Idée de bonté naturelle chez J.-J. Rousseau*. Paris: Rivière, 1929.

Moritz, Karl Philipp. *Anton Reiser: Ein psychologischer Roman*. Leipzig: Insel-Verlag, n.d.

Morley, John. *Rousseau*. 2 vols. London: Macmillan, 1873.

Mornet, Daniel. *Le Sentiment de la nature en France, de J.-J. Rousseau à Bernardin de Saint-Pierre*. Paris: Hachette, 1907.

———. *Le Romantisme en France au XVIIIᵉ siècle*. Paris: Hachette, 1912.

———. *Rousseau: L'homme et l'œuvre*. Paris: Boivin, 1950.

———. *La Nouvelle Héloïse: Étude et analyse*. Paris: Éditions Mellottée, 1950.

Mortier, Roland. *Diderot en Allemagne (1750–1850)*. Paris: Presses Universitaires de France, 1954.

Moser, Hans Joachim. *Goethe und die Musik*. Leipzig: Peters, 1949.

Mugnier, François. *Madame de Warens et J. J. Rousseau*. Paris: Calmann-Lévy, n.d.

Müller, Georg. *Goethe und die deutsche Gegenwart*. Witten/Ruhr: Luther-Verlag, 1955.

Münz, Bernhard. *Goethe als Erzieher*. Wien: Braumüller, 1904.

Muschg, Walter. *Tragische Literaturgeschichte*. Bern: Francke, 1948.

Muthesius, Karl. *Goethe und Pestalozzi*. Leipzig: Dürr, 1908.

———. *Goethe ein Kinderfreund*. 2nd rev. ed. Berlin: Mittler, 1910.

Nemo, Maxime. *L'Homme nouveau: Jean-Jacques Rousseau*. Paris: La Colombe, 1957.

Nourrisson, Jean-Félix. *Jean-Jacques Rousseau et le Rousseauisme*. Paris: Fontemoing, 1903.

Nowack, Wilhelm. *Liebe und Ehe im deutschen Roman zu Rousseaus Zeiten (1747 bis 1774)*. Bern: Francke, 1906.

Palissot de Montenoy, Charles. *Œuvres*. 6 vols. Paris: Collin, 1809.

Pange, Jean de. *Goethe en Alsace*, Cahiers Rhénans, No. 4. Paris: Société d'Éditions "Les Belles-Lettres," 1925.

Parker, L. John. *Christoph Martin Wielands dramatische Tätigkeit*. Bern: Francke, 1961.

Pascal, Roy. *The German Sturm und Drang*. Manchester, Eng.: Manchester University Press, 1953.

Peyre, Henri. *Literature and Sincerity*. New Haven: Yale University Press, 1963.

Pons, Amilda A. *Jean-Jacques Rousseau et le théâtre*. Geneva: Jullien, 1909.

Pougin, Arthur. *J.-J. Rousseau musicien*. Paris: Fischbacher, 1901.

Prang, Helmut. *Johann Heinrich Merck: Ein Leben für Andere*. Wiesbaden: Insel-Verlag, 1949.

Proal, Louis. *La Psychologie de Jean-Jacques Rousseau*. Paris: Alcan, 1923.

Rattner, Josef. *Grosse Pädagogen*. Munich & Basel: Reinhardt, 1956.

Raymond, Marcel. *Jean-Jacques Rousseau: La quête de soi et la rêverie*. Paris: Corti, 1962.

Reichenburg, Marguerite. *Essai sur les lectures de Rousseau*. Diss. Pennsylvania. Philadelphia: University of Pennsylvania Press, 1932.

Reinsch, Frank H. *Goethe's Political Interests prior to 1787*, UCPMP, Vol. 10, No. 3. Berkeley and Los Angeles, 1923.

Reiss, Hans. *Goethes Romane*. Bern: Francke, 1963.

Reynaud, Louis. *Histoire générale de l'influence française en Allemagne*. 2nd ed. Paris: Hachette, 1915.

————. *L'Influence allemande en France au XVIIIe et au XIXe siècle*. Paris: Hachette, 1922.

Rice, Richard A. *Rousseau and the Poetry of Nature in Eighteenth-Century France*, Smith College Studies, Vol. 8, Nos. 3 and 4. Northampton, 1925.

Ridderhoff, Kuno. *Sophie von La Roche, die Schülerin Richardsons und Rousseaus*. Diss. Göttingen. Einbeck: Schroedter, 1895.

Ritter, Eugène. *La Famille et la jeunesse de Rousseau*. Paris: Hachette, 1896.

Rod, Edouard. *Essai sur Goethe*. Paris: Perrin, 1898.

Roethe, Gustav. *Goethe: Gesammelte Vorträge und Aufsätze*. Berlin: Ebering, 1932.

Rolland, Romain. *Goethe et Beethoven*. Paris: Éditions du Sablier, 1930.

Roose, Adriana P. *Het Karakter van J.-J. Rousseau*. Diss. Groningen. The Hague: J. B. Wolters, 1919.

Rosenkranz, Karl. *Goethe und seine Werke*. 2nd ed. Königsberg: Bornträger, 1856.

Rossel, Virgile. *Histoire des relations littéraires entre la France et l'Allemagne*. Paris: Fischbacher, 1897.

Sainte-Beuve, Charles-Augustin. *Les grands écrivains français: Études des lundis*. Paris: Garnier, n.d.

————. *Causeries du lundi*. Paris: Garnier, n.d.

Sakmann, Paul. *Jean-Jacques Rousseau, Die grossen Erzieher, ihre Persönlichkeit und ihre Systeme*, Vol. 5. Berlin: Reichard, 1913.

Santayana, George. *Three Philosophical Poets: Lucretius, Dante and Goethe*. Cambridge: Harvard University Press, 1910.

Sauter, Hermann. *Goethe in Lob und Tadel seiner französischen Zeitgenossen.* Speyer: Dobbeck, n.d.

Schädelin, P. *Julie Bondeli, die Freundin Rousseaus und Wielands.* Bern: Jenni, 1838.

Schaeder, Grete. *Gott und Welt: Drei Kapitel Goethescher Weltanschauung.* Hameln: Seifert, 1949.

Scherer, Edmond. *Melchior Grimm: L'homme de lettres—le factotum—le diplomate.* Paris: Calmann-Lévy, 1887.

Scherer, Wilhelm. *Geschichte der deutschen Literatur.* Berlin: Knauer, n.d. (1st ed., 1883).

Schinz, Albert. *La Pensée religieuse de J.-J. Rousseau et ses récents interprètes,* Smith Coll. Studies in Modern Languages, Vol. 10, No. 1. Northampton, 1927.

Schinz, Albert. *La Pensée de Rousseau: Essai d'interprétation nouvelle.* 2 vols. Northampton: Smith College; Paris: Alcan, 1929.

Schlösser, Rudolf. *Rameaus Neffe, Studien und Untersuchungen zu Goethes Übersetzung,* Forschungen zur neueren Literaturgeschichte, No. 15. Berlin: Duncker, 1900.

Schmidt, Erich. *Richardson, Rousseau und Goethe: Ein Beitrag zur Geschichte des Romans im 18. Jahrhundert.* Jena: Frommann, 1875.

Schneider, Ferdinand Josef. *Die deutsche Dichtung der Geniezeit,* Epochen der deutschen Literatur, Vol. 3, Part 2. Stuttgart: Metzler, 1952.

Schöffler, Herbert. *"Die Leiden des jungen Werther": Ihr geistesgeschichtlicher Hintergrund.* Frankfurt/Main: Klostermann, 1938.

Schrempf, Christoph. *Goethes Lebensanschauung in ihrer geschichtlichen Entwicklung.* 2nd ed. Stuttgart: Frommann, 1932.

Schrimpf, Hans Joachim. *Das Weltbild des späten Goethe.* Stuttgart: Kohlhammer, 1956.

Schubart-Fikentscher, Gertrud. *Goethes sechsundfünfzig Strassburger Thesen vom 6. August 1771.* Weimar: H. Böhlaus Nachfolger, 1949.

Schubert, Hans von. *Goethes religiöse Jugendentwicklung.* Leipzig: Quelle und Meyer, 1925.

Sée, Henri. *Economic and Social Conditions in France during the Eighteenth Century.* Trans. Edwin H. Zeydel. New York: Knopf, 1927.

Seillière, Ernest. *Jean-Jacques Rousseau.* Paris: Garnier, 1921.

Sells, Arthur Lytton. *The Early Life and Adventures of Jean Jacques Rousseau (1712–1740).* Cambridge, Eng.: Heffer, 1929.

Semler, Christian. *Goethes "Wahlverwandtschaften" und die sittliche Weltanschauung des Dichters.* Hamburg: Richter, 1887.

Sengle, Friedrich. *Christoph Martin Wieland.* Stuttgart: Metzler, 1949.

Silz, Walter. *Hölderlin's "Hyperion": A Critical Reading.* Philadelphia: University of Pennsylvania Press, 1969.

Sime, James. *The Life of Johann Wolfgang Goethe.* London & Newcastle: Scott, n.d.

Simon, Lilli. *Verantwortung und Schuld in Goethes Romanen.* Diss. Erlang-
en. Erlangen: Palm und Enke, 1934.

Sommerfeld, Martin. *Goethe in Umwelt und Folgezeit.* Leiden: Sijthoff,
1935.

Spickernagel, Wilhelm. *Die "Geschichte des Fräuleins von Sternheim" von
Sophie von La Roche und Goethes "Werther."* Diss. Greifswald. Greifswald: Adler, 1911.

Spink, John S. *Jean-Jacques Rousseau et Genève.* Paris: Boivin, 1934.

Spranger, Eduard. *Goethe: Seine geistige Welt.* Tübingen: Wunderlich,
1967.

————. *Pestalozzis Denkformen.* Stuttgart: Hirzel, 1947.

Sprengel, Johann Georg. *Der Staatsgedanke in der deutschen Dichtung vom
Mittelalter bis zur Gegenwart.* Berlin: Junker & Dünnhaupt, 1953.

Staël-Holstein, Anne-Louise Germaine de. *Œuvres.* 3 vols. Paris: Lefèvre,
1838.

————. *Dix ans d'exil.* Paris: Garnier, n.d.

Stahl, Ernst L. *Schiller's Dramas: Theory and Practice.* Oxford: Clarendon
Press, 1954.

Staiger, Emil. *Goethe.* 3 vols. Zurich: Atlantis-Verlag, 1952–1956.

Stapfer, Paul. *Études sur Goethe.* Paris: Colin, 1906.

Steer, Alfred G. *Goethe's Social Philosophy as Revealed in "Campagne in
Frankreich" and "Belagerung von Mainz,"* UNCSGLL, No. 15, Chapel
Hill, 1955.

Steiner, Jakob. *Goethes "Wilhelm Meister": Sprache und Stilwandel.* Stuttgart: Kohlhammer, 1966.

Steinmetz, Felix. *Die pädagogischen Grundgedanken in Goethes Werken.*
Diss. Greifswald. Freienwalde: Battré, 1910.

Storz, Gerhard. *Goethe-Vigilien.* Stuttgart: Klett, 1953.

Strich, Fritz. *Goethe und die Weltliteratur.* Bern: Francke, 1946.

Susman, Margarete. *Deutung einer grossen Liebe: Goethe und Charlotte von
Stein.* Zurich: Artemis-Verlag, 1951.

Texte, Joseph. *J.-J. Rousseau et les origines du cosmopolitisme au XVIIIe
siècle.* Paris: Hachette, 1895.

Tiersot, Julien. *J.-J. Rousseau,* Series: Les maîtres de la musique. Paris: Alcan,
1913.

Unger, Rudolf. *Hamann und die Aufklärung.* 2 vols. Halle: Niemeyer, 1925.

Urzidil, Johannes. *Goethe in Böhmen.* Zurich: Artemis-Verlag, 1962.

Vallette, Gaspard. *J.-J. Rousseau, Génevois.* Paris: Plon-Nourrit; Geneva:
Jullien, 1911.

Van Tieghem, Phillippe. *"La Nouvelle Héloïse" de J.-J. Rousseau.* Paris:
Malfère, 1929.

Vial, Francisque. *La Doctrine d'éducation de Rousseau.* Paris: Delagrave,
1920.

Viëtor, Karl. *Goethe: Dichtung–Wissenschaft–Weltbild*. Bern: Francke, 1949.

Voisine, Jacques. *J.-J. Rousseau en Angleterre à l'époque romantique*. Thèse complémentaire Paris. Paris: Didier, 1956.

Voltaire, François-Marie Arouet de. *Œuvres complètes*. Ed. Louis Moland. 52 vols. Paris: Garnier, 1877–1885.

von den Steinen, Wolfram. *Das Zeitalter Goethes*. Bern: Francke, 1949.

von Gronicka, André. *The Russian Image of Goethe*. Philadelphia: University of Pennsylvania Press, 1968.

Vossler, Otto. *Rousseaus Freiheitslehre*. Göttingen: Vandenhoeck und Ruprecht, 1963.

Weineck, E. *Goethes pädagogische Gedanken in "Dichtung und Wahrheit."* Diss. Leipzig. Leipzig: Noske, 1911.

Weinhandl, Ferdinand. *Die Metaphysik Goethes*. Darmstadt: Wissenschaftliche Buchgesellschaft, 1965.

Weissenfels, Richard. *Goethe im Sturm und Drang*, Vol. 1. Halle: Niemeyer, 1894.

Weisstein, Ulrich. *Einführung in die Vergleichende Literaturwissenschaft*. Stuttgart: Kohlhammer, 1968.

Weitz, Hans-J., ed. *Briefwechsel Goethe-Willemer*. Frankfurt: Insel-Verlag, 1965.

Wellek, René. *A History of Modern Criticism, 1750–1950*. 5 vols. New Haven: Yale University Press, 1955–1967.

Wilson, Arthur M. *Diderot: The Testing Years, 1713–1759*. New York: Oxford University Press, 1957.

Witkowski, Georg. *Goethe*. 2nd ed. Leipzig: Seemann, 1912.

Wolff, Hans M. *Goethes Weg zur Humanität*. Bern: Francke, 1951.

———. *Goethe in der Periode der "Wahlverwandtschaften," 1802–1809*. Bern: Francke, 1952.

Wolff, Walter. *Wie denkt Goethe uber Erziehung und wie lassen sich seine pädagogischen Ansichten aus allgemeinen Anschauungen ableiten?* Diss. Erlangen. Borna-Leipzig: Noske, 1911.

Wundt, Max. *Goethes "Wilhelm Meister" und die Entwicklung des modernen Lebensideals*. Berlin and Leipzig: Göschen, 1913.

Wyneken, F. A. *Rousseaus Einfluss auf Klinger*, UCPMP, Vol. 3, No. 1. Berkeley, 1912.

Xylander, Oskar Ritter von. *Heinrich von Kleist und J.-J. Rousseau*. Germanische Studien, No. 193. Berlin: Ebering, 1937.

IV. Articles and Reviews

Anonymous. "Famous Biographies." *Edinburgh Review*, 214 (1911): 331–356.

Aron, Albert W. "The Mature Goethe and Rousseau." *JEGP*, 35 (1936): 170–182.

SELECTED BIBLIOGRAPHY

Atkins, Stuart P. "J. C. Lavater and Goethe: Problems of Psychology and Theology in *Die Leiden des jungen Werthers.*" *PMLA*, 63 (1948): 520–576.

Aulhorn, Edith. "Der Aufbau von Goethes Wahlverwandtschaften." *Zeitschrift für Deutschunterricht*, 32 (1918): 337–355.

Ayrault, Roger. "Schiller et Rousseau: Sur la genèse des *Brigands.*" *EG*, 10 (1955): 97–104.

Baldensperger, Fernand. "Goethes Lieblingslektüre 1826–1830: die Zeitschrift *Le Globe.*" *GRM*, 20 (1932): 166–173.

Bémol, Maurice. "Goethe et Rousseau, ou la double influence." *EG*, 9 (1954): 257–277.

———. "Goethe, Rousseau et *Faust.*" *EG*, 13 (1958): 1–17.

Benrubi, Isaac. "Goethe et Schiller continuateurs de Rousseau." *RMM*, 20 (1912): 441–460.

———. "Rousseau et les grands représentants de la pensée allemande." *Jean-Jacques Rousseau: Leçons faites à l'École des Hautes Études Sociales.* Paris: Alcan, 1912, pp. 201–249.

———. "L'Idéal moral chez Rousseau, Mme de Staël et Amiel." *AJJR*, 27 (1938): 7–304.

Bergstraesser, Arnold. "Erziehungsweisheit des alten Goethe." *Monatshefte* 37 (1945): 545–554.

Berselli, Paola Ambri. "Influences italiennes sur *La Nouvelle Héloïse.*" *AJJR*, 32 (1950–1952): 156–162.

Bettex, Albert. "Goethe und die Kunst des Reisens." *Goethe*, 11 (1949): 31–45.

Beutler, Ernst. "Corona Schröter." *Essays um Goethe.* 6th ed. Bremen: Carl Schünemann, 1957, pp. 460–505.

Bianquis, Geneviève. "Goethe et Voltaire." *Études sur Goethe.* Paris: Société d'Éditions: Les Belles Lettres, 1951, pp. 91–98.

Böschenstein, Bernard. "La Transfiguration de Rousseau dans la poésie allemande à l'orée du XIXe siècle: Hölderlin—Jean Paul—Kleist." *AJJR*, 36 (1963–65): 153–171.

Borcherdt, Hans Heinrich. "Die Entstehungsgeschichte von *Erwin und Elmire.*" *GJb*, 32 (1911): 73–82.

Bosanquet, Bernard. "Les idées politiques de Rousseau." *RMM*, 20 (1912): 321–340.

Bouvier, Bernard. "Rapport de la commission initiative." *AJJR*, 1 (1905): VII–XV.

Brandeis, Arthur. "Auf Goethes Spuren von Verona bis Rom," II. *Chronik des Wiener Goethe-Vereins*, 16 (1902): 49–54.

Browning, R. M. "The Humanity of Goethe's *Iphigenie.*" *GQ*, 30 (1957): 98–113.

Bruford, W. H. "Goethe's *Wilhelm Meister* as a Picture and a Criticism of Society." *PEGS*, n.s., 9 (1933): 20–45.

Bullock, Walter L. "On Re-reading Three Thwarted Romances: *La Nouvelle Héloïse, Die Leiden des jungen Werthers, Jacopo Ortis.*" *Goethe Centenary Papers.* Ed. Martin Schütze. Chicago: University of Chicago Press, 1932, pp. 65–74.

Burgelin, Pierre. "The Second Education of Émile." *YFS,* No. 28 (1962): 106–111.

Cahen, Albert. "La vie." *Jean-Jacques Rousseau: Leçons faites à l'École des Hautes Études.* Paris: Alcan, 1912, pp. 1–46.

Castle, Eduard. "*Pater Brey und Satyros.*" *JbGG,* 5 (1918): 56–98.

Caumont, Armand. "Goethe et la littérature française." *Programm des Städtischen Gymnasiums zu Frankfurt am Main.* Frankfurt: Mehlau & Waldschmidt, 1885, pp. 1–37.

Chapin, Chester F. "Johnson, Rousseau, and Religion." *TSLL,* 2, No. 1 (Spring, 1960): 95–102.

Chinard, Gilbert. "L'Influence des récits de voyages sur la philosophie de J.-J. Rousseau." *PMLA,* 14 (1911): 476–495.

Clark, Robert T., Jr. "The Psychological Framework of Goethe's *Werther.*" *JEGP,* 46 (1947): 273–278.

Collet, Georges-Paul. "Jean-Jacques Rousseau et Genève." *Symposium,* 18 (1964): 79–89.

Crocker, Lester G. "Julie ou la nouvelle duplicité." *AJJR,* 36 (1963–65): 105–152.

Dargan, E. Preston. "Goethe and France." *Goethe Centenary Papers.* Ed. Martin Schütze. Chicago: University of Chicago Press, 1932, pp. 45–64.

Dieckmann, Herbert. "Goethe und Diderot." *DVLG,* 10 (1932): 478–503.

Dowden, Edward. "Goethe and the French Revolution." *PEGS,* 5 (1889): 1–27.

Dumur, Louis. "Les détracteurs de Rousseau." *Mercure de France,* 67 (1907): 577–600.

Düntzer, Heinrich. "Ein böser Angriff auf Goethes *Hermann und Dorothea.*" *GJb,* 21 (1900): 239–240.

Durkheim, Émile, "La 'Pédagogie' de Rousseau." *RMM,* 26 (1919): 153–180.

Émery, Léon. "Rousseau and the Foundations of Human Regeneration." *YFS,* 28 (1962): 3–12.

Engel, Claire Éliane. "L'Abbé Prévost et Jean-Jacques Rousseau." *AJJR,* 28 (1939–40): 19–39.

Englert, Anton. "Über Entlehnungen Goethes aus dem Französischen." *Zeitschrift für vergleichende Literaturgeschichte,* 5 (1892): 119–121.

Fabre, Jean. "Réalité et utopie dans la pensée politique de Rousseau." *AJJR,* 35 (1959–62): 181–216.

Feise, Ernst. "Goethes Werther als nervöser Charakter." *GR,* 1 (1926): 185–253.

Fellows, Otis. "The Theme of Genius in Diderot's *Neveu de Rameau.*" *Di-*

derot *Studies*, Vol. 2. Syracuse: Syracuse University Press, 1952, pp. 168–199.

Ferrero, Guglielmo. "Genève et le *Contrat social*." *AJJR*, 23 (1934): 137–152.

Fischer–Lamberg, Hanna. "Frau von Stein—ein 'Bildungserlebnis' Goethes." *DVLG*, 15 (1937): 385–401.

François, Alexis. "Les provincialismes suisses-romands et savoyards de Jean-Jacques Rousseau." *AJJR*, 3 (1907): 1–67.

Franz, Arthur. "Die literarische Portraitzeichnung in Goethes *Dichtung und Wahrheit* und in Rousseaus *Confessions*." *DVLG*, 6 (1928), 492–511.

Franz, Erich. "Entweder—Oder? Bemerkungen zu dem Goethebuch von Richard Friedenthal." *Goethe*, 26 (1964): 136–143.

Frick, Reinhold. "Manon Lescaut als Typus." *GRM*, 7 (1915–1919): 445–464.

Friedländer, Max. "Goethe und die Musik." *JbGG*, 3 (1916): 275–340.

Fuchs, Albert. "Der *West-östliche Divan* als Buch der Liebe." *Goethe-Studien*. Berlin: de Gruyter, 1968, pp. 82–96.

———. "Le *West-östliche Divan*: Livre de l'amour." *PEGS*, n.s., 22 (1952–53): 1–30.

Gaiser, Konrad. "Goethes Auseinandersetzung mit der französischen Kultur." *Neue Jahrbücher für Wissenschaft und Jugendbildung*, 8 (1932): 113–127.

Gautier, Maurice. "Les *Institutions chymiques* de Jean-Jacques Rousseau." *AJJR*, 12 (1918–1919): 1–164, and 13 (1920): 1–178.

Gerhard, Melitta. "Goethes Erleben der französischen Revolution im Spiegel der *Natürlichen Tochter*. *DVLG*, 1 (1923), 281–305.

———. "Chaos und Kosmos in Goethes *Hermann und Dorothea*." *Monatshefte*, 24 (1942): 415–424.

Glaeser, Ernst. "Rousseau—fast ein Heiliger." *Merian*, 16 (1963): 65–69.

Gooch, G. P. "The Political Background of Goethe's Life." *PEGS*, n.s., 3 (1924): 8–20.

Grappin, Pierre. "Goethe et le mythe de Prométhée." *EG*, 20 (1965): 243–258.

Graul, Gaston. "Über Goethe, den kosmischen Menschen." *JbGG*, 8 (1921): 3–26.

Grünberg, I. "Rousseau joueur d'échecs." *AJJR*, 3 (1907): 157–174.

Guillemin, Henri. "Les affaires de l'Ermitage (1756–1757): Examen critique des documents." *AJJR*, 29 (1941–1942): 59–258.

Guinadeau, O. "Les Rapports de Goethe et de Lavater." *EG*, 4 (1949): 213–226.

Guthke, Karl S. "Zur Frühgeschichte des Rousseauismus in Deutschland." *ZDP*, 77 (1958): 384–396.

Hammer, Carl, Jr. "Goethe's Estimate of Oliver Goldsmith." *JEGP*, 44 (1945): 131–138.

————. "Wilhelm Meisters Wanderjahre and Rousseau." *Southwest Goethe Festival: A Collection of Nine Papers.* Ed. Gilbert J. Jordan. Southern Methodist University Studies, No. 5. Dallas: University Press in Dallas, 1949, pp. 34–50.

————. "Re-examining Goethe's Views of Corneille." *GR*, 29 (1954): 260–268.

————. "Goethe, Prévost, and Louisiana." *MLQ*, 16 (1955): 332–338.

————. "Holbach according to Goethe." *RomN* 1, (1959): 18–21.

————. "Goethe's Silence Concerning Ronsard." *MLN*, 75 (1960): 697–698.

————. "Jacobi's Memorial to Rousseau." *Die Neueren Sprachen*, No. 6 (Jahrgang 1965): 280–283.

————. "The 'Philosophers' Quarrel' as Seen by Goethe." *RomN*, 9, No. 2 (Spring, 1968): 232–234.

————. "Goethe and Marianne—after the *Divan.*" *SCB*, 27 (1968): 134–138.

Hankamer, Paul. "Zur Genesis von Goethes Wahlverwandtschaften." *Festschrift für Berthold Litzmann.* Berlin: Grote, 1921, pp. 36–52.

Harnack, Otto. "Briefe von und an Wilhelm von Humboldt." *Biographische Blätter.* Ed. Anton Bettelheim, 2 (1896): 52–71.

Havens, George R. "The Theory of 'Natural Goodness' in Rousseau's Nouvelle Héloïse." *MLN*, 36 (1921): 385–394.

————. "Voltaire, Rousseau, and the 'Lettre sur la Providence.'" *PMLA*, 59 (1944): 109–130.

Haymann, Franz. "La loi naturelle dans la philosophie politique de J.-J. Rousseau." *AJJR*, 30 (1943–1945): 65–109.

Hébert, Rodolphe-Louis. "Grimm and Rousseau." *FR*, 25 (1952): 262–269.

Hecker, Max. "Die Briefe Johann Friedrich Reichardts an Goethe." *JbGG*, 11 (1925): 197–252.

Hellersberg-Wendriner, Anna. "America in the World View of the Aged Goethe." *GR*, 14 (1939): 270–276.

Herrmann, Léon. "Jean-Jacques Rousseau traducteur de Sénèque." *AJJR*, 13 (1920–1921): 215–224.

Höffding, Harald. "Rousseau et la religion." *RMM*, 20 (1912): 275–293.

Hofmannsthal, Hugo von. "Wilhelm Meister in der Urform." *Corona*, 1 (1930): 633–641.

Jacobi, J. G. "Ueber J. J. Rousseau." *Der Teutsche Merkur*, 23 (1778): 201–218.

Jahn, Kurt. "Zu den Wanderjahren." *GJb*, 26 (1905): 275–278.

Jockers, Ernst. "Faust und Meister, zwei polare Gestalten." *GR*, 21 (1946): 118–131.

————. "Morphologie und Klassik Goethes." *Goethe und die Wissenschaften: Vorträge gehalten anlässlich des Internationalen Gelehrtenkon-*

gresses zu Frankfurt am Main im August 1949. Frankfurt: Klostermann, 1951, pp. 63–81.

———. "Soziale Polarität in Goethes Klassik." Mit Goethe: Gesammelte Aufsätze. Heidelberg: Winter, 1957, pp. 48–89.

Kneller, John W. "Jean-Jacques the Dynamist." YFS, No. 13 (Spring-Summer, 1954): 114–118.

Kohlschmidt, Werner. "Rousseau und Goethe." Zeitschrift für den deutschen Unterricht, 18 (1904): 139–140.

Lambeck, H. "J.-J. Rousseau und seine Nouvelle Héloïse mit einem vergleichenden Blick auf verwandte Erscheinungen anderer Literaturen." Programm, Stralsund, 1874, pp. 1–36.

Langkavel, Martha. "Eine Parallelstelle zu den Worten der Wette des Goetheschen Faust mit Mephisto." Archiv, 63 (1904): 156.

Lanson, Gustave. "L'Unité de la pensée de J.-J. Rousseau." AJJR, (1912): 1–32.

Lehmann, Rudolf. "Anton Reiser und die Entstehung des Wilhelm Meister." JbGG, 3 (1916): 116–134.

———. "Goethe und das Problem der Erziehung." JbGG, 4 (1917): 42–84.

Lévy-Bruhl, Lucien. "L'Influence de J.-J. Rousseau en Allemagne." Annales de l'École libre des sciences politiques, 2 (1875): 326–356.

Lienhard, Friedrich. "Goethes Elsass." JbGG, 7 (1920): 267–301.

———. "Klopstock und Rousseau." Wege nach Weimar, 3 (1907): 49–56.

Liepe, Wolfgang. "Der junge Schiller und Rousseau." ZDP, 51 (1926): 299–328.

Loiseau, Hippolyte. "Goethe en France." GRM, 20 (1932): 150–166.

———. "La légende de l'olympisme de Goethe." Mélanges Henri Lichtenberger. Paris: Stock, 1934, pp. 49–69.

Mann, Thomas. "Goethes Laufbahn als Schriftsteller." Leiden und Grösse der Meister. Berlin: S. Fischer, 1935, pp. 51–86.

———. "Zu Goethes Wahlverwandtschaften." Die neue Rundschau, 36 (1925): 391–401.

Maschek, Friedrich. "Goethes Reisen," II. Fünfzehnter Jahres-Bericht der k.k. Staatsmittelschule in Reichenberg. Reichenberg, 1887, pp. 3–27.

Mauzi, Robert. "La Conversion de Julie dans La Nouvelle Héloïse." AJJR, 35 (1959–62): 29–47.

May, Georges. "Rousseau and France." YFS, No. 28 (1962): 122–135.

Meessen, Hubert J. "Goethes Polaritätsidee und die Wahlverwandtschaften." PMLA, 58 (1939): 1105–1123.

———. "Clavigo and Stella in Goethe's Personal and Dramatic Development." Goethe Bicentennial Studies by Members of the Faculty of Indiana University. Ed. Hubert J. Meessen. IUHS, No. 22. Bloomington, 1950; pp. 153–206.

Mengod, Vicente. "Recordando a Goethe." ATENEA, 94 (1949): 289–309.

Meyer, Heinrich. "Der alte und der neue Goethe." *Merkur: Zeitschrift für europäisches Denken*, 3 (1949): 3–11.

Meyer, Richard M. "Literarhistorische Bemerkungen, I: Zu Goethe." *Euphorion*, 3 (1896): 101–108.

Minor, J. "Die Anfänge des *Wilhelm Meister*." *GJb*, 9, (1888): 163–187.

Montégut, Émile. "Types modernes en littérature: Werther." *RDM*, 11 (1855): 333–344.

Monty, Jeanne R. "The Criticism of Rousseau in the *Correspondance littéraire*." *MLQ*, 24 (1963): 99–103.

Morel, Louis. "L'Influence de la littérature française chez Goethe." *GJb*, 31 (1910): 180–188; 32 (1911): 83–100.

Morris, Max. "Über die Quelle der *Wahlverwandtschaften*." *Goethe-Studien*. Berlin: Skopnik, 1897, p. 129.

Müller, Walter. Review: "Erich Schmidt, *Richardson, Rousseau und Goethe* (Obraldruck der Auflage von 1875 [Jena: Biedermann, 1924])." *AJJR*, 16 (1924–1925): 267–268.

————. Review: "Elisabeth Caspers, *Goethes pädagogische Grundanschauungen im Verhältnis zu Rousseau* (Langensalza: Beyer, 1922)." *AJJR*, 16 (1924–1925): 251–252.

Neumann, Alfred R. "The Changing Concept of the *Singspiel* in the Eighteenth Century." *Studies in German Literature*. Ed. Carl Hammer, Jr. LSUSHS, No. 13. Baton Rouge, 1963; pp. 63–71.

Pange, Jean de. "Les voyages de Herder en France." *EG*, 2 (1947): 4–58.

Parodi, D. "Des idées religieuses de Rousseau." *RMM*, 20 (1912): 295–320.

Pascal, Roy. "Goethe's Autobiography and Rousseau's *Confessions*." *Studies in French Language and Literature Presented to R. L. Graeme Ritchie*. Cambridge, Eng.: Cambridge University Press, 1949, pp. 147–162.

Petersen, Julius. "Erdentage und Ewigkeit." *JbGG*, 18 (1932): 3–23.

Peyre, Henri. "Religion and Literary Scholarship in France." *PMLA*, 78 (1962): 345–363.

Price, Lawrence M. "Goldsmith, Sesenheim and Goethe." *GR*, 4 (1929): 237–247.

Raabe, August. "Das Dämonische in den *Wanderjahren*." *Goethe*, 1 (1936): 119–127.

Raymond, Marcel. "J.-J. Rousseau. Deux aspects de sa vie intérieure (intermittence et permanence du 'moi')." *AJJR*, 29 (1941–1942): 5–57.

Reiss, Hans. "*Die Leiden des jungen Werthers*: A Reconsideration." *MLQ* (1959): 81–96.

Remak, Henry H. H. "Goethes Gretchenabenteuer und Manon Lescaut: Dichtung oder Wahrheit?" *Formen der Selbstdarstellung: Festgabe für Fritz Neubert*. Berlin: Duncker & Humblot, 1956, pp. 379–395.

————. "Goethe on Stendhal: Development and Significance of his Attitude." *Goethe Bicentennial Studies by Members of the Faculty of In-*

diana University. Ed. Hubert J. Meessen. IUHS, No. 22. Bloomington,
1950; pp. 207–234.

Ritter, Eugène. "J.-J. Rousseau et Madame d'Houdetot." AJJR, 2 (1906):
1–36.

———. "Les douze métiers de Jean-Jacques." AJJR, 11 (1916–1917): 17–
34.

Roethe, Gustav. "Dichtung und Wahrheit." Goethe: Gesammelte Vorträge
und Aufsätze. Berlin: Ebering, 1932, pp. 1–24.

Rossmann, Kurt. "Goethe und der Geist der französischen Philosophie."
Goethe et l'esprit français. Ed. Albert Fuchs. Paris: Société d'Éditions:
Les Belles Lettres, 1958, pp. 195–210.

Rowbotham, Arnold H. "Rousseau and his Critics." SR, 38 (1930): 385–
397.

Sachs, C. "Goethes Beschäftigung mit französischer Sprache und Literatur."
ZFSL, 23 (1901): 34–68.

Sagave, Pierre-Paul. "Französische Politik in deutscher Dichtung." Jahresring
64/65. Stuttgart: Deutsche Verlagsanstalt, 1964, pp. 269–280.

Sauer, Eberhard. "Goethe und die französische Revolution." Jahrbuch des
Freien Deutschen Hochstifts, 1913, pp. 173–198.

Schaub, Edward L. "Goethe and Philosophy." Goethe Centenary Papers. Ed.
Martin Schütze. Chicago: University of Chicago Press, 1932, pp. 34–68.

Schaumburg, Max. "Sieben unbekannte Briefe des Grafen Reinhard an
Goethe." JbGG, 16 (1930): 121–148.

Schiff, Julius. "Mignon, Ottilie, Makarie im Lichte der Goetheschen Naturphilosophie." JbGG, 9 (1922): 133–147.

Schinz, Albert. "Le mouvement Rousseauiste du dernier quart de siècle:
Essai de bibliographie critique." MP, 20 (1922–1923): 149–172.

Schmid, Günther. "Goethes Metamorphose der Pflanzen." Goethe als Seher
und Forscher der Natur. Ed. Johannes Walter. Halle: Niemeyer, 1930,
pp. 208–226; 313–319.

Schröder, Rudolf Alexander. "Das politische Weltbild in Werk und Leben
Goethes." Goethe-Kalender auf das Jahr 1934. Ed. Ernst Beutler. Leipzig: Dieterich'sche Verlagsbuchhandlung, 1933, pp. 129–151.

Schulz, Günter. "Der ländliche Wesenszug des jungen Goethe." Goethe, 5
(1940): 115–137.

Seeber, Edward D. "Literature and the Question of Suicide: Werther in
France." Goethe Bicentennial Studies by the Faculty of Indiana University. Ed. Hubert J. Meessen. IUHS, No. 22 (1950): 49–59.

Seidlin, Oskar. "Georg Brandes." Essays in German and Comparative Literature, UNCSCL, No. 30, Chapel Hill, 1961, 1–29.

Smith, Herbert. "Goethe and Rousseau." PEGS, n.s., 3 (1926): 31–55.

Smith, John E. "Rousseau, Romanticism, and the Philosophy of Existence."
YFS, No. 13 (Spring-Summer, 1954): 52–61.

Sommerfeld, Martin. "Jean-Jacques Rousseaus Bekenntnisse und Goethes

Dichtung und Wahrheit." *Goethe in Umwelt und Folgezeit.* Leiden: Sijthoff, 1935, pp. 209–237.

———. "Goethes *Wahlverwandtschaften* im neunzehnten Jahrhundert." *Goethe in Umwelt und Folgezeit.* Leiden: Sijthoff, 1935, pp. 9–35.

Stahl, E. L. "*Die Wahlverwandtschaften.*" *PEGS,* n.s., 15 (1946): 71–95.

———. "Goethe as Novelist." *Essays on Goethe.* Ed. William Rose. London: Cassel, 1949, pp. 46–73.

Stapfer, Paul. "Werther." *Études sur Goethe.* Paris: Colin, 1906, pp. 73–96.

Strich, Fritz. "Goethe und die Schweiz." *CL,* 1 (1949): 289–308.

Süpfle, Theodor. "Goethe und Rousseau." *Zeitschrift für den deutschen Unterricht,* 21 (1907): 127–128.

Temmer, Mark J. "Art and Love in the Confessions of Jean-Jacques Rousseau." *PMLA,* 73 (1958): 215–220.

Torrey, Norman L. "Rousseau's Quarrel with Grimm and Diderot." *Essays in Honor of Albert Feuillerat.* Ed. Henri Payre, Yale Romanic Studies, No. 22 (New Haven, 1943), pp. 163–182.

Tresnon, Jeanette. "The Paradox of Rousseau." *PMLA,* 43 (1928): 1010–1025.

Trevelyan, Humphrey. "Goethe's Awareness of the Unconscious and the Elemental." *Gate,* 1 (1947): 28–36.

———. "Goethe's *Wahlverwandtschaften.*" *Gate,* 3 (1949): 13–22.

Tubach, Frederic C. "*Perfectibilité:* der zweite Diskurs Rousseaus und die deutsche Aufklärung." *EG,* 15 (1960): 144–151.

Ulrich, Joachim. "Goethes Einfluss auf Schillers Schönheitsbegriff." *JbGG,* 20 (1934), 165–212.

Vermeil, Edmond. "Arrière-plans révolutionnaires dans le *Faust* de Goethe." *EG,* 1 (1946): 360–383; 2 (1947): 60–71, 389–410.

———. "Goethe et Rousseau." *AJJR,* 36 (1946–1949): 57–77.

———. "Goethe: homme du milieu." *CL,* 1 (1949): 324–336.

———. "Goethe and the West." Trans. W. E. Delp. *MLR,* 44 (1949): 504–513.

———. "*La Nouvelle Héloïse* et son influence sur l'œuvre de Goethe." *Goethe et l'esprit français: Actes du Colloque International de Strasbourg, 23–27 Avril 1957.* Ed. Albert Fuchs. Paris: Société d'Éditions: Les Belles Lettres, 1959, pp. 57–68.

Vetter, August. "Wahlverwandtschaft." *JbGG,* 17 (1931): 98–113.

Voisine, Jacques. "L'Influence de la *Nouvelle Héloïse* sur la génération de *Werther.*" *EG,* 5 (1950): 120–123.

von der Hellen, Eduard. "Stackelberg bei Goethe, 1829." *GJb,* 13 (1892): 91.

Wachsmuth, Andreas B. "Ein neues Goethebild? Zu dem Buch von R. Friedenthal." *Goethe,* 27 (1965): 279–308.

Wahle, Julius. "Fünfzehn Briefe Goethes und ein Brief Schillers." *JbGG,* 1 (1914): 113–122.

Waidson, H. M. "Goethe and Klinger: Some Aspects of a Personal and Literary Relationship." *PEGS*, n.s., 23 (1954): 97–120.

Walzel, Oskar. "Goethes *Wahlverwandtschaften* im Rahmen ihrer Zeit." *GJb*, 27 (1906): 166–205.

Ward, Adolphus William. "Goethe and the French Revolution." *PEGS*, 14 (1912): 1–28.

Wasiliewski, Waldemar von. "War Goethe am Lago maggiore?" *JbGG*, 9 (1922): 182–198.

Weinhold, Karl, ed. "Anfang eines fantastischen Romans von Lenz, von dessen eigner Hand." *GJb*, 10 (1889): 46–70, 89–105.

Wilkinson, Elizabeth M. "Goethe's *Tasso*—the Tragedy of a Creative Artist." *PEGS*, n.s., 15 (1946): 96–127.

———. "Tasso—ein gesteigerter Werther," *MLR*, 44 (1949): 305–328.

Willoughby, L. A. "Literary Relations in the Light of Goethe's Principle of 'Wiederspiegelung.'" *CL*, 1 (1949): 309–323.

———. "Goethe—the Natural Philosopher." *Goethe After Two Centuries.* Ed. Carl Hammer, Jr., *LSUSHS*, No. 1 (1952): 3–19.

———. "The Image of the 'Wanderer' and the 'Hut' in Goethe's Poetry." *EG*, 6 (1951): 207–219.

Witte, William. "Goethe and 'Ius Naturale.'" *Schiller and Burns and Other Essays.* Oxford: Basil Blackwell, 1959, pp. 81–91.

Wolff, Hans M. "Der Rousseaugehalt in Klingers Drama *Das leidende Weib.*" *JEGP*, 39 (1940): 355–375.

———. "Rousseau, Möser und der Kampf gegen das Rokoko." *Monatshefte*, 34 (1942): 113–125.

———. "Der junge Herder und die Entwicklungsidee Rousseaus." *PMLA*, 57 (1942): 753–819.

———. "Satyros." *GR*, 24 (1949): 168–176.

Wood, Henry. "Die Faustromane F. M. Klingers und Goethes *Faust.*" *Faust-studien.* Berlin: Reiner, 1912, pp. 229–290.

Woodbridge, Benjamin M. "Rousseau and Faust." *MLN*, 55 (1940): 581–583.

Index